How to Be Like

Jackie Robinson

Life Lessons from Baseball's Greatest Hero

Pat Williams
with Mike Sielski

Health Communications, Inc.
Deerfield Beach, Florida

www.hcibooks.com

Library of Congress Cataloging-in-Publication Data

Williams, Pat, 1940–
    How to be like Jackie Robinson : life lessons from baseball's greatest hero / Pat
Williams with Mike Sielski.
        p. cm.
    Includes bibliographical references.
    ISBN 0-7573-0173-8
    1. Robinson, Jackie, 1919–1972.   2. Baseball players—United States—
Biography.   3. African American baseball players—Biography.   4. Conduct of
life.   I. Sielski, Mike, 1975–   II. Title.

GV865.R6W53 2005
796.357'092—dc22
[B]

                                                                    2005040261

©2005 Pat Williams
ISBN-13: 978-0-7573-0173-5 (pbk.)
ISBN-10: 0-7573-0173-8 (pbk.)

Publisher: Health Communications, Inc.
                3201 S.W. 15th Street
                Deerfield Beach, FL 33442-8190

R-04-13

Cover photo Copyright Bettman/CORBIS
Cover design by Larissa Hise Henoch
Inside book formatting by Dawn Von Strolley Grove

Praise for Jackie Robinson

"I'd run into some of Jackie's boyhood friends, and years later they'd remember how he had beaten them in marbles. He just had to win at everything. He was an intense competitor, but it was not to hurt you or damage someone. He was striving to be the best."

—**Rachel Robinson**
Jackie's widow

"Jackie faced more adversity in the big leagues than most people will ever face in their entire lives. It was rather remarkable how he handled all that adversity, his self-discipline. He held it all in, even with all of the terrible things he saw and heard."

—**Vin Scully**
Dodgers broadcaster

"He had a fire in him. His whole life, he believed if things were wrong, he wanted to change them. He had a strong belief in himself and what was right, and he was not going to tolerate any injustices to people. He couldn't stand being on the sidelines and being left out of the action."

—**Sharon Robinson**
Jackie's daughter

"Jackie Robinson was a man of enormous resolve and dignity. He was not a patsy. Through all his trials, he always maintained his dignity. Jackie showed all of us how to be courageous and keep moving forward."

—**Tom Brokaw**
author and former NBC News anchor

"Jackie Robinson's life was built around service to an idea, ideal, or a cause. He was always at the service of something or someone: UCLA, the U.S. Army, the Dodgers, the Republican Party, Branch Rickey, the NAACP. He was a champion that way to all people, not just blacks. Very few in history ever have had that."

—the late **Ralph Wiley**
author and sports journalist

"Jackie Robinson was a great man, polished and intelligent. But to me, his most unbelievable quality was his self-control in the face of the indignation he endured. Branch Rickey had prepared him well for the difficult times, but it's still amazing. You can search the papers and magazines of that time, and you will not find any reports that Jackie shoved anyone in a parking lot or pushed them—no reports of any altercations. It's a great lesson for young people: We can't control all that's said and done to us, but we can control how we'll react."

—Carl Erskine
former Brooklyn Dodger and Robinson teammate

"Jackie demonstrated all the great human virtues. However, I think among his most awesome talents was his ability to persevere. He stayed the course. He stuck it out. He held on. He endured. He preserved. He remained. He survived. In fact, he did better than survive. He thrived. And because of that, he is a role model for young women and young men the world over."

—Maya Angelou
poet and author

"Without Jackie Robinson, there would not be me. I would never have gotten an opportunity if Jackie hadn't played well and handled himself in the proper manner. I've always tried to take his way and apply it to what I do. I think about Jackie Robinson all the time and ask myself, 'What would he have done?'"

—Tony Gwynn
former San Diego Padres star

"With Jackie Robinson, it wasn't about baseball; it wasn't the playing part. It was the way he conducted himself and kept his mouth closed during those early years of abuse. That was difficult to do."

—Willie Mays
baseball immortal

"I grew up in Manhattan right near the Polo Grounds, but I was a Dodgers fan. Jackie Robinson was my hero. When I was deciding where to go to college, Jackie wrote me and encouraged me to go to UCLA, his alma matter. That meant a lot to me."

—Kareem Abdul-Jabbar
basketball immortal

This book is respectfully dedicated to Rachel,
Sharon and David Robinson.
Our admiration for them knows no bounds.

Contents

꧁꧂

Foreword

❧

As the commissioner of baseball, I firmly believe that baseball is an important social institution with enormous social responsibilities. This is most evident when you look back in our history and consider the impact that Jackie Robinson made on the lives, not only of African Americans, but all Americans. I have often stated that Major League Baseball's proudest moment and most powerful social statement came on April 15, 1947—the day Jackie Robinson set foot on a major-league baseball field. On that day, Jackie broke the color barrier that had existed for decades in the big leagues, and baseball, for the first time, became our true national pastime.

Fifty years to the day after that historic event, I had the privilege of joining Jackie's wife, Rachel, and former president Bill Clinton at Shea Stadium to remember Jackie and the history he made. That night, on behalf of Major League Baseball, it was my great honor to retire Jackie's number 42 in perpetuity. It was the first time any sport had bestowed such a gesture on an athlete. "No single person is bigger than the game of baseball, no one except Jackie Robinson," I said that night at Shea. "He remains bigger than the game."

It is vital that we never forget or minimize the significance of Jackie Robinson's legacy. His achievement predated the integration of the United States Army and the *Brown v. Board of Education* decision. Jackie Robinson changed the game of baseball, but more importantly, he changed the course of our country's social history.

Because of that legacy, and because of the imprint that he left on the lives of all Americans, each year on April 15, Major League Baseball celebrates Jackie Robinson Day throughout the major leagues. Every club that plays at home on that day honors Jackie's place in our nation's social history and also highlights how Jackie's contributions live on through programs such as the Jackie Robinson Foundation and the Breaking Barriers: In Sports, In Life educational program.

When I think of Jackie Robinson, my memories take me back to the summer of 1947. I was a teenager and an avid baseball fan, growing up in Milwaukee, Wisconsin. In time, Milwaukee would become a major-league baseball city—when the Boston Braves moved their franchise there in 1953—but in those days we had minor-league baseball. If you wanted to watch major-league baseball you had to go to Chicago. In May of that year, a friend of mine and I took a train to Wrigley Field to watch the Cubs, but also to get our first in-person glimpse of the National League's newest star. The Cubs were playing the Brooklyn Dodgers that day, and we were going to see Jackie Robinson.

Because he was the man who broke baseball's color barrier, Jackie was a curiosity. Back then, there was no ESPN. Television was brand new, and there weren't many television sets in people's homes. The opportunities to see Jackie play were rare. Your only option, other than to listen to games on the radio (and my radio was always tuned to baseball games throughout the Midwest), was to travel to a big-league ballpark. We arrived at Wrigley and bought the two cheapest tickets we could get—way back in the upper deck. We didn't care. This was the Cubs and the Dodgers, and this was Jackie Robinson. This was something special.

Then we went to sit down, and I noticed something that has stayed with me ever since. As we climbed to our seats, I looked at the people around us. We were the only white fans sitting in the entire section.

At that moment, even at my young age, I began to understand the impact that Jackie had made on his fellow African Americans—and on all Americans. I was proud to be there that day.

There is really no way to measure the courage of Jackie and Branch Rickey. They were a two-man civil-rights movement long before Martin Luther King Jr. entered the public consciousness. Their memories and their contribution to society should never die.

My friend Pat Williams and his coauthor, Mike Sielski, have performed a great service to all of us. Jackie Robinson was an extraordinary man. He had a loving wife and a devoted family to aid him, but I don't think we'll ever really know or comprehend what he went through in those early years of baseball's integration. Most people at that time wanted him to fail. He didn't, and we should always remember and celebrate him for that. Those who came after him—Willie Mays, Frank Robinson, Ernie Banks and Barry Bonds—could not have done so without Jackie. They needed him to succeed. We all did.

This book reminds us of that. Pat and Mike have done a marvelous job of researching Jackie's life, of capturing the essence of the man and of showing how you can apply the best qualities of his life to yours. Jackie's story needs to be told and retold frequently so that we never forget the importance of his life. There was only one Jackie Robinson, but we all should have a Jackie Robinson story to call our own.

They tell me that a bibliography of two hundred interviews and fifty books and periodicals constitutes a well-researched book. Well, there are more than 1,100 interviews and more than 160 books in this bibliography. What a resource this book is for those fortunate youngsters in classrooms all around America to use when they write their term papers on Jackie Robinson during Black History Month. It's also a marvelously inspirational book for anyone who wants to learn more about this great man and what he did for baseball, for American society, and for all of us. This is the ultimate work on Jackie Robinson's life, a treasure for young and old alike.

—*Allan H. "Bud" Selig*
Commissioner of Major League Baseball

Introduction: Consumed and Captivated

꿎

A FEW YEARS AGO, I started working on a book, and, well, there's no other way to put this: it consumed me.

Of course, that's the way it's supposed to be when you write a book. It's supposed to consume you. Otherwise, there isn't much point to writing it. Except that I tend to take "consumed" to another level.

The book was called *How to Be like Mike: Life Lessons About Basketball's Best,* and by the time I completed my research for it, I had interviewed, oh, fifteen hundred people or so, gathering their insights and opinions on Michael Jordan.

Once I finished the book on Jordan, my publisher, Peter Vegso, said I ought to think about other potential *Be Like* titles, about who else would serve as the right sort of subject for another book. The first person who came to mind was Jackie Robinson. To explain why, let me tell you a little bit about myself.

I grew up in Wilmington, Delaware, and during my youth Wilmington was a very segregated community. There were no African American students at my prep school, and Wake Forest University in Winston-Salem, North Carolina, had no black students during my four years as a student there from 1958 to 1962. But my mother and father, Ellen and Jim, were ahead of the times with respect to their attitudes on race, and their example shaped my attitude and perspective. One of the first big-league baseball games my father took me to see was at Shibe Park in Philadelphia in 1947. Phillies vs. Dodgers. I was seven. It was Jackie's rookie season, and he captivated me— the way he moved on a baseball field, the intensity he displayed.

My father did more to teach me about equality and dignity between blacks and whites than just by taking me to see Jackie play, however. He was one of the founders of Delaware's annual all-star high school football game, and a local prep school hosted the practices in 1956, when I was six-teen. All the players lived on the school's campus for two weeks while they practiced for the game—all the players except two, Al Hall and Joe Peters, who were from Howard High School in the northern part of the state. Al and Joe were black, and the school wouldn't let them stay on campus.

"Fine," my father said, "they'll stay at our house."

For those two weeks, I drove Al and Joe to practice each morning and picked them up each afternoon, and they joined us at the dinner table each night.

In 1962, after four years at Wake as a hotshot catcher, I signed a contract with the Philadelphia Phillies, who promptly sent me to Miami to play minor-league ball in the Florida State League. A few black players—includ-ing future Hall of Fame pitcher Ferguson Jenkins, future American League batting champion Alex Johnson and Wilmington native Fred Mason, a first baseman—were on the team, and every time we traveled to another town during the season, the routine was the same: the team bus would stop at a blacks-only hotel and drop off the black players, then continue to a whites-only hotel. Before each game, the bus driver would head from our hotel to the black hotel and pick up our teammates, and after each game, the driver would drop them back off again. Whenever we would stop to eat on the road, the black players stayed in the bus while we brought food to them.

At the end of that '62 season, I drove home from Miami with Fred Mason. We stopped at a gas station in Jacksonville, Florida, so I could fill the car's tank and Fred could use the restroom. As I was pumping the gas, Fred came running toward our car. Chasing him was the proprietor of the station, who was making it clear that Fred was not welcome at his establish-ment. He was screaming, his face was crimson and he was wielding a mon-key wrench high above his head.

Fred and I jumped into the car and pulled away. The next time we stopped for gas, Fred never left the front seat. As we continued driving home, mostly in silence, I remember asking Fred, "How did you control yourself back there?"

"Some of my friends back home," he said, "would have torn that place apart."

This was my introduction to professional sports—fifteen years after

Jackie Robinson had played his first game with the Dodgers.

So when Peter Vegso asked me who I wanted to write about next, these memories, for whatever reason, rushed back to me, and the decision to explore Jackie's life became an easy one. Though I had never met him, he had been a presence in my life. I knew that it was the right time to write about him.

But to write the right kind of book about Jackie, I first had to have the approval of his family. In the fall of 2001, I sent a letter to Rachel Robinson, asking for her permission to write the book. Soon, a letter arrived at my Florida office.

"I am pleased to bless your efforts," Rachel had written. "The few remaining people who knew Jack have been interviewed a lot. However, there are many who didn't know him but were strongly influenced by his life."

I was one of them, of course. Her words touched me, touched the boy who had seen Jackie play. Rachel Robinson is a beautiful, intelligent, talented eighty-two-year-old woman, and I am now proud to call her a friend.

So, with Rachel's blessing for the book, I became consumed again. I began my research. There were 870 ballplayers from the decade that Jackie played, 1947 to 1956, who were still alive, and I resolved to track down every one. Only 770 responded to my interview requests. (That's a facetious *only*.) Through the UCLA athletic department, I gathered information on Jackie's athletic career in college, particularly his time on the university's football and basketball teams. And I dug up almost every book that ever mentioned Jackie Robinson. The depth of research was there to accomplish my goal: presenting Jackie as a man and an athlete worthy of emulation.

I acknowledge Jackie Robinson is not perfect. No man is. He had his faults, but he had so many positive qualities that he stands as a model for how to live an upright life. I would argue he is one of the twenty most important Americans of the last century. Put simply, to be an American citizen, to understand the history of this country and our society's continuing growth, you have to know Jackie Robinson. It pains me when current players say they've never heard of Jackie. Whether we're baseball players or fans is not important. The attributes of his life apply to all of us—his guts, his sense of justice, his honesty. We don't need to know what his batting average was or how many bases he stole to savor the lessons of his life and pass them along to our children and grandchildren.

In that way, Jackie Robinson is the best kind of American hero—a man to be emulated, a life to be studied, a legacy to be treasured. We all need to know about him, and it was with that purpose in mind that I wrote this book. My hope is that it honors Jackie in the way he ought to be honored and plays its part in keeping alive his spirit, a flame that should never be extinguished.

Chapter One

❧

Courage in the Crucible

Jackie needed to quell his anger the first couple of years, a task which only someone of his inner strength and vision could have coped with at that moment. When I reflect and wonder what it must have been like for a man who should have been at the happiest of moments in his life to still have to deal with racial indignities on a daily basis, it is mind-boggling. Most moral men would have cracked.

—Carl Erskine, former Dodgers teammate

HE HAD BEEN HOODWINKED, lured to 215 Montague Street in Brooklyn under a false pretense. And now Jackie Robinson was in Branch Rickey's office, and Rickey, the general manager of the Brooklyn Dodgers, was standing in the middle of the room, calling Robinson a nigger.

This was August 18, 1945, and one of the most famous and most important meetings in baseball history—and perhaps the penultimate test of the courage of Jackie Robinson—had begun with a small lie and was continuing amid epithets and insults.

Robinson had suspected something was up from the moment he met Clyde Sukeforth at Comiskey Park in Chicago four days earlier. One of the Dodgers' top scouts, Sukeforth had come to see Robinson, then the

1

> *"I played against Jackie Robinson
> for four years. I thought
> he was the most courageous and
> disciplined player I had ever
> played with or against."*
>
> JOE PRESKO
> FORMER MAJOR-LEAGUE PITCHER

shortstop for the Kansas City Monarchs of the Negro Leagues, at Rickey's behest, telling Robinson that Rickey was starting a new all-black team, the Brooklyn Brown Dodgers. Rickey wanted to interview Robinson for a position on the team, Sukeforth said, and if Robinson was unable to get to Brooklyn for the interview, Rickey was willing to come to him. That last part—*Rickey was willing to come to him*—was what had made Robinson suspicious, had made him wonder what this meeting was *really* all about.

In Rickey's office, moments after Sukeforth introduced the two men to each other, Rickey asked Robinson a simple, direct question:

"Do you know why you were brought here?"

"To play for the Brown Dodgers," Robinson answered.

His answer was incorrect.

> *"The one regret I have in baseball
> is not writing Jackie Robinson
> while he was alive and telling him
> how much I respected and
> admired him for the way he
> played and the courage and
> strength he had."*
>
> ROY SMALLEY
> FORMER MAJOR-LEAGUER

"You were brought here," Rickey said, "to play for the Brooklyn organization."

Not the Brown Dodgers. Rickey was asking Robinson if he was interested in becoming a Brooklyn Dodger.

After a long silence, Robinson said yes. Rickey knew Robinson was a passionate, tempestuous man. During a three-year stint in the army, Robinson one day refused to sit in the back of an army bus, became involved in a dispute with the bus driver and faced a possible court-martial. But after being arrested by military police and charged with disobeying and showing disrespect to a superior officer, Robinson had been acquitted. Now, Rickey wanted to test him.

"I know you're a good ballplayer," he said. "What I don't know is whether you have the guts."

So Rickey rose from his chair and morphed into every foulmouthed, bigoted character his imagination could conjure. He was the sportswriter who teased Robinson with questions, the waiter who wouldn't seat him, the baserunner who spiked him and called him a "nigger boy." He did all this to gauge Robinson's reaction. If Robinson couldn't take such abuse from Rickey, he certainly wouldn't be able to take it from anyone else, and Rickey's great notion of breaking baseball's color barrier might fail. Never has there been more at stake in a game of make-believe.

Anger smoldered within Robinson, but he remained quiet for a while.

"Mr. Rickey," he said, "are you looking for a Negro who is afraid to fight back?"

"Robinson," Rickey shot back, "I'm looking for a ballplayer with guts enough *not* to fight back."

* * *

Consider that anecdote for a moment, and ask yourself this question: Could you have done what Jackie Robinson was being asked to do? Understand: Rickey was asking Robinson to do more than merely bridge the separation between blacks and Major League Baseball, to tolerate the slurs, the smears and the occasions when opponents deliberately tried to hurt him. He was asking Jackie to quell his very nature, to be the opposite of the fiery, combative person he had always been. Robinson was an eye-for-an-eye sort of man, and Rickey was asking him to turn the other cheek. He was asking him to conquer himself.

"Jackie was under pressure every minute," former Negro League great Buck O'Neil wrote in his autobiography, *I Was Right on Time*. "That's why

> "To see what is right and not do it is a lack of courage."
>
> CONFUCIUS
> CHINESE PHILOSOPHER

> "Courage is the main quality of leadership, in my opinion, no matter where it is exercised. Usually, it implies some risk, especially in new undertakings: courage to initiate something, to keep it going."
>
> WALT DISNEY

Branch Rickey picked him, because Jackie had been under pressure all his life, and the amazing thing was that, knowing Jackie's disposition, he did take the things he took. Because Jackie was fiery."

"It is important to remember that this was no docile foot-shuffler the Dodgers were going to put into the crucible," author Donald Honig wrote in his book *Baseball America*. "This was an angry, seething, highly competitive athlete with a razor-sharp resentment of ingrained, infuriating injustices. . . . For years, he was going to have to abide by the vow he made to Rickey to remain mute and passive no matter what came his way."

Imagine the courage required to take that vow. Imagine—when all you want to do is scream, shout, punch, kick, fight back—holding your tongue and unclenching your fist. Imagine subjugating your personality—everything that makes you *you*—for a greater good, for a higher cause, and imagine what Jackie Robinson went through while doing it. He did it for the entire 1946 season, with the Montreal Royals, and for his first two full seasons with the Dodgers. Almost every day for those three years, he had to withstand every scenario Rickey had acted out that day in Brooklyn.

And he still was named the National League's Rookie of the Year in 1947.

And its Most Valuable Player in 1949.

And was inducted into the Baseball Hall of Fame in 1962.

"Courage," actress Ruth Gordon once said, "is very important. Like a muscle, it is strengthened by use." Robinson's courage, then, had to be stronger than any muscle in his body, or any muscle in anyone else's body.

"He teaches us that, at the moment of our challenge, we can duck from it or walk up to the challenge and win," David Robinson, Jackie's son, told me. "We face those moments daily, so it's important to seize them. It's not easy, but you have to do what you feel is right."

"When I think of Jackie Robinson, I think of courage," author Roger Kahn, who wrote *The Boys of Summer* and numerous other books about baseball and the Brooklyn Dodgers, told me. "I saw him take so much garbage, but yet he stood up to it. He would get angry, but later when I spent time with him at his home, he

> *"One man, with courage,*
> *makes a majority."*
>
> PRESIDENT ANDREW JACKSON

was a lovely, sweet guy—just wonderful to be around."

After the space shuttle *Columbia* crashed in February 2003, author Peggy Noonan wrote: "We forget to notice the everyday courage of astronauts. We forget to think about all the Americans doing big and dangerous things . . . members of the Armed Forces, cops and firemen, doctors in public hospitals in hard places." Noonan is right, of course. We do forget about the people who, each day, display courage grandly: running into a burning building, risking themselves for the sake of exploration and knowledge, working long hours to heal and help the less privileged. "Most forms of courage aren't especially visible," sportswriter Frank Deford said. We get wrapped up in ourselves, in our jobs and our pursuit of material things, and we pay no mind to the daily displays of bravery all around us. Noonan could as easily have written the same words about Jackie Robinson—a man who showed courage every day just by showing up at the ballpark, who carried that courage into every aspect of a life spent pursuing equality and justice.

* * *

It would be a mistake to think everyone in the Dodgers' organization initially regarded Robinson with the same respect that Rickey did. When Robinson joined the Montreal Royals in 1946 for his single season of minor-league play before joining the Dodgers, he walked through the clubhouse doors and was spotted by his new manager, Clay Hopper.

"Well," Hopper said, "when Mr. Rickey picked one, he sure picked a black one."

Hopper's attitude was indicative of the insults and attacks Robinson put up with throughout his season at Montreal and his first few seasons

> *"The true meaning of courage is to be afraid and, then, with your knees knocking and your heart racing, to step out anyway."*
>
> OPRAH WINFREY

> *"Fate saves a warrior when his courage endures. If you keep fighting, blindly, in a positive and courageous way, sometimes change will rescue you."*
>
> PAT SUMMIT
> UNIVERSITY OF TENNESSEE WOMEN'S BASKETBALL COACH

with the Dodgers. When Robinson was called up to the Dodgers, Dixie Walker, Brooklyn's most popular player, threatened to circulate a petition among Robinson's teammates to protest his presence on the team. It was the rare game that the opposing pitcher didn't send a fastball sizzling past Robinson's scalp, or a baserunner didn't try to take him out on a double play by charging with spikes high into second base. Opponents routinely went out of their way to injure him. Once, with Robinson at bat, an opposing catcher, while supposedly attempting to pick off a baserunner, purposely held onto the ball and struck Jackie in the back of the head.

> *"Courage is a quality that few can define, but most recognize [it] when they see it. It is, unquestionably, a kind of strength that allows men to perform extraordinary feats in the face of overwhelming opposition. It cannot be taught, though it can be inspired, and it normally springs from something like faith or resolve . . . a commitment to something larger than oneself."*
>
> STEPHEN MANSFIELD
> AUTHOR

"The throwing at Robinson was more persistent and more vicious than anything I had seen or my father had seen before me, and by that measured, persistent, malevolent viciousness, beanballs hurled by brawny whites at the black recruit appeared new and ugly," Roger Kahn once wrote. "One day a rangy Philadelphia right-hander named Al Jurisich knocked Robinson down and on the next pitch cracked him with a fastball near the elbow. Jurisich was behind in the count. The pitch made no baseball sense. Its purpose was to injure, and Robinson clutched his right elbow and jumped and spun in pain."

> *"Courage is the most important of all the virtues, because you cannot be sure that you can practice any other virtue with consistency without courage."*
>
> MAYA ANGELOU
> POET

Yet, if you were to talk to any of Robinson's teammates or to any of the many opponents who grew to respect him, each would tell you that Jackie stood up and stood in time after time, never allowing fear of a fractured skull or shattered kneecap—or something worse—to overcome him. As Mark Twain put it: "Courage is not lack of fear, absence of fear. It is control of fear . . . mastery of fear." It wasn't that fear didn't exist within Robinson; it did. He simply possessed the strength to master it.

"Making the double play, they didn't move him," Pee Wee Reese, the Dodgers' Hall of Fame shortstop, once said. "He'd get over that darn bag. He didn't care how big you were, how hard you slid. He challenged you, and he had those big legs and, playing alongside him seven, eight years, I don't remember seeing the guy knocked down."

> "A man full of courage
> is also full of faith."
>
> CICERO
> PHILOSOPHER

"I admired Jackie Robinson so much for all he had to go through in those early years," former major-league player and manager Bill Virdon told me. "He was forced to put up with more abuse than any other player in history. He set an example for so many people to follow."

As the Dodgers' center fielder, Duke Snider had a clear view of what Robinson had to withstand on the field. "Torment seems almost too mild a word to describe what Jackie went through," Snider wrote in his autobiography, *The Duke of Flatbush*. "Torture would be more like it. . . . Right from the start of his rookie season all the way through his first year, and for years after that, Jackie endured what no other mere mortal could or should."

One player who came after Robinson who had an inkling of what Robinson went through was Henry Aaron. As Aaron chased Babe Ruth's career home run record, he was inundated with hate mail, letters whose writers told him that, as a black man, he was not worthy of being baseball's home run king. The letters wounded Aaron to his soul, but he withstood their hatefulness and ultimately

> "Ted Williams looks like
> John Wayne, and when I asked
> him about Jackie Robinson,
> he looked at me like Wayne would
> and said, 'That man had tons
> and tons of guts.'"
>
> KEN BURNS
> FILMMAKER

triumphed, breaking Ruth's record in 1974.

"Jackie Robinson had to be bigger than life," Aaron once said. "He had to be bigger than the Brooklyn teammates who got up a petition to keep him off the ball club; bigger than the pitchers who threw at him . . . bigger than the bench jockeys who hollered for him to carry their bags and shine their shoes; bigger than the so-called fans who mocked him with mops on their heads and wrote him death threats. . . . He was a fighter—the proudest, most competitive person I've ever seen."

In 1946, Duane Pillette was in his first year of professional baseball, a green pitcher for the Newark Bears of the AAA International League. The Montreal Royals came south to play the Bears during the second week of the season, and Robinson tore up Newark's pitching. "He must have hit .800 off of our pitchers," Pillette told me. "I was fortunate I didn't pitch in that series."

When the series ended, the Newark manager told his pitching staff: "I don't know or care who will pitch our first game when we play them again, but it will cost that pitcher fifty dollars if he doesn't drill Robinson good." Given that Pillette was earning only $400 a month, the fifty bucks was a pretty heavy price for disobedience.

> *"Whatever you do, you need courage. Whatever course you decide upon, there is always someone to tell you that you are wrong. There are always difficulties arising that tempt you to believe your critics are right. To map out a course of action and follow it to an end requires some of the same courage that a soldier needs. Peace has its victories, but it takes brave men and women to win them."*
>
> RALPH WALDO EMERSON
> WRITER/PHILOSOPHER

Later that season, the Bears faced Jackie and the Royals again, and lo and behold, Pillette was the starter. He retired the first hitter, then up came Robinson. Newark's manager gave Pillette the signal to throw at Jackie.

"I thought it was wrong," Pillette said, "so I came close with my first three pitches, but Jackie, thank God, moved good. My next pitch was in the dirt at his feet."

After drawing the walk, Robinson took his typically large lead at first.

Pillette threw to first to keep him close—and accidentally hit Robinson in the ankle.

"When I retired the side," Pillette said, "I said to the manager, 'Skip, I missed at home plate, but I got him at first.' He looked at me with a very unbelieving eye and said, 'Yeah, I guess you saved fifty bucks, kid.'

> *"Courage is endurance of the soul."*
>
> SOCRATES
> PHILOSOPHER

"What a relief."

At no time during Robinson's career with the Dodgers was his courage put to a greater test than on April 22, 1947, when the Philadelphia Phillies came to Ebbets Field for their first series against Brooklyn in Jackie's rookie season. If you grew up in the Philadelphia area and cared about baseball at all, as I did, you knew the story of Ben Chapman. You knew the history of how the Phillies manager sat in the visitors' dugout that day and unleashed the most virulent torrent of racist obscenities Robinson would hear in his major-league career. (You'll read more about Chapman and this incident throughout this book, for I consider it the defining moment in Jackie Robinson's career, and in his effect on history and American society.)

Here's what came from the Phillies dugout:

"Hey, nigger, why don't you go back to the cotton field where you belong?"

"They're waiting for you in the jungles, black boy!"

"Hey, snowflake, which one of those white boys' wives are you dating tonight?"

"We don't want you here, nigger."

"Go back to the bushes."

It was as close as Robinson would come to quitting.

> *"Heroes and cowards feel exactly the same fear; heroes just react differently."*
>
> CUS D'AMATO
> BOXING TRAINER

"I have to admit that this day, of all the unpleasant days in my life, brought me nearer to cracking up than I ever had been," Robinson wrote in his autobiography, *I Never Had It Made*. "I felt tortured, and I tried just to play ball and ignore the insults. But it was really getting to me. What did the Phillies want from me? What, indeed, did Mr. Rickey expect of me? I was, after all, a human being. What was I doing here turning the other cheek as though I weren't a man . . . ?

"For one wild and rage-crazed minute, I thought, 'To hell with Mr. Rickey's noble experiment. It's clear it won't succeed. I have made every effort to work hard, to get myself into shape. My best is not good enough for them.' I thought what a glorious, cleansing thing it would be to let go. To hell with the image of the patient black freak I was supposed to create. I could throw down my bat, stride over to that Phillies dugout, grab one of those white [bleeps] and smash his teeth in with my despised black fist. Then I could walk away from it all. . . ."

Except he didn't.

"The strongest, most generous and proudest of all virtues is courage."

MICHEL DE MONTAIGNE
PHILOSOPHER

"Then, I thought of Mr. Rickey—how his family and friends had begged him not to fight for me and my people. I thought of all his predictions, which had come true. Mr. Rickey had come to a crossroads and made a lonely decision. I was at a crossroads. I would make mine. I would stay."

* * *

That was the thing about Robinson, and that's the thing about courage. Because Robinson was brave in standing up for himself and his race, his peers gradually felt emboldened enough to stand up for him. Courage begets more courage. "Courage is contagious," the Reverend Billy Graham once said. "When a brave man takes a stand, the spines of others are stiffened. A show of courage, by any person, encourages others."

Indeed, from the moment Robinson's professional baseball career began, his courage either rubbed off on others or encouraged others to show the courage they always had. At their annual winter meeting in January 1947, Major League Baseball's owners voted fifteen to one against letting Robinson play for the Dodgers. Giants owner Horace Stoneman actually said during the meeting that if Robinson were allowed to play, blacks

"The essence of sport is courage."

THOMAS MCGUANE
WRITER

would riot and burn down the Polo Grounds. After the meeting, Rickey visited commissioner Happy Chandler at Chandler's home in Kentucky and asked him where he stood on the prospect of having Robinson play in the majors.

"Mr. Rickey," Chandler said, "I'm going to have to meet my maker some day. If He asked me why I didn't let this boy play, and I answered, 'Because he's a Negro,' that might not be a sufficient answer."

Chandler approved Robinson's transfer from Montreal to the Dodgers. In 1951, the owners refused to renew Chandler's contract as payback for his decision to cross them. He had lost his job, but he had kept his integrity.

So Robinson joined the Dodgers, and his teammates, led by Dixie Walker, promptly planned the petition against him. The players had one problem, though: Manager Leo Durocher found out about the petition. He called a team meeting and said, among other things that were a bit more profane, "I don't want to see your petition. I don't want to hear anything about it. . . . The meeting is over. Go to bed."

The Dodgers weren't the only National League team that considered making a collective stand against Robinson that year. In May, Stanley Woodward, the great sports editor of the *New York Herald Tribune,* learned that the St. Louis Cardinals were threatening to strike during their games against the Dodgers. The Cardinals' hope was that other teams would follow suit and Robinson

> *"Whenever two teams or players of equal ability play, the one with the greater courage will win."*
>
> PETE CARRIL
> FORMER PRINCETON UNIVERSITY
> MEN'S BASKETBALL COACH

would be drummed out of Brooklyn. Woodward broke the story in his newspaper, and National League president Ford Frick cabled a letter to the Cardinals. It read in part: "I do not care if half the league strikes. Those who do it will encounter quick retribution. All will be suspended. . . . This is the United States of America, and one citizen has the right to play as another." Author James N. Giglio once wrote: "Never had the wishy-washy Frick acted so forcefully." And in 1962, the Cardinals' organization showed how far it had come with respect to matters of race. That year, the team's owner, August Busch, threatened to move the team from its

St. Petersburg, Florida, spring-training site because the community treated St. Louis's black players so poorly.

> *"Courage is the willingness to embark on a new course of action, with no guarantees of success. In fact, you must expect to suffer temporary failure and defeat, over and over again, if you are really serious about being a big success."*
>
> MARK TWAIN
> AUTHOR

Such was the effect Robinson's courage had on others. That was the wonderful thing about his rookie year in Brooklyn and the remainder of his career: time after time, his courage rubbed off on people. During spring training in 1949, the Dodgers played several games in Georgia, and Sam Lacy, the renowned sportswriter for the Baltimore *Afro-American,* followed them as part of his coverage of Robinson. Lacy knew Robinson as well as any writer in the country and had seen everything Jackie had gone through.

While the Dodgers were in Georgia, Dr. Samuel Green, the grand dragon of the Ku Klux Klan, threatened to cause chaos at the games. So Lacy went to Green's house, requesting an interview. When asked why a black man would knock on the door of a Klansman, Lacy said: "I wanted to know if he was going to start any crap at the ballpark."

> *"On some positions, cowardice asks the question, 'Is it expedient?' Then, expedience comes along and asks the question, 'Is it politic?' Vanity asks the question, 'Is it right?' There comes a time when one must take a position that is neither safe, nor polite, nor popular, but one must take it, because it is right."*
>
> MARTIN LUTHER KING JR.

Lacy's action was, in a way, a precursor to Robinson's life after baseball. Jackie became a crusader for civil rights, traveling into the teeth of the segregationist South to deliver speeches and march with the likes of Dr. Martin Luther King Jr. In August 1962, for instance, he spoke in Albany, Georgia, at King's request, only days after two black churches there had been burned to the ground. In that moment, with that decision to speak in the aftermath of such a tragedy, with danger still lingering, Robinson cemented his place as a leader in the civil rights movement.

"Sometimes, you have to rise to the occasion and be daring and courageous," U.S. congressman and civil rights leader John Lewis told me. "When I was young, I asked my parents and grandparents, 'Why do we have to have segregation?' They'd reply, 'Don't get in the way. Stay out of trouble.' Well, Jackie was willing to 'get into trouble,' a good kind of trouble. He set a noble example for all of us."

That's what courage often comes down to: one choice, one decision, one evaluation of your values and your commitment to them. A leader needs courage in the way a hitter needs a bat: without it, he's useless. This is true in any organization: the coach or captain of a sports team, the CEO of a business, the pastor of a congregation. In his book, *Listen Up, Leader!* David Cottrell offers seven ways that courage serves a true leader. After each of Cottrell's tenets, I offer some ideas for how Cottrell's tenets applied to Robinson's life and career.

1. *Have the courage to accept responsibility. If we are looking for excuses or someone to blame, we'll never get to where we're trying to go.* After their initial meeting, Robinson and Rickey never lost sight of their ultimate goal: proving black men could bring honor to the national pastime. They accepted help from others, but they didn't expect help from others. "Through Robinson's ordeal in Montreal," author Peter Golenbock once wrote, "his teammates were never more than mere spectators. They expressed neither opinions nor feelings about what Robinson was going through. They made no overtures of support for him." And still, Robinson continued on his crusade.

2. *Have the courage to seek the truth. Things are not always as they seem. If you don't use all your resources to understand the real truth, you may make bad decisions. The higher you are on the organizational chart, the more difficult it is to discover the truth.* Both Robinson and Rickey had the courage to seek the truth about baseball's color barrier: it was immoral, and it needed to be demolished.

3. *Have the courage to take risks, as long as they are well thought-out and the end result is worth the price we have to pay. But remember: The more we fail, the closer we are to success.* Has a sports executive ever taken a bigger risk

than Rickey by introducing a black man into an all-white game in the late 1940s? Has a professional athlete ever taken a bigger risk than Robinson simply by playing?

4. *Have the courage to stand up for what's right. Set the example.* If Jackie Robinson didn't embody this principle—before, during and after his baseball career—no one did.

5. *Have the courage to reject cynics. There are plenty of cynical people in our world. If you allow them to spread their cynicism, it will eventually take over. Comfort the cynics and take action to prevent them from destroying your organization.* Remember: Rickey threatened to trade or release Dixie Walker, the Dodgers' most popular player, and anyone else who didn't go along with his decision to have Robinson join the team.

6. *Have the courage to persevere. When faced with adversity, often the easiest path is to surrender. . . . Yet one of the keys to success is to hang in there longer than everyone else. Don't give up. What separates winners from losers is the courage to persist.* Imagine what might have happened if Jackie Robinson had said in 1947, "This is too tough. I can't take the abuse. I quit." Imagine how much different baseball history—and American history—might be. And how much worse.

7. *Have the courage to accept responsibility for your role. You are a leader everywhere you go and in everything you do. Don't waste your time asking, "Is anyone watching?" Rather, ask, "What are they seeing, and in what direction am I leading?"* This principle hearkens back to Rickey's initial demand of Robinson—that no matter how fierce the physical and verbal attacks on him those first three years in Montreal and Brooklyn, he was not to retaliate. He was to turn the other cheek, carry himself in silent grace. And so he did.

And, again, imagine what he had to endure to do it. Imagine the courage it required. Of course, as Steven Goldberg points out, "You can only imagine being such a person." The chairman of the City University of New York's sociology department, Goldberg grew up in New York City and had only two heroes as a child: the Lone Ranger and Jackie

> *"It takes courage to think alone, to resist alone, to stand alone, especially when the crowd seems so safe, so right."*
>
> CHARLES SWINDOLL
> AUTHOR

Robinson. Why Robinson? Because Goldberg, an intellectual kid who felt a bit ostracized from his peers, felt he could identify, on a small, small scale, with Robinson, who was courageous enough to stand alone.

"But the wonderful thing in imagining," Goldberg told me, "is that, in so imagining, you become a little more like that person, a very little bit more to be sure, but even this little bit matters a lot. Jackie's been gone a long time now and we miss him terribly, but he's here every time we have to be reminded that when courage is necessary, courage is possible."

* * *

Rickey's test of Robinson that August day in 1945 lasted three hours. At one point, Rickey brandished a copy of *The Life of Christ* by Giovanni Papini and read Robinson an excerpt:

> *Ye have heard that it hath been said, An eye for an eye and a tooth for a tooth: But I say unto you that ye resist not evil: But whosoever shall smite thee on the right cheek, turn to him the other. There are three answers men can make to violence: revenge, flight, turning the other cheek.*

So there was Rickey, setting up Robinson's choice. When confronted with the racist actions of his opponents, with the violence they would inflict on him, Jackie could seek revenge. He could strike back in the way his antagonists might expect him to—by allowing them to see his anger, by cursing at them, by fighting them with his fists. Or, he could simply run and avoid the confrontation altogether.

> *The first is the barbarous principle of retaliation. Flight is no better than retaliation. The man who takes flight invites pursuit.*

Rickey's message became clear in the next three sentences.

> *Turning the other cheek means not receiving the second blow. It means cutting the chains of the inevitable wrongs at the first link. Your adversary is ready for anything but this. . . .*

Rickey understood that this was not a time for euphemisms, for softening or minimizing the importance of the task that he and Robinson faced. For his role in Rickey's plan, Robinson would have to summon from deep within himself a courage few men possessed. As he finished reading from Papini, Rickey cut to the core of what Robinson must face and must do.

Every man has an obscure respect for courage in others, especially if it is moral courage, the rarest and most difficult sort of bravery. It makes the very brute understand that this man is more than a man. The results of nonresistance, even if they are not always perfect, are certainly superior to resistance or flight. To answer blows with blows, evil deeds with evil deeds, is to meet the attacker on his own ground, to proclaim oneself as low as he. Only he who has conquered himself can conquer his enemies.

And with that, their courageous crusade began.

After Robinson's first two years with the Dodgers, Rickey removed the invisible restraints from him, told him he could fight back if he felt the need. "I realized the point would come when my almost filial relationship with Jackie would break with ill feeling if I did not issue an emancipation proclamation for him," Rickey once wrote. "I knew . . . that while the wisest policy for Robinson during those first two years was to turn the other cheek and not fight back, there were many in baseball who would not understand this lack of action. They could be made to respect courage only in the physical sense. So I told Robinson that he was on his own. Then I sat back happily, knowing that, with the restraints removed, Robinson was going to show the National League a thing or two."

> *"It's a measure of the man when he's courageous when it's not absolutely required of him."*
>
> GARRISON KEILLOR
> AUTHOR

Did he ever. But then, of course, he already had.

Chapter Two

A Hero and
His Influence

I was a kid playing high school football in Birmingham when word came that the Dodgers had signed Jackie Robinson. That gave me hope that, someday soon, there might be an opportunity for me in baseball.

—Willie Mays

YOU START WITH HIS GRAVE.

If you want to understand Jackie Robinson's influence on this country and on this culture, if you want to appreciate how he continued his crusade for justice and equality until the days before he died, you have to begin at Cypress Hills Cemetery in Brooklyn, only blocks from the place where he made so many memories, Ebbets Field, once stood. You have to begin with the words on his headstone. You have to begin with his epitaph.

It reads:

"A life is not important except in the impact it has on other lives."

In so many ways, in almost every aspect of his life, Jackie Robinson embodied that axiom—not only by excelling as a baseball player and by working to improve American society, but through the elementary acts of his daily existence. He was a son. He was a husband. He was a father. He was a ballplayer. He was a black man. He was an activist. He was a hero.

"I loved Jackie Robinson. You remembered him if you ever met him. He left that kind of an impression on you for the rest of your life. If you list the fifty or one hundred most significant Americans of all time, Jackie Robinson has to be on the list."

DAVE ANDERSON
NEW YORK TIMES SPORTS COLUMNIST

And in all of those roles, he touched people—those who knew him and those who never met him—through measures great and small.

It might have been something as great as his base running, so daring and compelling that it forced television to adopt the "split screen" so viewers at home could watch him. It might have been something as simple as a handshake and autograph to a young fan.

It might have been something as great as a speech in the heart of the South, risking himself for the sake of his cause. It might have been something as small as his collecting three hits on a day a father took his son to his first ball game.

"He was blessed with extraordinary talent, but he had a grace and a personality that transcended baseball. He reached people and touched them and brought out all sorts of emotions in them. He still does to this day."

SHARON ROBINSON
JACKIE'S DAUGHTER

"Jackie Robinson wanted to be remembered for more than just being a baseball player," Brooklyn radio and television producer Tom Villante told me. "He transcended sports and was really an international figure."

Indeed, as great a baseball player as he was, Robinson was more influential as a symbol and champion of civil rights. He opened up the struggle for equality to thousands who otherwise might not have appreciated or understood what blacks were fighting for and why.

"The story of Jackie Robinson is the story of a man and an era," his son, David, told me. "The nation was segregated and filled with racial problems. Then, in 1947, here comes a man who is going to break right through it like a race car going through a big piece of cardboard. Baseball was the national sport, so his efforts impacted all phases of American society."

"When I look at the world today, with its racism and color barriers and an attitude of not accepting others who look like you, I think of Jackie Robinson," former major-league pitcher Dave Stewart told me. "He had it a lot tougher than anybody today, and it was because of him that so many of us have received these opportunities."

Chicago Cubs manager Dusty Baker grew up in Riverside, California. When Baker was a boy, his father made him watch the film *The Jackie Robinson Story.* To this day, Baker keeps two framed photographs of Jackie in his home. "I try to put into practice what Jackie stood for—tolerance without acceptance," Baker told me. "As the Cubs manager, I get a lot of derogatory racial mail, and I simply think of all that Jackie went through and how he would respond."

Day after day, game after game, Robinson presented an image of controlled intensity, intelligence and dignity that persuaded people of the rightness of the civil-rights movement. Martin Luther King Jr. once said Jackie was more important to the movement than he was. One night in 1968, only a month or so before James Earl Ray murdered him, King was having dinner with former Dodgers pitcher Don Newcombe, and King said he appreciated how much easier Robinson, Newcombe and Roy Campanella had made his job by excelling on the baseball field. All those moments when King had to stand up for equal rights, all those times when he was sprayed with water hoses and clubbed with nightsticks and sent to jail, and Newcombe couldn't believe what he was hearing: *We* made it easier for *him.*

"My God," Newcombe once said, "How hard would his job have been without us in baseball? And all of this came from the efforts of my idol, Jackie Robinson."

> *"Live your life in the manner that you would like your kids to live theirs."*
>
> MICHAEL LEVINE
> AUTHOR

"Martin Luther King had his dream, but he didn't know how to start it," Willa Robinson Walker, Jackie's sister, once told Stan Hochman of the *Philadelphia Daily News.* "And then he became aware of Jack, in baseball. And he said, 'This is what I want to do in other areas.' And the black minister from South Africa, Bishop Desmond Tutu—I went to dinner with him. And he told me that Jack was his inspiration. He told me he had seen a copy of *Ebony* magazine in a dentist's office and read about Jack and what he endured. And he said that if Jack could go through what he did, others could follow."

Robinson's effect on King and Tutu and on their crusades shows that in any endeavor, we all have a role to play. By carrying himself with class and playing with such skill and flair, Robinson reached and influenced those people who read the sports pages but didn't read much else in the newspaper. Those who might have turned off their televisions when the networks showed footage of one of King's speeches or the March on Washington were still aware of the struggle for civil rights because of Robinson. Even before King emerged as the movement's public spokesman, the struggle played out every summer day for a decade in Dodgers box scores—first with Robinson, then with Newcombe and Campanella, and before long with the rest of Major League Baseball.

"In 1947, black and handsome, athletically gifted but also cool and astute in his play, stoically enduring insult and injury, Robinson had revolutionized the image of the black man in America," Arnold Rampersad wrote in his book *Jackie Robinson*. "He had supplanted the immensely popular image projected during World War II by Joe Louis, that of the physically powerful but uneducated, perhaps even weak-witted, black man uplifted by humility and patriotism—a modern African American version of the noble savage."

Or, as Professor Richard Zamoff put it to me, "Babe Ruth changed baseball. Jackie Robinson changed America."

> *"My father used Jackie Robinson as a model for me when I was a kid growing up. My senior year at Yale, I met Jackie. I'd heard that he ate peanuts with the shells on, so for about twelve years I'd done the same. I asked him if that was true, and he told me he didn't eat them that way. Oh, well. I'd gotten to like the taste by then, so I still eat them with the shell on."*
>
> CALVIN HILL
> FORMER NFL STAR

* * *

Before we go any further, let's settle on a working definition of "influence." Why? Because it can mean a lot of things—some good, some bad. A drug dealer might exert influence over young men in an urban neighborhood, or a bully might have influence in a playground, or an abusive father might influence his children. But those aren't the kind of influences that caused me to write this book, and they definitely aren't the kind of influences that Jackie Robinson displayed.

So . . . when I say "influence," what do I mean? Well, as Andy Stanley, the pastor of North Point Church in Atlanta, Georgia, has said, "Influence is a funny thing. It's hard to define. It is even hard to describe it." But, fortunately, Pastor Stanley is a sharp man, and he does a pretty good job of pinning down a working definition:

> *"I don't know any other way to lead but by example."*
>
> DON SHULA
> FORMER NFL COACH

"It is the alignment between convictions and behavior that makes a person's life persuasive," he says. "The phrase that best captures this dynamic is 'moral authority.' Moral authority is the credibility you earn by walking your talk. It is the relationship other people perceive between what you say and what you do, between who you claim to be and who you are."

OK. If we're going to stick with Pastor Stanley's definition, then it's hard to imagine someone who has had more influence than Jackie Robinson. Think about it. Persuasive? By his words and actions on and off the baseball diamond, Jackie persuaded much of the United States that blacks were the equals of whites—not just in sports, but in their humanness. Credibility? If breaking baseball's color barrier and doing it so courageously didn't give him credibility, then his work in the civil-rights movement during and after his baseball career certainly did. And as for who Jackie Robinson claimed to be and who he was, well, there was no difference between the two. Who he claimed to be was exactly who he was. As the saying goes, "What you see is what you get."

All these years after his father, Dodgers shortstop Pee Wee Reese, put his arm around Jackie in a public symbol of loyalty and solidarity, Mark Reese talked to me about how Pee Wee grew up in Louisville, Kentucky, in a tightly segregated city. Segregation was all Pee Wee knew in his youth. "Dad was probably closer to the 'Dixie Walker thought process' than people realized," Mark told me. "But Jackie impressed my dad by the way he conducted himself and the tremendous courage he showed. Dad saw something in this man that was unusual, and that's why he stood up for Jackie. The other players saw what Jackie had in the way of intelligence and class, and that's why they made a quick turnaround, as well."

It wasn't just the players who turned around. No matter how they felt about blacks during that difficult, complex time, the people Robinson came in contact with routinely came away from the encounter marveling at him. During Robinson's first spring training at Daytona Beach, before he began his season with the Montreal Royals, his manager, Clay Hopper, and Branch Rickey sat watching a morning game together. Robinson made a great defensive play at first base, diving to his left for a ground ball and starting a double play, and Rickey said, "Clay, I haven't seen a play to beat that in years! Where are you going to go to see a fellow who can make that play?" But when Robinson made another terrific play later in the game, Hopper grabbed Rickey by the lapels of his coat and said, "Mr. Rickey, do you really believe that a *nigger* is a human being?"

> *"Tell me, and I'll forget; show me, and I may remember; involve me, and I'll understand."*
>
> CHINESE PROVERB

Months went by, and in the first week of October, after Montreal had won the International League pennant and Hopper had spent an entire season managing Robinson, Hopper knocked on the door to Rickey's office. When Rickey let him in, Hopper said, "You remember when we talked about Jackie Robinson in spring training? Well, I want to tell you something. I think that he'll make your club. But if he doesn't, I'd like to have him back. He's not only a great player, he's a great gentleman."

Ed Charles, an African American and third baseman with the Kansas City Royals and the New York Mets, was thirteen years old when Robinson signed to play with the Montreal Royals. When he learned that the Royals were coming to Daytona Beach, Florida, for spring training, he and his friends couldn't wait to watch him play.

"I was like a little boy waiting for Christmas and Santa Claus to see what kind of toys he was going to bring us," Charles once said. "We were waiting on Jackie, because this was the first time we were going to have any kind of socialization of the races in the Deep South, and if he succeeded, he was going to open the door to blacks as well as other minorities in baseball.

> *"The young are moved by greatness. They are inspired by it. Children need heroes. They need them to lift life, to suggest a future you can be hungry for."*
>
> PEGGY NOONAN
> AUTHOR

"That Jackie Robinson had signed and was coming down here, I looked at that and said, 'OK, maybe now we're going to begin to start living the American dream like the rest of the citizens, maybe now we're going to make some headway to right what I had seen to be these types of wrongs, the inhuman treatment of our people, the hardships on blacks.' And it gave me a little hope that perhaps we were on the right track as far as living the type of American dream, this freedom of opportunity we were supposed to have in this country."

Of course, Robinson didn't merely influence the people he met. As with any star athlete, there were millions of little boys—tuning in on their radios, watching on their televisions, streaming into Ebbets Field and the other National League ballparks—who wanted to emulate Jackie on the diamond. Regardless of his skin color, Robinson was *sui generis*—completely unlike any ballplayer before him, with his own unique style and flair. He could beat you in any number of ways: a home run, a great defensive play, a bunt, a stolen base. And the best part of his uniqueness was that it wasn't fakery. It was just him, the way he was.

> *"Example is the school of mankind, and they will learn at no other."*
>
> EDMUND BURKE
> POLITICAL PHILOSOPHER

"I grew up in Brooklyn, and Jackie Robinson was my hero, and not because he was black," sports broadcaster Spencer Ross told me. "It was because I loved him as a player."

Before he coached the Detroit Pistons to the 2004 NBA championship,

Larry Brown confessed to me just how much Jackie Robinson had meant to him as a kid growing up in Brooklyn. During Brown's six years coaching the Philadelphia 76ers, his combination to open the gate to the parking lot at the team's practice facility was 4–2—Jackie's uniform number.

Former Major-Leaguer Jim Brady never got the chance to play against him, but as a child Brady watched Robinson, as a Montreal Royal, play against the Jersey Giants in Brady's hometown of Jersey City.

"He literally terrorized pitchers and catchers when he'd get on base," Brady told me. "His mere presence on any base distracted a pitcher, causing him to lose composure and focus. In short, his daring, aggressive and fearless base running made him a force. Those who respected and loved him as childhood fans and sandlot players would imitate his baseball style by using thicker bats, running pigeon-toed, drag-bunting and taking larger-than-normal leads off of first base. What an exciting athlete and human being he was."

A friend of mine, a businessman in Orlando named Harris Rosen, grew up in New York City and was one of those childhood fans of whom Brady spoke. When Harris was seven years old, his parents started to worry about him because he walked in such an odd way—pigeon-toed, actually. So they took him to an orthopedic specialist.

After he examined Harris's feet closely, the doctor asked Mr. and Mrs. Rosen to leave the room.

> "What you do speaks so loudly that I cannot hear what you say."
>
> RALPH WALDO EMERSON
> POET

"Why are you walking like you are?" the doctor asked.

"Because," Harris said, "I want to be like Jackie Robinson."

The doctor couldn't help but laugh. "The reason I asked," he said, "is because I've been treating a lot of boys with the same problem as you!"

There is a lesson to be learned from these boys-turned-men who emulated and admired Robinson. You never know who is watching you. You never know who you might be influencing at any time, no matter who you are, no matter what you do. Joe DiMaggio, the great Yankee center fielder, was once asked why he always did his best to move so gracefully in the outfield, to never show any outward displays of anger during a game. In response, DiMaggio said that at every game there was always someone who was seeing him play for the first time, so he always wanted to be at his best for that person.

That principle applies to every one of us. It would be a mistake to think that you have to possess the stature of someone like Jackie Robinson—a big-league ballplayer, an astronaut, a famous entertainer— to have a positive influence on the people around you. Nothing could be further from the truth. Think of the movie *It's a Wonderful Life*. The character of George Bailey, played by Jimmy Stewart, has no idea how he has touched so many people in his little town of Bedford Falls until an angel comes along to show him. But just because George didn't know he was so loved by his friends and family didn't mean that he wasn't loved. Broadcaster Joan Lunden carries around a chain e-mail in her wallet that illustrates this point perfectly:

> *"Don't expect a role model to come along all by him or herself. There are plenty of classy people out there who want to help. Instead of waiting for someone to take you under their wing, go out there and find a good wing to climb under."*
>
> DAVE THOMAS
> FOUNDER OF WENDY'S RESTAURANT

- Name the five wealthiest people in the world.
- Name the last five Heisman Trophy winners.
- Name the last five winners of the Miss America contest.
- Name ten people who have won the Nobel or Pulitzer Prize.
- Name the last dozen Academy Award winners for best actor or actress.
- Name the last decade's worth of World Series winners.

How did you do?

The point is . . . none of us remembers the headlines of yesterday. These are no second-rate achievers. They are the best in their fields, but the applause dies. Awards tarnish. Achievements are forgotten. Accolades and certificates are buried with their owners.

Here's another one. See how you do on this one.

- List a few teachers who aided your journey through school.
- Name three friends who have helped you through a difficult time.

- Name five people who have taught you something worthwhile.
- Think of a few people who have made you feel appreciated and special.
- Think of five people you enjoy spending time with. Name a half-dozen heroes whose stories have inspired you.

Easier?

Of course. It is through everyday acts that we touch people most deeply, and it is those everyday acts that too often pass in and out of our memories—lending a friend a couple of bucks, complimenting a coworker for a job well done, smiling at someone who is having a rough day. We forget about them, and we never realize the help we have given and care we have shown to someone. President John Quincy Adams once said, "The influence of each human being on others, in this life, is a kind of immortality." Sure, every boy who likes sports wants to dunk like Michael Jordan, and every girl wants to score goals like Mia Hamm. But the simple acts are what often form the most lasting impressions.

Joe Carrieri, a former Yankee batboy, interacted with Robinson during the several World Series in which the Yankees and Dodgers met. Often, Robinson would tell him, "Be persistent. Don't ever give up. That's been the secret of my success."

> "How often do we come in contact with men and women in whose presence we may dwell only for a short time, but we can never look upon their countenances or be in any way associated with them without being made better or lifted up?"
>
> BOOKER T. WASHINGTON
> CIVIL RIGHTS LEADER

"Jackie Robinson was one of many great ballplayers who, in my seven years with the Yankees, helped ease my transition to the adult world," Carrieri once wrote. His "mere presence on the field represented a sea of change in the great American pastime. In the world I grew up in, there were few people of color. To me, integration meant that Irish kids and Italian kids were attending the same parochial school for the first time."

Robert C. Cope was a twelve-year-old boy in 1965, the year his entire Little League team, the Wilco Pirates, piled into a bus and drove from Gary, Indiana, to Comiskey Park in Chicago for a big-league game on a sunny Saturday afternoon. When the team got to Comiskey, Cope, Coach Bill Ronchi and several of Cope's teammates strolled around the park in search of players who might sign a few autographs. Near a locker room, Cope noticed an NBC sign—the network was broadcasting the game as its "Game of the Week"—and he noticed something else. He noticed a man walking along a catwalk into the locker room. He noticed Jackie Robinson, there to work the game for NBC.

Cope pleaded with Ronchi to find a way for the team to meet Robinson. So the coach approached an usher and whispered in his ear, and the usher disappeared into the locker room. Five minutes later,

> *"Live in such a way that you would not be ashamed to sell your parrot to the town gossip."*
>
> WILL ROGERS
> HUMORIST

Robinson emerged from the locker room, walked across the catwalk and met Cope and his teammates. The boys tore a cardboard drink holder into little pieces so that Robinson could sign them. And he did. Every one.

"I suppose the other kids were disappointed at getting an autograph from an older black man with gray hair," Cope told me. "To tell you the truth, I don't think they even knew who he was. But I did. I can still see him to this day, signing the pieces of paper with his own ballpoint pen. I even reached up and touched his blue NBC blazer. I was truly thrilled. Even in 1965, I knew this was a very special moment."

How long could it have taken for Robinson to sign those autographs? Ten minutes? Twenty? How long could it have taken him to give Robert Cope a memory that would last a lifetime? How many special moments have those teachers, those mentors and those friends who are referenced in Joan Lunden's favorite e-mail created for children? How easy is it to have a positive influence on someone? Sometimes, all it takes is a matter of minutes: A handshake. A "How are you?" A "What can I do to help?"

Sometimes, you just have to be you. You just have to do what you always do.

"The main reason I play football," Curtis Martin, the New York Jets' star running back, once said, "is to light up the face of a sick child or someone less fortunate, for that makes my heart sing. If football were just for the money and the fame, I believe, in my heart, that I wouldn't play. I go through the pain on the field so that I can somewhat relieve another person's pain off it."

> *"To know what people really think, pay regard to what they do rather than what they say."*
>
> RENÉ DESCARTES
> PHILOSOPHER

As an executive in the NBA, I see many of our league's players—multimillionaires who often come from impoverished backgrounds—forgetting how much impact and influence they can have on young people. It's as if they forget that these children and teenagers look up to them, emulate them, and watch what they do and how they do it. I once read a newspaper article about Rasheed Wallace, now of the Detroit Pistons. The column described how a boy approached Wallace at an airport and asked him for an autograph. Wallace snubbed him, and the boy's mother told him, "You broke my boy's heart."

The columnist argued that since Wallace was such a "sullen jerk," a person with "no grace, no class, no empathy," no one should even bother approaching him for an autograph ever again. Since Wallace won't grow up, the columnist wrote, his fans have to. They have to understand who Wallace is, accept that he's not a particularly charitable person, and move on. Well, I'm too much of an optimist and an idealist to surrender just yet, to argue that our children should stop looking for heroes among professional athletes because professional athletes aren't capable of being heroes, and I'd like to share an anecdote that, I think, justifies my position.

> *"I was nine years old, and, when the game was over, I rushed over with a scrap of paper and beseeched Phil Ruzzuto to sign it. He did, gave it back and smiled. I lost the paper, but I still have the smile."*
>
> PAT JORDAN
> AUTHOR

In May 1997, my team, the Orlando Magic, and our star player, Anfernee "Penny" Hardaway, were in the midst of a pretty rough time. The previous season, 1995–96, we had won sixty games, finishing first in the Atlantic Division, and had advanced to the Eastern Conference Finals, where we were swept in four games by the Chicago Bulls. (Losing to the Bulls was hardly an embarrassment, though. In Michael Jordan's first full season back after his brief retirement, Chicago had won an NBA-record seventy-two games. Seventy-two games!)

Anyway, the 1996–97 season wasn't quite as fun as the 1995–96 season. We had lost our big man in the middle, Shaquille O'Neal, to the Los Angeles Lakers. Penny had been hurt for a good portion of the regular season; he played in only fifty-nine games, and our record was only 45–37. Finally, we lost in the first round of the play-offs to the Miami Heat. Needless to say, we were all disappointed.

So you can imagine my pleasure as I sat in my office one day after the season ended and read a letter dated May 27, 1997, from one Mr. John Morris. His letter said:

Dear Mr. Williams:

Like many Orlando Magic fans, I read the sports pages on a regular basis. As a result, some of the things put in print by columnists and fans sometimes amuse, but other times irritate me, especially when they are inaccurate. Some of these comments have been directed toward Penny Hardaway. You, as well as the entire Magic organization, need to know of a recent incident that occurred involving Penny.

Each year, I serve as committee chairman for a chairman for a golf tournament known as the Pastor's Masters, that raises money for our church, Faith Lutheran Church, located in Pine Hills. The funds are used for youth programs for our kids and the kids of surrounding communities.

Because of the socioeconomic factors in the area, we strive to use this money in the best way possible. For example, every other year there is a National Christian Youth Gathering for kids across the country. This summer's event will be held in New Orleans. Registration for the gathering is $275 per child. Many of the parents would be unable to afford this amount, so the funds from the tournament will subsidize the cost, and the actual cost for the parents will be $50.

We hold this tournament each year at Metro West Country Club. On May 10, we were about to raise $4,700, which was our best result in the six years we have been organizing this event. Coincidentally, Penny also happened to be playing there that morning. Although he teed off prior to our event's getting started, everyone knew he was out on the course, which created a predictable amount of excitement, particularly among our youth volunteers; therefore, we instructed the kids to behave themselves and to respect Penny's privacy if they encountered him while out on the course.

Well, Pat, it happened. One of our foursomes (four dads and their "caddies," their children) was waiting to tee off when Penny and his group were coming off their green on a distant hole. Although definitely out of his way to the next hole, Penny, when he spotted the kids, went out of his way to drive his cart up to our foursome, completely unsolicited, to spend a few minutes to talk to the youth. Our group was flabbergasted, and the impact he made on the children was immeasurable. One of the Dads talked my ear off for twenty-three minutes afterward, and his young daughter received the thrill of her young life. What an act of caring and class!

I could have addressed this letter to Penny; however, I decided to write to you instead because you and the organization need to know what one of your players, **your star player,** is doing to make a difference in the community and the random act of kindness he committed. Please thank him, for me, on bchalf of the Faith Lutheran Church. This is one Magic fan who hopes Penny stays in Orlando for a long, long time.

> *"My life is my message."*
>
> MAHATMA GHANDI
> POLITICAL LEADER AND PHILOSOPHER

I have to say, that letter made my day. I was proud of Penny, and as I look back on Mr. Morris's letter, I can't help but think Jackie Robinson would have done exactly what Penny did.

* * *

There may be no way to quantify Robinson's early influence on blacks, baseball and society. How do you measure something like that? How do you measure the impact one man, particularly Jackie Robinson, has on the people around him?

Perhaps these words from Rachel Robinson answer the question: "The day Jackie finished the season in Montreal, Sam Malton in the *Pittsburgh Courier* wrote a story saying it was the first time a mob had chased a Negro to love him instead of to kill him. And it literally happened. He was running because he had to catch a plane, and fans were chasing him down the street."

Perhaps you need to picture the scene that would play out at ballpark after ballpark whenever the Dodgers were in town: crowds of blacks filling the parking lots, eating their lunches or dinners. They might have ridden the train up from the South, or walked to the park from their neighborhoods. They carried picnic baskets. The men wore straw hats. The women dressed as if it were Easter. "When Jackie Robinson and the Dodgers came to Cincinnati," former Reds player Chuck Harmon told me, "it was like a holiday in town. That was instrumental in breaking down many barriers in racial matters. With those huge crowds going to Cincinnati to see Jackie and the Dodgers, the restaurants and hotels finally had to break down and admit blacks. They didn't want to miss out on all that green. Money talks, you know."

As Harmon suggested, attendance soared whenever and wherever Jackie played. For instance, in Robinson's first season, the Dodgers drew a National League–record 1,807,526 fans to Ebbets Field and drew 1,863,542 fans on the road.

That season was the nation's first real chance to see Robinson in person—and it was his first real chance

> "I talk and talk, and I haven't taught people, in fifty years, what my father taught, by example, in one week."
>
> FORMER NEW YORK GOVERNOR MARIO CUOMO

to influence not only blacks, but whites, too. The Dodgers traveled to St. Louis that summer to play the Cardinals, and a teenaged boy from Commerce, Oklahoma, accompanied by his father and his best friend, drove all night in the family LaSalle to Sportsman's Park to see one of the games. They got to the park at 8 A.M., and they saw thousands of blacks lined up around the park, waiting for the chance to buy tickets to the game.

> *"Perhaps the most important element of moral training, in a child's life, is the example parents set themselves. As Aesop explained it, a mother crab was scurrying across the sand, with her son following in her tracks. The mother chastised her child, saying, 'Stop walking sideways. It's much more becoming to stroll straight ahead.' The young crab replied, 'I will, Mother, just as soon as I see you showing me how.' You have to walk it like you talk it."*
>
> BILL BENNETT
> AUTHOR AND SPEAKER

That teenager was Mickey Mantle. Seeing that crowd "was a completely new experience for Mickey," author Tony Castro wrote. "Race relations and integration were not everyday topics in Commerce."

Gene Verble, a Major-Leaguer from Robinson's era, was playing for the minor league Atlanta Crackers when he watched an exhibition game in 1950 that featured the Dodgers. "What a sight!" he told me. "There were 12,000 black fans in the outfield stands and 12,000 white fans in the grandstand."

One day during Robinson's rookie season, 35,000 settled into the stands at Wrigley Field in Chicago, and Harold Parrott, who served for years as the Dodgers' traveling secretary, estimated that "20,000 of them must have been black, come to hail their trailblazer." Dodgers first baseman Gil Hodges looked toward the bleachers and asked Robinson: "All your friends in on passes you left for 'em, Jack?"

Even at his career's end, when he refused to play for the Giants in 1957 and retired from baseball, Robinson held great cachet with the public.

> *"Without heroes, we are all plain people and don't know how far we can go."*
>
> BERNARD MALAMUD
> AUTHOR

Buzzie Bavasi, the longtime Dodgers executive, wrote that "if Jackie had elected to play for the Giants, the club might not have moved from New York to San Francisco. That's how much Robinson would have helped them at the gate."

While Robinson was pulling black fans to Dodgers games, however, he was pulling them away from the Negro Leagues. Because Robinson's debut was so successful, scouts were now flooding the Negro Leagues, looking for the next big fish to catch. More importantly, now that a black had broken into the big leagues and was earning respect among the white establishment of Major League Baseball, a separate league for black players was no longer necessary—not for practical reasons, and not for philosophical reasons. As sportswriter Sam Lacy put it, "After Jackie, the Negro Leagues [became] a symbol I couldn't live with anymore."

"This was the first real step toward integration," Negro League great and Hall of Famer Buck O'Neil once wrote. "The scouts were there, looking for the next Jackie Robinson, and that inspired us. And so now we were being discovered yet again."

And so it was that Negro League teams began selling off their best players in a last-ditch attempt to keep themselves afloat. For $15,000, the New York Giants bought an eighteen-year-old center fielder named Willie Mays from the Birmingham Black Barons. The Milwaukee Braves bought Henry Aaron from Indianapolis; the Cubs got Ernie Banks from the Kansas City Monarchs. By 1954—the year Mays won his first National League MVP award and the Giants beat the Cleveland Indians in the World Series—the Negro Leagues were gone, a tangible symbol of segregation done away with because of one man. Because of Jackie Robinson.

Has there ever been another baseball player who caused an entire league to fold? Such was Robinson's power, his effect on an entire sport and an entire society.

Now *that's* influence. By any definition.

* * *

As I close this chapter, it is vital to remember something about the quality of influence: at its core, influence is a two-way street. As much as we might want to influence someone, to have a positive effect on other lives, those people must be willing to be influenced. They must be open to the possibility of learning, of growing, of broadening themselves. If

> *"The only rational way of educating is to be an example."*
> ALBERT EINSTEIN

those people aren't so willing, aren't so open, it won't matter if they meet a

Jackie Robinson. Because of their nearsightedness, they will derive nothing from the encounter.

For example, before Game Two of the 1972 World Series between the Oakland A's and the Cincinnati Reds, Bowie Kuhn, then the commissioner of Major League Baseball, arranged a tribute for Robinson to celebrate the twenty-fifth anniversary of his Dodgers debut. His diabetes and his blindness worsening, Jackie died only days after the ceremony, but still he participated in the day's festivities.

"Philadelphia has a black mayor now, a black superintendent of schools. Only the color of money decides where a person stays while visiting. If you don't know that Jack Roosevelt Robinson, and the way he played the game, helped make that possible, then you don't understand the history of baseball or the history of this nation."

STAN HOCHMAN
PHILADELPHIA DAILY NEWS
SPORTS COLUMNIST IN 1987

Before the game, he was led into the A's clubhouse. According to former Dodgers broadcaster Red Barber, who was the master of ceremonies at the event, it was assumed that Oakland's black players would want to meet Robinson, the man who had paved their way into baseball.

"I heard," Barber once wrote, "that the Oakland black players paid no attention, were not interested in coming over to greet him, and Jackie was quietly led away. It is terrible when human beings forget their blessings and fail to say thank you."

The episode serves as a reminder that we shouldn't miss an opportunity to draw on another—someone older, someone wiser—for assistance, for just a word that might shape us in some way. In truth, we're never alone in anything we do or become.

Someone, some time along the way, has helped us. Maybe by teaching us something new. Or by taking a chance and hiring us for a new job. Or by serving as a symbol of strength and courage by suiting up every day and playing baseball as hard as he could. We are all influenced, and we all can influence others, in the best of ways. We shouldn't let those moments pass us by.

In his autobiography, *Cosell,* famed sports broadcaster Howard Cosell

described a touching scene he witnessed at Gil Hodges's funeral.
Robinson struggled to climb the
steps of the church. He held onto the
arm of Ralph Branca, his onetime
teammate with the Dodgers. "For a
fleeting moment," Cosell wrote, his
life as a young adult flashed through

> *"Influence is like a savings
> account. The less you use it,
> the more you've got."*
>
> ANDREW YOUNG
> CIVIL RIGHTS LEADER

his mind, and he remembered the importance and influence of Jackie
Robinson. He remembered "an age when baseball . . . symbolized to all the
world that America could cope with its most terrible of problems—
the problem of race.

"This was what Jackie Robinson symbolized. He helped inspire the
image that this nation was capable of racial amity instead of racial anguish,
and that was the best thing that ever happened to baseball."

And maybe to all of America, too.

Chapter Three

The Pursuit of Victory

I can't tell the difference between dark and light skin. I'm inter-
ested enough to know the likes and dislikes of men, but it never
occurred to me that it was necessary to select a team because of
race, creed or color. I'll go down on that. I'm out to win a
pennant.

—Branch Rickey

On March 14, 2003, I returned to Philadelphia to celebrate the twentieth anniversary of my greatest professional triumph to date. The 76ers
were playing the Portland Trailblazers that night, and at halftime of the
game, the Sixers were honoring their 1983 NBA Championship team, the
last of the city's four major sports teams to win a title.

What a glorious night! I was the general manager of the Sixers in '83,
and it was wonderful to see all the coaches and players and to relive that
season for a few moments. First, there was a reception before the game for
the team, and we all got to catch up: Coach Billy Cunningham and Julius
Erving and Moses Malone and Bobby Jones and everyone who made the
championship possible. There were so many hugs and hellos and fond
memories, I walked around the room with a silly little smile on my face. I
was just so happy to see everyone. At halftime of the game, they dimmed

the lights of the First Union Center and introduced each of us one by one. The building was filled with people, and they stood and cheered for us until all anyone could hear was just one long, loud sound. It was a powerful, emotional event, and it touched all of us.

Then, just as the night was ending, a tiny moment took place that I'll remember forever. The team was finishing a bus ride from the arena to our hotel, and as the bus pulled up, Clint Richardson turned toward me. Clint was the third guard on the '83 Sixers, behind point guard Mo Cheeks and shooting guard Andrew Toney, but he was essential to our success. He was a terrific defensive player, and he gave us a boost on offense every time he entered a game. Plus, he's a sweet person, still wide-eyed and almost innocent after all this time.

"I'm sure glad we won," he said to me. "They wouldn't have had this event if we hadn't, you know."

Now, I'm sure that, at first reading, Clint's words that night seem obvious and even childlike. However, he touched on a pretty profound concept. Winning is important in life, and giving everything you have in the pursuit of winning is a noble, sometimes necessary goal. Only by putting all of yourself into that pursuit, and then succeeding, can you truly taste how sweet life can be. Clint was right. They wouldn't have held that event for us if we hadn't won, because second place is never as sweet as first.

And Jackie Robinson knew that truth well.

"It kills me to lose," he once said. "If I'm a troublemaker—and I don't think that my temper makes me one—then it's because I can't stand losing."

I was talking on the telephone one

> *"The first step toward victory is to position your idea so that your victory is everyone's victory."*
>
> MICHAEL WARSHAW
> AUTHOR

> *"Jackie Robinson was a great man. He was polite and friendly, but he'd do anything to beat you. He'd get on base, and the other team knew he was going and still couldn't stop him. I respected him as a man and a leader."*
>
> PAUL MINNER
> FORMER MAJOR-LEAGUE PITCHER

day with Rachel Robinson about Jackie's competitive nature, and she said something that showed how ingrained in him the need to win was.

"I'd run into some of his boyhood friends," she told me, "and years later they'd remember how Jackie had beaten them in marbles. He just had to win at everything. He was an intense competitor, but it was not to hurt or damage someone. He was striving to be the best."

It is hard to conceive of someone—be it a professional athlete, a great poker player or anyone at all—who was more competitive than Robinson. "Jackie Robinson was not the best player I ever saw," former Dodgers executive Buzzie Bavasi once said, "but he was the greatest competitor. He could beat you in so many ways. . . . As a competitor, he was without equal. The best I have ever seen."

There are so many anecdotes of what Robinson did in the pursuit of victory, so many I-never-saw-that-before stories, that it's difficult to cat-

> *"Jackie teaches all of us you have to get in and do what you have to do to be successful. The results will be worth it. I see so many young men in my neighborhood who don't want to do anything. Not working is almost a status symbol. They have no motivation. That's not the way we were raised."*
>
> RAYMOND ISUM
> RACHEL ROBINSON'S BROTHER

alog them. Everyone who played with him, played against him or watched him play seems to have one, a tale of how Jackie Robinson's competitiveness, his abhorrence of losing, spurred him to another fantastic athletic feat. It is plain to see why Branch Rickey chose Robinson for his "great experiment" in the first place. Take a moment and go back to the quote with which I began this chapter. "I'm out to win a pennant," Rickey said. So was Robinson. Every day. Every year. And nothing would get in his way.

In compiling the research for this book, I spoke with hundreds of ballplayers, and almost every one testified to Robinson's all-consuming desire to win. When I spoke to former pitcher, pitching coach and manager Roger Craig, I could hear the awe in his voice.

> *"There's nothing more fun than winning."*
>
> DON ZIMMER
> MAJOR-LEAGUE PLAYER, MANAGER AND COACH

"I have never seen a competitor like Jackie," Roger told me. "After the game was over, you could not talk to him. It was like he was still in the game. Everything he had in him had been drained out of him."

Now, if we could live our lives like that, finish every day totally drained, knowing we had done our very best and given everything we had in everything we had done, wouldn't that be something special?

* * *

It's particularly startling how many of the stories I collected involve Robinson stealing home, the most daring feat in baseball—so daring that, nowadays, no one tries it. Not the way Robinson did it. He stole home nineteen times in his career.

Listen, for instance, to Andy Pafko, the former center fielder for the Chicago Cubs: "One day at Wrigley Field, Jackie gets on first base. Bob Rush is the Cubs' pitcher. He had a big motion, so on the first pitch Robinson steals second. On the next pitch, he steals third. I go to the mound and say, 'Bob, you've got to be careful or he'll go home on you.' I mean, I just got back to my position, and, boom, Jackie is stealing home. He's safe. Three pitches and the Dodgers have a run—the most amazing sight I ever saw in baseball."

In fact, Robinson made such a habit of stealing bases off Rush that former Cub Hank Sauer once said, "Why don't we just put Robinson on

> *"Competition is easier to accept if you realize it is not an act of aggression or abrasion. I've worked with my best friends in direct competition. Whatever you want in life, other people are going to want it, too. Believe in yourself enough to accept the idea that you have an equal right to it."*
>
> DIANE SAWYER
> TELEVISION JOURNALIST

> *"The winning mentality is partly optimism, but, mostly, it's a combination of focus, pride, competitive anger, relentlessness, hardness, fitness and courage. . . . This type of mentality is not about your skills or tactics. What it comes down to is intense desire."*
>
> —ANSON DORRANCE, UNIVERSITY OF NORTH CAROLINA WOMEN'S SOCCER COACH

third base and get it over with?"

"The Pirates feared him," former Pittsburgh pitcher Bob Friend told me. "You could be in Ebbets Field and be up by five or six runs and you never felt safe. He stole home on me twice. In Pittsburgh, he timed my windup and beat the pitch. Then, at Brooklyn, I went into the stretch. He broke for the plate and still got there."

There's a famous black-and-white highlight from Game One of the 1955 World Series—the only Series that Robinson and the Brooklyn Dodgers ever won—that shows Robinson stealing home against the Yankees and catcher Yogi Berra. Based on the footage, it appears Robinson is out, and Berra to this day tells anyone who asks, "He's out—and he's still out." It was perhaps Robinson's most memorable steal against Berra, but not his only one. Robinson stole bases so frequently against Berra in the 1947 World Series that Berra alternated between catching and playing the outfield the following season, so skeptical were the Yankees of his ability behind the plate.

In 1955, Robinson was nearing the end of his career, and the Yankees actually won Game One of that Series, but neither of those facts

In December 1997, as one stop on a book tour for The Magic of Teamwork, *I visited my alma mater, Wake Forest University, and spoke to the school's student-athletes and coaches. Jim Caldwell, who was Wake's football coach at the time, attended, and I chatted with him after my speech.*

During our conversation, I mentioned that having Florida State in the ACC had messed up the entire scene in the conference because the Seminoles were so dominant. "Not at all," Jim said. "Florida State is the best thing that has happened to ACC football. The competition they provide has forced all the other schools to push their programs to a higher level. The brand of football is better because Florida State has forced us up to its level."

"Of course the game is rigged. Don't let that stop you. If you don't play, you can't win."

ROBERT HEINLEIN
AUTHOR

matters to Berra. To him, that steal of home only reflected Robinson's desire to spark his team. "That was Jackie," Yogi told me. "He hated to lose. He was just one heck of a competitor. He did more to change the course of a game than anyone I ever played against."

But it wasn't just by stealing home that Robinson displayed how competitive he was. He showed his competitiveness every time he played golf, played hearts, played checkers.

> "You have to learn to win without bragging and lose without excuses."
>
> EDDIE ROBINSON
> FOOTBALL COACH

During an exhibition game in Japan, Robinson complained to Jocko Conlan, one of the best-known and most well-respected umpires of Robinson's era, because Conlan called an overmatched Japanese hitter safe on a grounder to short when the hitter was clearly out. "It was the only time in my career that I ever called a man safe when I knew he was out," Conlan once said. "He was such a fine little fellow." Every other Dodger on the field knew why Conlan had called the hitter safe, yet Robinson yelled at Conlan so vehemently that Conlan threw him out of the game. An *exhibition game.*

But that was Robinson. On the baseball field, he would do almost anything to win, would use his brain and his mouth and his feet in ways other players couldn't or wouldn't, and he respected only those who shared his passion.

> "Jackie Robinson was the best baseball player I've ever seen because he could win a game so many different ways—with a single or a home run, with an inning-ending catch, with a stolen base or by rattling the pitcher into a balk, or sometimes with his competitive fire that inspired his teammates."
>
> DAVE ANDERSON
> SPORTS COLUMNIST, *NEW YORK TIMES*

Against the Boston Braves one day, Robinson was on third in a tie game with less than two outs when Duke Snider laid down a bunt toward Braves third baseman Eddie Matthews. Robinson neither broke for home nor retreated to the bag. He followed Matthews down the line, staying one step behind the third baseman. When Matthews fielded the ball, he glanced back at Robinson, who froze. When Matthews threw to first, Robinson took off for home, scoring the winning run.

"Just the play you make in that situation," Robinson told Roger Kahn after the game. "As long as I'm a step behind him, he can't tag me. He can't reach that far. And he can't catch me. I'm quicker than he is. So he can do two things. He can hold the ball. Then I stay at third and Duke is safe at first. Or he can throw. Then I go home. But there's no way they can get an out without giving up the winning run."

Such a play takes incredible athleticism, certainly. It also takes a sharp baseball mind to evaluate the situation so quickly and understand the best base running strategy. But most of all, it requires a desire to score that crucial run—a desire that is so strong, it supercedes the risk of failing and making the final out.

"He was a living flame," sportswriter Frank Graham Jr. told me. "Whenever the Dodgers were lagging, Jackie would do something to rouse the team. He would steal home, lay down a bunt, argue with an umpire."

No opponents stoked that fire within Robinson the way the Yankees and the New York Giants did. Year after year, the Giants and Dodgers battled for the National League pennant, and in those years the Dodgers won, they challenged the Yankees in the World Series. These were meaningful games, and they often featured Robinson at his most competitive and most creative.

Dodgers pitcher Clyde King once had to face Willie Mays in the top of the ninth inning during a game at Ebbets Field. Brooklyn was up a run with runners at first and third. There were two outs. King got two strikes on Mays, and Robinson approached the mound from second base.

> "I'm convinced the only thing that separates champions is the individual's competitive drive. The people who survive and then flourish are the ones who love to compete . . . maybe even live to compete."
>
> JOE MONTANA
> NFL GREAT

"Clyde," Jackie said, "try your quick pitch on this guy."

So that's what King did. He came set, and when Mays tapped the plate with his bat, King quick-pitched and threw a called third strike.

"I wasn't ready!" Mays screamed.

"Sorry," the umpire replied, "but you were in the batter's box, and there was no time-out called, so the pitch is legal."

In the clubhouse, Robinson said to King: "This tells me that you and I have something in common. We'll do anything to win a game, as long as it's legal and within the rules."

> *"The first biological lesson of history is that life is competition. Competition is not only the life of trade, it is the trade of life."*
> HISTORIANS WILL AND ARIEL DURANT

Jack Lang, a former sportswriter for the *Long Island Press,* told me when Jim Hearn, a pitcher for the New York Giants, was on the verge of winning the Jimmy Burns Golf Tournament in Miami, he missed a putt on the eighteenth hole and lost the tournament. Robinson learned about the missed putt, and one day he used it to his advantage.

"The Giants were at Ebbets Field," Lang said. "It's extra innings. Hearn has pitched the whole game for the Giants. Jackie leads off with a walk. He steals second. The throw goes into center field, and Jackie ends up on third. He starts dancing off third, and he's yelling at Hearn, 'You're going to blow this game like you blew that putt.'

"Hearn loses his focus, balks, and the game is over."

There is perhaps no better example of Robinson's will to win than his performance on September 30, 1951, in the heat of the most famous pennant race in Major League Baseball history. Though the Dodgers had built a thirteen-and-a-half-game lead by early August, the Giants charged back over the season's final two months to catch

> *"I have been up against tough competition all my life. I wouldn't know how to get along without it."*
> WALT DISNEY

them. Each team had a 95–58 record entering the season's last day, and with the Dodgers trailing the Phillies in the sixth inning in Philadelphia, 8–5, Robinson looked at the scoreboard in Shibe Park and noticed that the Giants had beaten the Boston Braves, 3–2, to take a half-game lead in the National League.

Playing second base, Jackie already had committed an error in the game that led to two runs for the Phillies, and in his two at bats he had grounded into a double play and taken a called third strike. But in the fifth inning, he had tripled and scored to cut the Phillies' lead to 6–5, and in the eighth, the Dodgers scored three runs to tie the game at 8.

The game went to the bottom of the twelfth inning, and the Phillies loaded the bases with two outs. First baseman Eddie Waitkus came to the plate and . . . and, well, maybe it's better to let a pair of Pulitzer Prize–winning sports columnists from the *New York Times* tell you what happened next.

First, Dave Anderson, in his book *Pennant Chases*:

"With a quick swing, [Waitkus] lashed a low liner between Robinson and second base. Robinson dove, snaring the ball backhanded. Face first, he skidded across the infield's hard dirt, his right elbow knifing into his solar plexus. As umpire Lon Warneke signaled the third out, Robinson, thinking the ball might fall out of his glove, flipped it toward [shortstop Pee Wee] Reese, then collapsed."

Second, Red Smith, writing in the *Times* on the occasion of Robinson's death:

"Of all the pictures he left upon memory, the one that will always flash back first shows him stretched at full length in the insubstantial twilight, the unconquerable doing the impossible."

Robinson then faced Robin Roberts, the Phils' future Hall of Famer, in the top of the fourteenth, the game still tied. He drove a 1–1 fastball into the upper deck in left field. The Dodgers won, 9–8, to set up a three-game play-off with the Giants and pit baseball's two most competitive people—Robinson and Leo Durocher, then the Giants' manager—against each other.

> *"Larry Bird always wanted the last shot. He believed he would make it. . . . It was more than just confidence. To take the last shot when that one shot means victory or maybe defeat is to expose yourself to the possibility of pain. It is a proposition so frightening to many folks that they find ways to avoid it."*
>
> DAVE KINDRED
> SPORTSWRITER

"He's my kind of player," Durocher once said of Robinson. "He don't just come to beat you. He comes to kill you."

"In spring training 1949, I was a young pitcher at Vero Beach. One night, I watched Jackie, Gil Hodges and two other guys in a game of hearts. It was very intense, and they were playing for twenty-five cents. You would have thought they were competing in the seventh game of the World Series."

BOB ROSS
FORMER DODGERS PITCHER

Durocher was supposed to be the Dodgers' manager in 1947, Robinson's rookie year, but he was suspended for the season for associating with gamblers. Still, upon seeing Robinson play for the Montreal Royals, he told his players: "I'm the manager of the ball club, and I'm interested in one thing: winning. I'll play an elephant if he can do the job, and to make room I'll send my own brother home." In a way, Robinson and Durocher were kindred spirits— two aggressive, intense men whose similarities almost guaranteed there would be conflict between them. And there was. At the start of the 1948 season, Durocher left the Dodgers, and he and the emotion that bubbled within him went to Harlem, to the Polo Grounds, to the Giants.

"It was Leo who set the tone, and that rubbed off on all of us," Giants outfielder Bobby Thomson once wrote, "He was always out in front, always on top of everything. You could always *hear* him. He never walked around with his head down. If he had some-

"Jackie Robinson was two years older than me, but I played basketball against him in the summer. He was terrific and ran circles around the rest of us. One day, he said, 'Winters, I'm going to kick your tail today.' And he did."

TEX WINTERS
FORMER NBA COACH

thing on his mind he would tell you and we all appreciated that. . . . There was something else, as well. Anytime you're playing for a pennant, you're not thinking about yourself; you're thinking about the ball club. When you played for Durocher, you had to *learn* to subordinate yourself to the ball club. That's one of the things I learned from him that I'll never forget."

Thomson, of course, hit "The Shot Heard 'Round the World" in the third game of that play-off series, a game-winning, three-run homer off Ralph Branca in the bottom of the ninth inning at the Polo Grounds to give the Giants a 5–4 victory and the NL pennant.

But all you need to know about Jackie Robinson's competitive nature is this:

While the Giants mobbed the field and his teammates held their heads in their hands, Robinson watched Thomson jog around the bases. Only when he was certain Thomson had stepped on every base did Jackie Robinson finally leave the field.

* * *

"In any game, they'll call you names if they think they can rile you. That's just competition."

—Jackie Robinson

Like so many timeless athletes, particularly Michael Jordan, Robinson used whatever he could to motivate himself, to give himself a competitive edge. There is no athlete who withstood as many insults as Robinson, yet every derogatory word piled on top of the others as some kind of invisible kindling, fuel for his competitiveness. "You don't razz great players," former Major-Leaguer Randy Jackson told me, "because it makes them play better." The razzing almost always made Robinson play better.

The words of some of Jackie's former teammates and opponents provide a bit insight into Jackie' greatness.

Durocher: "When I went over to the Giants, Jackie and I were always needling each other. And . . . the more I needled him, the more he killed me."

Former Phillie Sam Nahem: "The more Ben Chapman and the guys insulted Jackie Robinson, the better he played. It was an ironic twist that Ben Chapman, who was the leader of

"The ultimate victory in competition is derived from the inner satisfaction of knowing that you have done your best and that you have gotten the most out of what you had to give."

HOWARD COSELL
SPORTS BROADCASTER

the racist business, had to tell them to stop getting on Jackie Robinson because he was killing us on the ball field."

Dodgers broadcaster Red Barber: "The most eloquent answer to abuse, bench jockeying and insults in baseball is a base hit."

Former Dodger Don Zimmer: "Branch Rickey had to have been a very brilliant man to pick this guy as the first black player to play in the big leagues. Jackie had an inner fire about him like nobody else, but how he was able to contain it while being subjected to all that racial abuse when he first came up, I'll never know. In later years, once he was established, he was able to retaliate—in the best way he knew how, with his God-given abilities."

In any competitive situation, whether it's sports or business or a personal struggle, that's the true test of someone's character: How does the person respond when everyone is against him? How does he or she perform under pressure? If you can succeed in those moments, everything else is pretty easy. As author John C. Maxwell put it, "Whiners achieve only when they feel like it. Winners achieve even when they don't."

> *"In business, the competition will bite if you keep running. If you stand still, they'll swallow you."*
>
> WILLIAM KNUDSEN JR.
> CHAIRMAN OF FORD MOTOR COMPANY

Often, in fact, successful people will create obstacles for themselves where none previously existed. They will manufacture opponents or impediments so their competitive juices start flowing. Now Jackie Robinson, of course, didn't have to do this. He encountered more obstacles, opponents and impediments than any athlete before or after him. But few of us undergo the external pressures and demands that Jackie experienced, so our success—our striving, our desire, our competitiveness with respect to our well-being—has to come from inside ourselves.

Michael Jordan was famous for creating hurdles for himself out of thin air. Once, a journeyman player for the Washington Bullets named LaBradford Smith scored thirty-seven points in a game against Jordan's Bulls in Chicago, and afterward, Jordan claimed Smith trash-talked to him during the game. So Jordan said that when the teams played the next night in Washington, he wanted to show Smith how great a player he really was.

And he did, torching Smith and leading the Bulls to a win. Except, in reality, Smith had never said a word to Jordan. Jordan simply used the story to push himself into a great performance.

From his days as a youth in Kingfeather, Oklahoma, until his death, Sam Walton carried with him an ambition that led to his becoming one of the greatest American entrepreneurs of the twentieth century. He once said that he always had to be pressing ahead, always doing things immediately and not later. He saw life as a competition, a season, and every act was a game, and every game, he had to win. That's how Wal-Mart came to emerge and thrive, and that's what I mean about creating pressure and finding your motivation.

"I've always asked, 'How do you inspire people, motivate people?'" Pat Riley, former coach of the Los Angeles Lakers and the Miami Heat, once said. "You only motivate people by having someone who inspires you to inspire them. I have to find someone to motivate me." *You* have to find that someone to motivate you, to push you toward success. Maybe, like Jordan and Walton, that someone is you.

> *"He was a fantastic competitor, the greatest I've seen. And it was infectious."*
> DUKE SNIDER
> ON JACKIE ROBINSON

It's important to remember, too, that by success, I'm not necessarily talking about fame, fortune, a new promotion or anything else of great material value. Those goals have their place in our lives and in the world, but they can also be highly superficial and, if we allow them, all-consuming. We have to remember to be "competitive" when it comes to our family, our friends and our faith, as well. How often do we postpone time with our children because we can't fit it into our schedule? How often do we skip church each week because we just don't feel like getting up early in the morning? How often do we forget important dates—a spouse's birthday, a wedding anniversary, a daughter's piano recital—because we're so busy with things that, in the long run, aren't quite as important?

"There is something that can happen to every athlete, every human being," Jesse Owens, the great track and field star, once said. "It's the instinct to slack off, to give in to the pain, to give less than your best. . . . Defeating those negative instincts that are out to defeat us is the difference between winning and losing, and we face that battle every day of our lives." Consider a father and a son, for instance, having a catch in the backyard. Maybe the father would rather be inside, on the sofa, watching television, but the son wants to have a catch. He wants to be a better pitcher for his Little League team. So the father obliges him. And sure, having the catch may, down the road, be one

> "To be your best, you must compete with yourself."
>
> RICHARD C. HALVERSON
> CLERGYMAN

small step in helping the son to become a better pitcher, but maybe what's more important is that the father didn't pass up a chance to spend time with his son. The boy will remember he improved his baseball skills. He'll win some big games and cart home a few trophies, and his achievements will be well earned and wonderful. But he'll also remember that it was his father who took the time to help him, and their love will be stronger for it.

That scenario, I think, gets to the heart of what competition is really all about. The father uses his son as motivation to win the battle against indifference within himself. Plus, the scenario touches on what former UCLA basketball coach John Wooden once said: "I've learned that winning games, titles and championships isn't all it's cracked up to be, and that getting there, the journey, is a lot more than it's cracked up to be." This from a coach whose teams won eighty-eight straight games and ten NCAA championships in twelve years!

I understand that we usually think of competition as a struggle against an outside force or person. But sometimes, being a competitive person means not succumbing to the little voice inside your head that's telling you to quit, to allow your fear to overtake you, to take the easy way out.

> "Anyone who believes that the competitive spirit in America is dead has never been in a supermarket when the cashier opens another checkout line."
>
> ANN LANDERS
> ADVICE COLUMNIST

Which is what made Jackie Robinson so competitive—and so successful. He never took the easy way out in any situation.

There is a famous story about an at bat Robinson had against the great

Sal Maglie when Maglie was pitching for the Giants. Maglie brushed Robinson off the plate by throwing a pitch near Robinson's head. On the next pitch, Jackie bunted the ball down the first-base line—so Maglie would have to field the ball.

"Jackie ran right over him," sportswriter Sam Lacy once said, "which tells you all you need to know about Jackie as a competitor."

"No pitcher ever backed me up—no one—and they all tried," Robinson once told Roger Kahn. "Near the end Sam Jones—you remember him with that big sidearm stuff—brushed me, and I got up and hit the hell out of his curve."

Life's going to throw a lot of sidearm stuff at you, too.

Are you going to stand in there and hit it?

* * *

"Jackie Robinson was a real winner. He wanted to beat you and win for the Brooklyn Dodgers."

—Johnny Podres, former Dodgers pitcher and teammate of Jackie Robinson

To be truly competitive is to be unselfish. For all the talk we hear in society about "wanting to win for myself," no one exists in a fishbowl. Even a CEO whose competitive nature has pushed him to the top of the business world benefits others by his competitiveness. His business creates jobs, stimulates the economy and the stock market, and provides goods and services to the public. If he is an ethical businessman, he is not succeeding merely for himself, but for "his team."

In the same way, a truly competitive athlete doesn't play the game for individual statistics, for money or for any selfish reasons. He does whatever he can to benefit the team. He plays for his teammates. He plays to win. He plays like Jackie Robinson.

It's no coincidence that in Robinson's ten seasons in Brooklyn, the Dodgers won six National League pennants and a World Series.

"After I played for Andy [Seminick], my entire approach and outlook of how the game of baseball should be played changed dramatically. I learned from him that there are two types of players: 'winners' and 'losers.'

"Winners have both 'seen' and 'unseen' stats. The 'seen' stats are individual ones that show up on paper. The 'unseen' are team stats that never make it in print and involve doing something for the team. 'Unseen' stats win games, and only a good manager and/or other knowledgeable baseball people see them. They hurt batting averages, demolish egos, cause countless little cuts and scrapes and never draw interviews from reporters. 'Losers' usually have only 'seen' stats and care less about anything else. Andy taught me how much of winning baseball is unselfishness, intelligence and consistently executing fundamentally and making routine plays routinely. In 1962, the year after I played for Andy, a representative from McGregor Sporting Company, who Andy introduced me to in 1961, approached me during batting practice in Indianapolis. Andy came up in the conversation, and the gentleman said, 'Seminick told me last year that the Vassie kid is a winner.' I considered that a tremendous compliment, especially coming from Andy Seminick."

LOU VASSIE
MINOR LEAGUE BASEBALL PLAYER
ON MANAGER ANDY SEMINICK

When I called Bobby Thomson to interview him for this book, I talked with him about those Giants-Dodgers battles of the '50s, and even though he admitted "We basically hated them," he had nothing but respect for the way Robinson played.

"Now that so much time has passed," Thomson told me, "I realize Jackie is the greatest competitor I ever faced. I can't say enough about him. He had a great combination—tremendous talent and desire. He had something special."

The great ones always do. A reporter once asked Yankees manager Joe McCarthy why he thought so much of his second baseman, Hall of Famer Joe Gordon. McCarthy called Gordon over.

"Joe," McCarthy said, "what's your batting average?"

"I don't know," Gordon said.

"Well, then, what's your fielding average?"

"I don't know that, either."

Gordon walked away.

"That's what I mean," McCarthy said to the reporter. "All he cares about is beating you."

It was all Jackie Robinson cared about, too. He once set the long-jump record for Pasadena Junior College, then drove forty-five miles to Glendale for the school's baseball game, got there in time to pinch-hit in the seventh inning and singled to win the game. Jackie would do just about anything for the sake of victory.

Which brings me back to Clint Richardson and the anecdote with which I began this chapter. As I write this book, Philadelphia is in the midst of a championship drought of more than twenty years; none of the city's four major sports teams—the

> *"One day we were walking to spring practice and walked by the track. Two varsity sprinters were lined up for a 100-yard dash. Jackie lined up next to them with no blocks and beat them both."*
>
> PAUL HUNTER
> JACKIE ROBINSON'S TEAMMATE
> ON THE UCLA FOOTBALL TEAM

Sixers, the Eagles, the Phillies, the Flyers—has won a title since the '83 Sixers. The entire town—every athlete, every sports fan—is waiting to win, to savor the sweet taste of the ultimate fruit of competition. There is nothing else like it, and Jackie Robinson knew it.

"That's the way I am about winning," he once said. "All I ever wanted to do was finish first."

Chapter Four

❧

A Man of Action

There is no comparison between that which is lost by not succeeding and that which is lost by not trying.

—Francis Bacon, philosopher

THESE DAYS, AS I WRITE, I am surrounded by examples of boldness, of people daring to be different. All I have to do is pick up a newspaper and skim through any of its sections to find an example of someone succeeding or striving for success by being aggressive, or bold, or both.

I look at the front page of the paper, and President Bush speaks of the viability of landing a man on Mars—a call to exploration that hearkens back a generation to John F. Kennedy's goal of sending a man into space to walk on the moon. I read of people criticizing Bush for daring to reach so far and for focusing too much on such a concept as a man on Mars, and I wonder if these same people were saying the same thing when Neil Armstrong stepped on the moon's surface on July 20, 1969.

I look at the business section, and I read a profile of Trish McDermott, the "vice president of romance" in the San Francisco office of Match.com, the matchmaking Web site. I wonder how such a popular and lucrative venture came to be. The Internet, after all, is still really in its infancy. Who had the foresight and guts to start the site? Who understood how powerful a tool the Web would become? And what exactly does a "vice president of romance" do?

> "We have to understand that the world can only be grasped by action, not by contemplation. . . . The most powerful drive in the ascent of man is his pleasure in his own skill. He loves to do what he does well and, having done it well, he loves to do it better."
>
> JACOB BRONOWSKI
> AUTHOR

I look at the sports section, and I read about the NFL play-off games that took place last weekend, about New England Patriots coach Bill Belichick and St. Louis Rams coach Mike Martz. The Patriots defeated the Tennessee Titans, 17–14, in part because Belichick decided to have his offense go for a first down on fourth-and-three late in the fourth quarter. The Rams lost to the Carolina Panthers, 29–23 in overtime, in part because, with his team down by three points and deep in Carolina territory late in the fourth quarter, Martz decided to run down the clock and settle for a game-tying field goal. He didn't try to win the game in regulation, and he lost it in overtime.

It's funny. There are hundreds of stories about Jackie Robinson's daring base running, his will to win, the lengths to which he would go to reach base and score a run and inch the Dodgers closer to victory. But after all the research and all the interviews I did for this book, I couldn't find a single story or anecdote in which Jackie was overly cautious, or hesitant, or was just sitting somewhere moping or lost in a daydream. Always, he was *doing*. Always, he was bold. He stole home nineteen times in his career because he didn't fear being caught. There is nothing bold about standing on first base. There's nothing bold about sitting around the house. The catch-phrase of the science-fiction television show *Star Trek* wasn't, "To *meekly* go where no man has gone before."

> "One day, the Reds were at Brooklyn when Rogers Hornsby was managing the Reds. Our pitcher knocked Jackie Robinson down. Jackie got up and walked over to our dugout and said to Hornsby, 'If I go down again, I'm coming after you.'"
>
> HOBIE LANDRITH
> FORMER MAJOR-LEAGUER

During a discussion with me, former baseball star Tommy Holmes got right to the nub of the matter when he said: "Jackie taught all of us that you can't reach home standing on third. In other words, go for it. Don't hold back. When the pressure is on, don't hold back and don't go into a shell. Jackie got knocked down like we all do, but face the pressure, and don't quit."

"Iron rusts from disuse," Leonardo da Vinci once said. "Stagnant water loses its purity and, in cold weather, becomes frozen. So does inaction sap the vigor of the mind."

Branch Rickey didn't wake up one day, decide to break baseball's color barrier and call Jackie Robinson on the phone to inform Jackie of his brilliant idea. Rickey's decision took years of planning, of action, of weighing the risk of failure against the precious possibility of success.

The same principles apply to our careers, our loves, our lives. If we simply wait on a dream to come true, if we don't do what's necessary to position ourselves to be happy, we're really just wasting time. Yes, there's that famous saying: "All good things come to those who wait." But I prefer what journalist Eudora Welty wrote: "All serious daring starts from within." In reality, the simple act of twiddling our thumbs—without a plan or a way

> *"Leap, and the net will appear."*
> ROBIN CROW
> AUTHOR

to execute the plan—gets us nowhere. "All growth depends on activity," President Calvin Coolidge once said. "There is no development, physically or intellectually, without effort, and effort means work." You can afford to be patient and wait for the good things of life once you've laid the groundwork necessary for attaining those good things—a happy, stable relationship with your spouse; contentment with your career; fulfillment in your family life.

To lay that groundwork, though, you have to follow a four-pronged process within yourself. Here's what I mean:

1. BE A PERSON OF ACTION

"Greatness stems from faith in one's ability, and you get faith by action, by doing, and by trying something out."

—Branch Rickey

In April 1942, Jackie Robinson was drafted into the United States Army. Both were changed forever.

At the time Robinson joined the army, it was, of course, still segregated. When Robinson was assigned to Fort Riley, Kansas, he could not play on the camp baseball team. He was restricted to segregated facilities. And officers' candidate school was not an option for him. Nevertheless, he worked his way to the rank of lieutenant, all the while arguing and campaigning for better conditions for blacks at the camp.

That's being a person of action.

"If opportunity doesn't knock, build a door."

MILTON BERLE
COMEDIAN

After he was transferred to Fort Hood, Texas, Robinson boarded a military bus on July 6, 1944. Texas's Jim Crow segregation laws would have required Robinson to sit in the back of a civilian bus, but in June 1944, the army had banned segregation on its military bases. Robinson knew this. When he noticed a woman he knew sitting in the middle of the bus, he sat down next to her. The driver ordered him to the back of the bus. Robinson refused. The two began to argue. Heatedly.

"Jackie was passionate about justice and fairness for everybody," Rachel Robinson told me, "and if he didn't see that, he'd take action and try to correct it."

Eventually, the military police arrived to investigate, and eighteen days later, on July 24, Robinson was arrested and charged with "behaving with disrespect" to a superior officer and "willful disobedience of lawful command."

Had Robinson been found guilty of those charges in his court-martial, he could have been dishonorably discharged from the army. But the jury rightly acquitted him, and the entire incident served as both a turning point in his life and a prelude of what lay ahead of him in baseball and beyond.

"I don't think Jack ever looked for a fight," his mother, Wilma Rae, once said, "but I don't think he ever walked away from one, either."

In speaking to author Arnold Rampersad for his biography of Jackie, Rachel Robinson said that Jackie's willingness to be bold came from Wilma Rae, his Christian upbringing and his faith in God. She explained that Wilma Rae instilled this faith in Jackie by reminding him, "You are a child of God, made in God's image. Because God is there, nothing can go wrong with you. You can allow yourself to take risks because you just know that the Lord will not allow you to sink so far that you can't swim."

They were words that Jackie took to heart.

In a game against the Cubs, Robinson was on first base when the Dodgers put on a hit-and-run play. The batter slapped a ground ball to Don Johnson, the Cubs' second baseman, who flipped the ball to shortstop Bobby Sturgeon.

"A self-made millionaire who gives seminars on success demonstrates an important principle from time to time in his classes. Standing in front of the room, he holds up a $100 bill and asks, 'How many of you would like to have this $100 bill?' Naturally, every hand goes up, but the millionaire does nothing. After a few moments, he says, 'Come on. Doesn't anyone out there really want this bill?' Eventually, a few people get the idea. Instead of waiting for the millionaire to give them the money, they walk up to get it from him. But he doesn't hand it to anyone. He stands there until someone physically takes it from his hand. Then, he asks, 'What did that person do that the rest of you didn't?' The answer, of course, is that while everyone else sat passively hoping they'd get the money with no effort, one person took action."

JASON OMAN
AUTHOR

However, Sturgeon wasn't interested in completing the double play. He threw the baseball squarely into the center of Robinson's chest.

> *"I was in spring training with the Pirates, and one day we played the St. Louis Browns in an exhibition game. I stole second base and third base consecutively and then tried to steal home. I was called out. That night at dinner, Branch Rickey beckoned me over to his table and had me sit down. He took his pen out and started marking all over the tablecloth on how to steal home. All I could think was, 'I bet he did the same thing with Jackie Robinson.' There was only one word to describe Jackie: daring."*
>
> BRANDY DAVIS
> FORMER MAJOR-LEAGUER

Robinson did nothing except jog off the field.

Six weeks later, the Cubs and Dodgers again met, and again, Robinson reached first. This time, he took off for second on the first pitch, and when Sturgeon moved over from short to cover the bag, Robinson didn't bother to slide. He charged into Sturgeon, knocking him clear off the base and breaking two of Sturgeon's ribs. Neither man said anything.

Frank Smith, a former pitcher with the Cincinnati Reds, told me about a 1951 game at Ebbets Field in which he faced Robinson. With 1–2 count, Smith threw a high, inside fastball to back Robinson away from the plate. Robinson hit the deck. But on the very next pitch, he bunted the ball up the first-base line.

"I had to field the ball and flip it to first for the out," Smith told me. "As I was doing this, Jackie and I collided, and he went right over me. He went back to the dugout, and I went back to the mound—not a word spoken, and no fighting. We both knew exactly what it meant. That's the type of player Jackie Robinson was—a tough, aggressive competitor, but a pro."

"Jackie played aggressively and lived the same way," former baseball executive John McHale told me. "When I was in the Tigers front office, he would get on me about our not having any black players or front-office people. He was right because we were slow."

Six years after his playing career

> *"Unless people undertake more than they can possibly do, they will never do all they can do."*
>
> HENRY DRUMMOND
> AUTHOR/EVANGELIST

ended, in January 1962, Robinson began writing a column for the *Amsterdam News, a* weekly black newspaper in New York, . He wasted no time in proving to his readers that civil rights—African Americans' battle for equality—was the foremost item on his agenda. When President John F. Kennedy delivered his 1962 State of the Union address and made barely any mention of civil rights, instead engaging the steel industry in a confrontation over steel prices, Robinson challenged the president's commitment to the civil-rights movement in one of his columns: "Mr. President, don't you believe that the explosive situation in the South and the sneaky, covered-up prejudice in the North are as damaging to the public interest, to democracy and to world peace as a $6 raise in steel prices?"

Not bad for a rookie columnist. I mean, once you take on the president of the United States, where do you go from there?

Someone once asked baseball great Frank Robinson, the first black manager in major-league history, if those who lord over baseball today would have embraced Jackie, making sure he had some role as an executive.

"No," Robinson replied. "He was too controversial, too honest. He'd create too many problems by speaking up and speaking out."

When you think about it, Frank Robinson's response is saddening and heartening at the same time. On the one hand, anyone would want Jackie Robinson, if he were still alive,

> *"Remember, people will judge you on your actions, not your intentions. You may have a heart of gold, but so does a hard-boiled egg."*
>
> ANONYMOUS

involved in baseball in some capacity, and it's sad to think people wouldn't want him to have a place in the game. On the other hand, Frank Robinson's point is that Jackie wouldn't have stayed in the shadows when it came to correcting baseball's problems. He would have been speaking his mind and telling hard truths. That's the heartening part.

Sharon Robinson, Jackie's daughter, told me: "He had a fire in him. His whole life, he believed if things were wrong, he wanted to change them. He had a strong belief in himself and what was right, and he was not going to tolerate injustices to people. Jackie Robinson couldn't stand being on the sidelines and being left out of the action."

"You don't have to see the whole staircase to take the next step."

MARTIN LUTHER KING JR.

That's the core of being a person of action: You have to learn to deal with the consequences, good and ill, of what you do. You have to be prepared for anything—for praise, for criticism, for outrage. For the sake of yourself and the people who count on you, you can do no less.

2. TO BE A PERSON OF ACTION, YOU MUST BE BOLD

"There is a tide in the affairs of men which, taken at the flood, leads on to fortune; omitted, all the voyage of their life is bound in the shallows and in miseries . . . and we must take the current when it serves, or lose our ventures."

—William Shakespeare

In October 2003, I visited the site of an old cattle trail north of Dallas. At the site, cut into the trees and signposts, were quotes from cowboys. One of those quotes stayed with me: "If you have a hill to climb, waitin' won't make it smaller."

As Shakespeare said, take the current when it serves. Get on with it. Don't wait. Climb the hill. Of course, it's simple to say that, harder to do. Excuses are always easy to find for why we stay in a job we dislike, keep quiet when we ought to speak out, or, as Henry David Thoreau wrote, live "lives of quiet desperation." But you don't have to live such a life if you're willing to make some sacrifices and some bold, "loud" choices.

"I have not looked back on one decision I have made and wished I had made it a different way. I don't spend a lot of time theorizing or agonizing. I get things done."

PRESIDENT GEORGE W. BUSH

These were the only kinds of choices Robinson knew how to make. Talk-show host Larry King explained it to me this way: "Jackie teaches us about grit and determination. Jackie grabbed life by the throat and was never afraid to live boldly. Jackie's life was not easy, but he went about his business and didn't complain."

King told me Robinson's attitude reminded him of an interview he did with the great attorney Edward Bennett Williams. During the interview, Williams told King, "There is only one reason we take geometry while in school: It teaches us to do things in life you don't want to do."

Or maybe there are things in life you'd like to do, goals you want to accomplish, but you hesitate to try. Why? What's stopping you? Insecurity? Fear of failure? Fear of upsetting someone else? You think Jackie Robinson worried about such things? Of course he didn't. That's what made him such an intimidating ballplayer and such a militant crusader.

"He was the only base runner of his time who could bring a game to a stop just by getting on base," Red Smith once wrote. "When he walked to first, all other action ceased."

Except, oftentimes, the action of Robinson's mouth. Particularly against the Yankees, Robinson was a perpetual source of chatter on the field, an antagonist in every sense. In an exhibition series against the Yankees early in Robinson's career, the Dodgers won all three games, and Robinson so taunted the Yankees' pitchers with his large leads on the bases that manager Casey Stengel told the Yanks after the final game: "All of you guys, when you get into the locker room I want you to check your lockers. He stole everything out there he wanted today, so he might have stolen your jocks as well."

"Robinson was awfully good, precisely the talented all-around player that Stengel admired and would love to have on his own team," Stengel's biographer, Robert W. Creamer, once wrote. "The fact that Robinson was not on his team, that he was the enemy—and an irritating, overbearing enemy—goaded him. He had a thing with Jackie Robinson, an ongoing thing. And it really didn't have to do with race. It had to do with Jackie Robinson's abrasive style of play."

> "Defensive strategy never has produced ultimate victory."
>
> GENERAL DOUGLAS MACARTHUR

Abrasive. The word conjures up visions of sandpaper, of roughness, of someone who is nasty or irritating. True enough. But like sandpaper, an abrasive person can shave a rough situation until it is smooth, can see a situation that needs to be fixed and, by his unwillingness to compromise, help fix it. For instance, in the era of the Negro Leagues, sportswriters such as Wendell Smith, Sam Lacy and Shirley Povich pressured Major League Baseball's owners to give tryouts to black players. The tryouts, as Buck O'Neil called them, were "just a show," but they started the movement toward Robinson's entrance to the big leagues.

The same goes for Branch Rickey. He had the crusader gene in his DNA, too, and he was every bit as daring as Robinson. He was once described as having "an evangelical fervor" to him. But think about how strong he had to be in his mind and soul to have such conviction. Granted, he felt good about his choice of Robinson as the man to break baseball's color barrier, but how could he know for certain?

> "How far would Moses have gone if he had taken a poll in Egypt?"
>
> PRESIDENT HARRY S. TRUMAN

Answer: He couldn't. Something might go wrong. Robinson might not have proved up to the task. Rickey would have suffered public humiliation, and his goal of integrated baseball might have been set back for years.

"He knew that baseball was perceived as public property, that the public was content with the game as it existed," baseball historian Donald Honig once wrote, "and that before one proclaimed the rights of man above the indifference of the public, one had better not only be ready to endure the firestorm that could rip from that indifference, one had better be pretty damned sure he had the right man to go forth with it. . . . By 1945 his genius had created disciples and enemies. He knew who would follow, who would oppose. And most importantly for any calculating man, he knew the strengths of his enemies, he knew the weaknesses of indifferent people, and he trusted the basic decency of the masses."

You can never go wrong doing that. No matter what your profession, your endeavor, your goal, you can never go wrong trusting peoples' basic decency.

3. TO BE BOLD, YOU MUST TAKE RISKS

"Happiness comes from the capacity to feel deeply, to enjoy simply, to think freely, to risk life, to be needed."

—Margaret Storm Jameson, novelist and critic

On February 5, 1947, Rickey addressed more than thirty black leaders from New York on Robinson's impending debut with the Dodgers. You'll have to pardon the antiquated language—1947 was a different time, with different standards for what constituted a racial slur—but this is what Rickey told them:

"I'm not going to tell you what you hope to hear. . . . Someone close to me said I didn't have the guts to tell you what I wanted to; that I didn't have the courage to give it and that you wouldn't be able to take it.

> *"He that dare not grasp the thorn should never crave the rose."*
>
> ANNE BRONTE
> AUTHOR

. . . If Jackie Robinson does come up to the Dodgers, the biggest threat to his success—the one enemy most likely to ruin that success—is the Negro people themselves!

"I say it as cruelly as I can to make you all realize and appreciate the weight of responsibility that is not only on me and my associates, but on Negroes everywhere. For on the day Robinson enters the big leagues—if he does—every one of you will go out and form parades and welcoming committees. You'll strut. You'll wear badges. You'll hold Jackie Robinson Days . . . and Jackie Robinson Nights. You'll get drunk. You'll fight. You'll be arrested. You'll wine and dine the player until he is fat and futile. You'll symbolize his importance into a national comedy . . . and an ultimate tragedy—yes, tragedy!

> *"You don't concentrate on risks. You concentrate on results. No risk is too great to prevent the necessary job from getting done."*
>
> CHUCK YEAGER
> TEST PILOT

"For let me tell you this: If any individual group or segment of Negro society uses the advancement of Jackie Robinson in baseball as a triumph of race over race, I will regret the day I ever signed him to a contract, and I will personally see that baseball is never so abused and represented again!"

Now, if that's not taking a risk—the possibility of alienating the very people who most wanted Robinson to succeed—I don't know what is. And that possibility was only one of many risks Rickey and Robinson assumed in their quest. Rickey banked on the idea that owners would get on board with integration because it would increase their profits, but he didn't know for certain that it would. Fans might riot. Players might revolt. Racists might threaten Jackie's life. Robinson might not be able to handle the taunts, the dirty play from his opponents or even a big-league fastball. There were several scenarios that jeopardized their alliance, their plan to integrate baseball and their hopes of success. They could have given up before they even began.

But then, to call on Will Shakespeare again, "All glory comes from daring to begin."

In a way, Shakespeare's words encapsulate Robinson's career as a baseball player. The praise and glory bestowed on him by his peers came because he played so aggressively, because he was so eager to take chances on the bases, because he was always trying to do whatever he could to shake up an opposing pitcher. After Gil Hodges drove in Robinson with the only run in Game Three of the 1949 World Series, Yankees pitcher Vic Raschi said, "I had just never seen anything like him before, a human being who could go from a standing start to full speed in one step. He did something to me that almost never happened: He broke my concentration, and I paid more attention to him than I did to Hodges. He beat me more than Hodges did."

"If no one ever took risks, Michelangelo would have painted the Sistine floor."

NEIL SIMON
PLAYWRIGHT

Here's a story from former Dodgers pitcher Clyde King: "In a night game at Ebbets Field, I came in to relieve with runners on first and third, two outs, in the ninth inning, Dodgers leading by one run—a very tight situation.

"Jackie came to the mound and said, 'Clyde, I think we can pick off this runner. Do you want to try it?'

"'Sure,' I said.

"I made a couple of pitches to the batter, then Jackie gave me the sign to throw over. I did, we picked off the runner, and the game was over. Jackie was responsible for that victory because he encouraged me, a young pitcher, to try something."

"Jackie's life teaches us that when we're presented with a challenge, don't back down or run from it," Sharon Robinson told me. "Take the risk, and if it's beyond you, don't be afraid to reach for it."

By the way, remember the audience that Rickey addressed that night in 1947?

When he finished speaking, they stood up and applauded.

> *"If the Creator had a purpose in equipping us with a neck, He surely meant us to stick it out."*
>
> ARTHUR KOESTLER
> AUTHOR

4. TO TAKE RISKS, YOU MUST FIGHT THROUGH YOUR FEARS

"He who fears being conquered is sure of defeat."

—Napoleon Bonaparte

It would be fair to say that, in the 1950s, few major-league pitchers were more feared than the Yankees' Ryne Duren. He was one of the American League's hardest throwers, and no one—not even Duren himself—knew where the ball was going when he let it go. He was notoriously wild. Batters' knees knocked as they stood in against him. And his appearance was of no comfort to hitters, either. He wore thick glasses, like Buddy Holly in a baseball uniform, and the spectacles only added to his image as an intimidator who pitched as if he couldn't see home plate.

> *"You gain strength, courage and confidence by every experience in which you really stop to look fear in the face. You are able to say to yourself: 'I lived through this horror. I can take the next thing that comes along.' You must do the thing you think you cannot do."*
>
> ELEANOR ROOSEVELT

In 1955, the Yankees and Dodgers played an exhibition game. When the teams posted their early lineups, all of the Dodgers' regulars were in the starting nine, including Roy Campanella, Gil Hodges, Duke Snider, Carl Furillo and Jackie Robinson.

Then they learned who the Yankees' starting pitcher would be.

"When the Dodgers found out I was pitching, they all got scratched from the lineup," Duren told me.

"Except Robinson. He stayed in the lineup. He was one tough guy."

Former Giants pitcher Al Worthington told me he drilled Robinson in the ribs with a fastball during a 1956 game. Robinson just walked to first. He never rubbed his ribs, never even flinched. "As he stood on first base," Worthington said, "I thought to myself, 'I know it hurts.'"

"Jackie was afraid of nobody on the field," former Yankee Tommy Henrich told me.

Bruce Jenner set the world record in the decathlon in winning the gold medal at the 1976 Montreal Olympics. Afterward, he said: "Fear is part of the process. If you weren't scared, you'd be in trouble. I was scared to death, but I made fear score points for me. Fear is right behind me; fear is six inches off my back. That's where fear is. It's there. It's present. I can feel its presence. It's not going to catch me. When I'm running, fear is right behind me, and I'm not going to let it catch me. If I did, it would slow me down. It could even make me stop."

And he wasn't afraid of anything or anyone off the field, either. When the Dodgers traveled to St. Louis in the early 1950s to play the Cardinals, the last hotel to allow blacks to register for rooms was the Chase Hotel. Instead of staying in a black motel, Robinson made a point of staying in the Chase. Once his playing career ended, he gave civil-rights speeches in the most dangerous parts of the South, in places such as Birmingham, Alabama, and Albany, Georgia, where black churches were burning and federal troops tried to maintain order.

"He teaches us to confront our challenges by facing them head on," author and historian Jules Tygiel told me. "His ultimate prize was to make a social contribution and make a better society. He understood that being a baseball star could be a stepping-stone to more important things."

His mentor understood it, too. Robinson and Rickey couldn't afford to be afraid in going forward with their "great experiment." Fear of failure on the field. Fear of injury. Fear of having an entire social movement take a step backward if he didn't make it in the major leagues. Fear of disappointing an entire race of people who were counting on him to prove blacks were equal to whites. Fear that baseball's owners would ostracize Rickey. Fear that Robinson's promotion wouldn't offend other Negro League stars, some of whom were considered better ballplayers. Fear that Robinson's quick temper might lead him to break his promise to Rickey to be stoic, that it might cause him to explode in anger.

They conquered every one.

During Robinson's rookie year, National League president Ford Frick even suggested to Rickey that Robinson skip the Dodgers' first series against the New York Giants, who played at the Polo Grounds in

> *"Walk in fear, and fear will gobble you up. Fear is always hungry for cowards."*
>
> SPARKY ANDERSON
> FORMER REDS AND TIGERS MANAGER

the middle of Harlem. The crowds will grow too wild, Frick argued. Rickey, of course, said no. Robinson would play.

"Jackie broke the color line, but if he blew his assignment—if he lost his temper, got in a fight, struck back at the men who were riding him—the barrier would have gone right back up again," Mickey Mantle once said. "Jackie not only had to prove himself as a major-league player, which is a pretty tough job all by itself, as you can find out by asking any ballplayer who ever had a shot at the big leagues, but he had to prove it fast. There wasn't time for a second or third chance. If he failed the first time and had to be sent back down to the minors, Rickey's experiment would have been called a failure, and no telling how many years it would have been before another Negro got a chance."

Like Mantle, I wonder . . . if Robinson and Rickey had succumbed to any of these fears, if they had decided any one of them was too much to overcome, if they had quit their endeavor before it was completed, where would baseball be now? Where would we as a society be?

"Be not afraid to go slowly; be only afraid of standing still."

JAPANESE PROVERB

In truth, baseball and America were fortunate Rickey chose such a man with so strong a personality as Robinson. Robinson was the first black to jump from the Negro Leagues to mainstream major- and minor-league baseball, but few remember the second. John Wright, a right-handed pitcher, was Robinson's teammate on the Montreal Royals in 1946, but Wright never made it to the majors. He bounced around the minors for a while before returning to the Homestead Grays. In Robert W. Peterson's book *Only the Ball Was White,* Robinson explained why:

"John had all the ability in the world, as far as physical abilities were concerned. But John couldn't stand the pressure of going up into this new league and being one of the first. The things that went on up there were too much for him, and John was not able to perform up to his capabilities. . . . Because John was the first Negro pitcher, every time he stepped out there he seemed to lose that fineness, and he tried a little bit harder than he was capable of playing. He tried to do more than he was able to do, and it caused him to be a lot less of a pitcher than he actually was. If he had come in two or three years later when the pressure was off, John could have made it to the major leagues."

Maybe. Maybe John Wright would have made the majors if he had come along later. But often in life, we don't have the luxury of choosing whether to face pressure. Often, we just have to face our pressure, our fear, at that moment. The question is, how will we face it? Do we have the strength to handle it? Jackie Robinson did. He

"Jackie Robinson was not afraid of anything."

SAM LACY
SPORTSWRITER

faced and handled more pressure than any athlete before him or since. He never backed down. He never stopped daring to live and play on his terms.

There is a lesson here. For all of us.

Chapter Five

❧

The Strength Within

*I'm not concerned with you liking or disliking me. All I ask is
that you respect me as a human being.*

—Jackie Robinson

THERE WAS SOMETHING RIGHT, something fitting, in having the six-foot,
ten-inch retired basketball player carry the coffin of the baseball pioneer.
On October 29, 1972, Bill Russell, the great center for the Boston Celtics,
was one of six athletes to serve as a pallbearer for Jackie Robinson. Russell
and five ex-Brooklyn Dodgers—Don Newcombe, Joe Black, Junior
Gilliam, Ralph Branca and Pee Wee Reese—lifted the casket out of
Harlem's Riverside Church and carried it into the funeral hearse.

"Jackie and I were soul mates,"
Russell told me. "Jackie was very
strong physically and mentally. He
was not a victim despite all he went
through. He always acted out of
strength. He believed he was the

> *"No man is great by imitation."*
>
> SAMUEL JOHNSON
> AUTHOR

master of his own fate and was not at the mercy of others."

Rachel Robinson had asked Russell to be a pallbearer for Jackie, a gesture that acknowledged how similar the two men were as athletes and as

people. They shared a certain pride, a commitment to excellence, teamwork and social justice. Russell, by almost any standard, is the greatest winner in the annals of team sport: He won eleven NBA championships in his thirteen seasons with the Celtics, two NCAA titles at San Francisco and a gold medal in the 1956 Olympics. But perhaps the more revealing detail about Russell came to light in a 1999 profile by *Sports Illustrated's* Frank Deford.

Deford began the piece with an anecdote about a car ride he shared with Russell in 1969. On that trip, Russell told Deford that they were not friends, and they could not be friends.

"But," Deford said, "I thought we were friends."

"No," Russell said, "I'd like to be your friend, and we can be friendly, but friendship takes a lot of effort if it's going to work, and we're going off in different directions in our lives, so, no, we really can't be friends."

> *"You have a unique message to deliver, a unique song to sing, a unique act of love to bestow. This message, this song, and this act of love have been entrusted exclusively to the one and only you."*
>
> JOHN POWELL
> CLERGYMAN AND WRITER

It takes a special sort of person to place such a high premium on friendship. Such a man must have high standards and must hold himself to them. More importantly, he must understand himself, accept himself and possess an unwillingness to compromise his beliefs and values for any reason.

> *"Your only obligation, in any lifetime, is to be true to yourself."*
>
> RICHARD BACH
> AUTHOR

Bill Russell, who said he was taught by his mother, Katie, to "just be yourself," was such a man.

So was Jackie Robinson.

"I never cared about acceptance," Robinson once said, "as much as I cared about respect."

No one ever gains respect by acting, unless that someone is Robert DeNiro. A person who doesn't learn to stand on his or her own, to acknowledge his or her respective perfections and flaws, can't be successful in any facet of life. Industrialist Charles Schwab said: "A man who trims himself to suit everybody will soon whittle himself away."

When I first moved to Orlando, a real estate agent sold me on a two-story house. He gave one story before I bought it . . . and another after I bought it.

You don't ever want to be the subject of that joke. You want to be genuine. And Jackie Robinson always was.

In the spring of 1954, Robinson began a correspondence with a boy named Ronnie Rabinovitz, who lived in Sheboygan, Wisconsin. In one of his letters to Ronnie, Jackie wrote, "I learned a long time ago that a person must be true to himself if he is to succeed. He must be willing to stand by his principles even at the possible loss of prestige. He must first learn to live with himself before he can hope to live with others. I have been fortunate. God has been good to me, and I intend to work as hard as I can to repay all the things people have done for me."

The only way Jackie could live with himself, as he said in that letter to little Ronnie Rabinovitz, was to say what was on his mind and to expect the same from others. Open, honest communication was the foundation of his dealings with people, whether they were his family members, his friends, his teammates or his opponents. It was less important to Jackie whether someone agreed with him or disagreed with him. What was of primary importance to Jackie was that people expressed their thoughts

> *"One day during my first spring training as manager of the San Francisco Giants, a magazine reporter sat down beside me in the dugout and asked me who I admired most as a youngster, which ballplayer I tried hardest to emulate when I was starting out in baseball. 'Frank Robinson,' I replied without hesitation. 'C'mon,' he said with a chuckle, 'who was it really?' 'Frank Robinson,' I repeated. The guy cocked his head to one side and stared at me with this blank expression. He knew I was serious, but he wasn't altogether sure what I meant. 'Look,' I said, 'the most important person any player should work to be as good as is himself. Your own excellence, success and greatest pride comes from only one person—you.'"*
>
> FRANK ROBINSON
> BASEBALL HALL OF FAMER

In one of my several conversations with Jackie's daughter, Sharon, she told me how rigid he was in his tastes. He liked certain things in certain ways.

"In the car, he listened to the same gospel tape by the Edward Hawkins Singers," Sharon said. "He ate the same breakfast: grits, eggs and bacon. Dad made the grits. And he ate at just a few restaurants: a steak restaurant in Greenwich, Connecticut; an inn in Stamford, Connecticut, that served great roast beef with popovers, and Mama Leone's in New York City."

and feelings honestly, that they treated him like a man and didn't hold anything back.

Early in Robinson's rookie season with the Dodgers, Eddie Stanky, a tough, veteran second baseman, approached him.

"I want you to know something," Stanky said to him. "You're on this ball club, and as far as I'm concerned that makes you one of the twenty-five players on my team. But before I play with you I want you to know how I feel about it. I want you to know I don't like it. I want you to know I don't like you."

Obviously, the "it" Stanky was talking about was Robinson's mere presence on the team. Stanky didn't like the idea of a black man playing for the Dodgers, and while it seems crude and antiquated that someone would earn respect for saying such a thing, in the context of that era, Stanky was simply being up front with Robinson.

"All right," Jackie said back to Stanky. "That's the way I'd rather have it. Right out in the open."

"Do not wish to be anything but what you are, and try to do that perfectly."

St. Francis de Sales
Sixteenth-Century French Bishop

By the end of that season, the Dodgers were the National League champions, and Robinson had turned Stanky's thinking around—which he had a habit of doing with people. As Dodgers manager Charlie Dressen put it, "When they see it's Robinson getting them World Series money, he's going to look awful white awful fast." Eventually, those who came in contact with Robinson had to accept him as he was. They didn't see him as "white" as much as they saw that he was an individual and deserved treatment as such. There was no other way to deal with him.

"If I did anything constructive in the Robinson situation, it was simply in accepting him the way I did—as a man, as a ballplayer," broadcaster Red Barber once said. "I didn't resent him, and I didn't crusade for him. I broadcast the ball."

Even in the Negro Leagues with the Kansas City Monarchs, Robinson was his own man, breaking from the norms of his peers. He couldn't be labeled. He was a ballplayer who didn't smoke, didn't drink and, as historian Jules Tygiel once wrote, didn't enjoy "what [Satchel] Paige called the 'social ramble.' Robinson never really fit in among the Monarchs."

He was so straitlaced in private and such a rabble-rouser in public, never afraid to speak out on any important topic in American society or to take an unpopular stand. In 1960, he endorsed Richard Nixon for the presidency over John F. Kennedy, explaining his decision this way: "I wanted to be fair about things, so I went to see both Kennedy and Nixon. Now, Nixon seemed to understand a little bit of what had to be done. John Kennedy said, 'Mr. Robinson, I don't know much about the

"I know I am heading for trouble in Florida next month when I must train with Montreal. . . . I know I'll take a tongue-beating, but I think I can take it. . . . These days keep reminding me of something my mother told me when I was a little kid. She told me that the words they say about you can't hurt you. And when they see that, they'll quit saying them. I've had plenty of nasty things said about me from the stands, especially in basketball, where you can hear everything they shout. I never let it get to me. I think it made me play better. I'll always remember what my mother taught me, and I think I'll come through."

JACKIE ROBINSON, 1946

"Make the most of yourself, for that is all there is of you."

RALPH WALDO EMERSON
POET AND ESSAYIST

problems of colored people since I come from New England.' I figured, the hell with that. Any man in Congress for fifteen years ought to make it his business to know colored people."

"One piece of advice I would pass on to a young coach, or a corporation executive or even a bank president, is this: Don't make them in your image. Don't even try. My assistants don't look alike, think alike or have the same personalities, and I sure don't want them thinking the way I do. You don't strive for sameness. You strive for balance."

BEAR BRYANT
COLLEGE FOOTBALL COACH

Johnny Most, the legendary play-by-play man for the Boston Celtics, watched a nationally televised interview with Robinson in 1954. During the interview, Jackie was asked if prejudice still existed in baseball.

"Do you want me to answer that diplomatically or do you want the truth?" Jackie said. "If you want the truth, yes, there's prejudice in baseball."

"Because of that frank and correct statement, Robinson was criticized by the media," Most wrote in his autobiography, *High Above Court-side*. "But Jackie could not have cared less because he had his self-respect and his honesty, which is why I admired him as a person. If he liked you, you knew it. If you were his enemy, you knew that, too."

"I don't know what the key to success is, but I know what the key to failure is: trying to please everybody."

BILL COSBY
ENTERTAINER

Understand: Jackie never saw himself strictly as a ballplayer. He saw himself as a man, whole and complete, with interests and passions beyond the field, and he demanded that others see him the same way. He never put on a facade for anyone, and he couldn't tolerate those who did.

"When you're a ballplayer, that's what you are—a ballplayer," former Dodger Clem Labine once said. "This is what you do, that's all there is." But with Robinson, "there were other things to talk about aside from baseball. It was interesting to hear about his life, about his joys and his fears."

Robinson once told Labine: "I want to be accepted for who I am, and not what I stand for."

After retiring from baseball, in March 1957 he became the vice president of the Chock Full o' Nuts company, and a newspaper writer visited him a month into his tenure. There was not a single piece of sports memorabilia in Robinson's office—no bats or balls, no Dodgers caps, no bronzed football shoes (though he eventually would put one from his playing days at UCLA on his desk).

"Most people call me Jackie," he told the reporter. "Sometimes the employees call me Mr. Robinson, but if they call me Jackie, I don't mind. They like to kid with me, and I enjoy kidding them back. . . . This is a team operation. To gain the confidence of employees, you must be willing to discuss their problems openly with them. Then, when you're looking for their cooperation, you will find it working for you."

> *"The privilege of life is being who you are."*
>
> JOSEPH CAMPBELL
> AUTHOR

PLAY THE WAY YOU KNOW HOW

Robinson's individuality was never more apparent than when he was on a baseball field. He was instantly recognizable to anyone watching a game. His swing was different from everyone else's. His running style—that pigeon-toed dash so many boys tried to copy—was different from everyone else's. But those differences made him the player he was, and any manager or coach who might have tried to change him would have been a fool. Sometimes, the very thing that makes a player, or a person, unorthodox is what makes him great.

"Most of the older fellas, especially the pitchers, never thought he would hit, because he was a lunger," former

> *In the 1998 Boston Marathon, my wife, Ruth, and I ran with a man from Ohio wearing a T-shirt that said, "Everybody loves a nut." He juggled four balls while running the entire 26.2 miles. It was quite the attraction. The sad part is, Ruth and I still couldn't beat him.*

Dodger Spider Jorgensen once said. "They'd throw him fastballs inside, and he'd fight them off and hit them on the fist, foul them back, but he could always hit the breaking ball, and he was one of those guys who was a better hitter with two strikes.

"The older guys didn't think he'd hit for average, but he had so much speed that you might hit him on the fist, but he'd hit a blooper over the infield for a base hit, and he'd get one hit bunting, and then he'd cream a couple of curveballs. And he did hit for average."

Think about what might have happened if a coach or manager had started tinkering with Robinson's swing and, in doing so, ruined him as a hitter. The ramifications would have gone well beyond the damage to the Dodgers' lineup.

"Sports is a societal testing ground in this country, and as time goes on we realize how important that 1947 season really was," MSNBC broadcaster Keith Olbermann told me. "Jackie hit .297, but what if he'd hit .197 or .247 and been released in July? Then the critics could've claimed that no black man could stand the pressure of Major League Baseball. If Jackie had failed, when would the next black man have received another chance? What would have happened to this country in this whole area of integration? It boggles the mind to think of this nation if Jackie had stumbled and fallen."

DON'T BE AFRAID TO FIGHT BACK

Above all else, Robinson set himself apart from every other ballplayer of his generation, and successive generations, with his intense competitiveness. That was why it was such a difficult, courageous act for him to follow Branch Rickey's request that he turn the other cheek in the face of the taunts, insults and dirty play he was sure to encounter. Robinson was not a passive person, and even after his promise to Rickey, he still couldn't completely quell his fiery nature. Rickey didn't want him to fight back, but that didn't mean Jackie didn't want to fight back. He was not someone to hold in his emotions.

"Once a writer came up and said I better start saying thank you if I wanted to be Most Valuable Player," he once said. "I said if I have to thank *you* to win MVP, I don't want the thing."

"You knew where Jackie stood on everything," former Major-Leaguer and former National League president Bill White told me. "He didn't pull punches on any subject."

In an incident during his rookie year, Robinson was playing first base for the Dodgers, and St. Louis Cardinals catcher Joe Garagiola was trying to beat out a double-play ground ball. Garagiola was out at first, but as he crossed the bag he accidentally stepped on Robinson's foot.

The next inning, when Robinson came to the plate, he and Garagiola began jawing at each other. Only umpire Beans Reardon's quick move to step in between the men and separate them prevented a full-scale brawl. There was no fight, but this much was clear: Rickey's request for restraint was merely masking the person Robinson really was. In his remaining years in the majors, Robinson would never be afraid to show his true personality, or the win-at-all-costs mind-set that came with it.

"To be nobody but yourself . . . in a world which is doing its best, night and day, to make you like everybody else . . . means to fight the hardest battle that any human being can fight."

E.E. CUMMINGS
POET

"Know yourself. Don't accept your dog's admiration as conclusive evidence that you are wonderful."

ANN LANDERS
ADVICE COLUMNIST

"Robinson wouldn't take as much abuse as he had as a rookie," my minor-league manager, former Phillies catcher Andy Seminick, told me. "Now, he'd talk back to umpires and talk back to players, just like other players would. He was a tough cookie."

"He was a high-spirited guy, would fight at the drop of a hat," former Negro Leaguer Gene Benson once said. "He had no patience. There were a lot of ballplayers had better tempers than Jackie's. He fought just about everybody he could fight. I know at least three fights he had while he was in our league. . . . Another time Jackie jumped up and knocked the umpire out, cold knocked him out. But they hushed that up."

As much as Robinson wanted to win, though, he was more concerned with remaining his own man. He did not have to be surrounded by

> *"No one can possibly achieve any real and lasting success . . . by being a conformist."*
>
> J. PAUL GETTY
> FOUNDER OF GETTY OIL

teammates at all times, and he was not above taking time for himself, being a solitary man. "He always hung by himself," Paul Hunter, one of Robinson's teammates on the UCLA football team, told me. "He was a nice guy, but he was a private person."

When Robinson first joined the Dodgers, Pee Wee Reese told him: "I'm not going to be your great white father." He did not mean it as an insult, and Robinson did not take it that way. Reese meant that he was not going to be overprotective of Robinson, that Jackie would have to stand up and stand on his own to make it in the majors and earn the respect of his teammates and opponents.

> *"I don't have to be what anyone else wants me to be. I am free to be who I want to be."*
>
> MUHAMMAD ALI

"It was never said that Pee Wee Reese was the protector of Jackie Robinson," Don Newcombe once said. "Jackie didn't need any protector. He needed someone to understand. Pee Wee understood, or tried to. Jackie wanted to show everyone that he was the same as everyone else."

But even to do that, he would have to have great inner strength. He would have to be a man who could stand alone. He would have to be the man Branch Rickey wanted to find when he sent three scouts, each unaware of the others' presence, to watch the Kansas City Monarchs and pinpoint the best black ballplayer to bring up to the majors. In addition to ability, each scout was to take mental and emotional strength into consideration when making his evaluation.

Each of the three scouts picked Jackie Robinson.

DON'T BE AFRAID OF CLEAN LIVING

Living in today's world can be hard because so much comes so easily. There's temptation everywhere: temptation to drink too much, to waste time, to dishonor our spouses, to lie, to cheat, to steal, to be gluttonous. Or just to fit in with whatever seems to be the latest trend, the thing to do at that moment. We experience peer pressure during our adolescence, even after we grow into adulthood, and every day we face pressure from our family, our job, our finances and from who knows where else. Those pressures are often what lead people to fall into the traps of addiction, infidelity and unwholesomeness.

But it might help us to remember sometimes how Jackie Robinson lived, and what he lived through. It might make our problems and pressures seem so small.

"There were now other blacks in baseball," Newcombe said of his playing days, "and we suffered much abuse ourselves, but he was still the man who integrated baseball, and he lived under more pressure than any human being I met in my life, and that included Martin Luther King Jr. Yet he never drank or smoked."

> *"I passionately hate the idea of being 'with it.' I think an artist has to always be out of step with his time."*
>
> ORSON WELLES
> ACTOR AND DIRECTOR

In this way, Robinson and Branch Rickey were quite similar. Rickey had grown up in Ohio in a devoutly Methodist house. The Rickey family never drank alcohol, valued education and often spent their evenings discussing religious topics and values among themselves or with friends and neighbors.

> *"Don't let other people tell you what you want."*
>
> PAT RILEY
> BASKETBALL COACH

I firmly believe that maintaining a strong sense of discipline in your life is essential to being truly happy, and finding that proper level of self-discipline is one of the most important processes you'll ever go through. The more you do what you believe to be second-best, or wrong or sinful, the more you will drop in your view of "self," causing a kind of self-sabotage. No amount of money, good experiences or blessings can alter this. Only you can. The process requires asking a lot of tough questions of yourself: When am I at my happiest? When am I at my most productive? What

"I've traveled around the world. I've walked in Moscow's Red Square and been through Checkpoint Charlie in Berlin. A lot of kids my age party and try to be cool. They haven't found where they want to be. Most teenagers figure if they don't do what other people do, they won't be accepted. Well, if you like yourself, it doesn't matter what anyone thinks, as long as you're happy. Twice a day, I push my body to the limit, test my self-discipline. I know what I want out of life. I have a good sense of myself."

OLYMPIC SWIMMER AND
GOLD MEDALIST JANET EVANS
SPEAKING WHEN SHE WAS
SEVENTEEN YEARS OLD

is stopping me from achieving my goals? And, once you've answered those questions for yourself, it requires that you stick to those answers.

It can be a scary process, too, but remember what writer Johann Wolfgang von Goethe said: "Just trust yourself. Then you will know how to live."

PLACE HIGH DEMANDS ON YOURSELF AND OTHERS

As Robinson's career with the Dodgers neared its end, he came into Buzzie Bavasi's office one day and asked, "Buzz, do you think I'd make a good manager?"

"No," Bavasi, the longtime Dodgers executive, said. "You're a perfectionist, and the players would drive you crazy."

After a long pause, Robinson answered.

"Yeah," he said. "You're probably right."

INDEPENDENCE IS IMPORTANT

Perhaps the most interesting relationship Robinson had with a Dodger teammate wasn't the one he had with Reese. It was the one he had with Roy Campanella.

The truth is, as author Michael Shapiro points out in his book *The Last Good Season,* Robinson and Campanella weren't the best of friends by the time Robinson's playing career was nearing its end. In fact, they didn't get along well at all. Their personalities were complete contrasts. "The rift should not have been surprising," Shapiro wrote. "They had nothing in common but baseball and race."

Campanella tried to get along with everyone. Robinson didn't care if people liked him or not. Campanella generally did not challenge the status quo when it came to race relations in the 1950s. Robinson was perhaps the loudest voice on the subject of that era, and he continued lobbying and crusading after he retired from baseball. They respected each other, but they were as different as different could be.

> "My mother said to me, 'If you become a soldier, you will be a general. If you become a monk, you will end up as Pope.' Instead, I became a painter, and wound up as Picasso."
>
> PABLO PICASSO

Which is exactly why their relationship is so interesting. At that time in American society, most white Americans couldn't or wouldn't conceive that two black men could be so different, could be such *individuals*. It was a convention Robinson flaunted for most of his life. According to historian Jules Tygiel, he was so steadfast in his belief that blacks must work hard within the framework of American society to progress that some black militants regarded him as an "Uncle Tom."

> "The best advice I ever got came from my dad. He told me, 'Always be yourself.'"
>
> TIGER WOODS, PRO GOLFER

It is a label Jackie Robinson must have laughed at. He laughed at every label that anyone ever tried to put on him. He learned the same life lesson that Bill Russell, his friend and pallbearer, learned. He was beyond labels. He was himself.

Chapter Six

❧

"I Am the Right Man for the Test"

Self-confidence is the hallmark of a champion, any champion.
　　　　　　　　—Grantland Rice, sportswriter

I wear a lot of hats and make a lot of trips. Whether it's as an NBA executive, a public speaker or a father, I spend a substantial portion of my life in airports, on airplanes or in rental cars. I don't mind the travel. I enjoy it, in fact. But there can be one small drawback: When you travel, you can't help but turn your comfort and safety over to others. You relinquish some control over your life, and sometimes that can be a scary thing.

For example, I heard a story about a gentleman who attended a convention in Hot Springs, Arkansas. Once the convention ended, he had to fly to Memphis, change planes and then continue on to Atlanta. But the weather throughout most of

> *"Skill and confidence are an unconquered army."*
>
> GEORGE HERBERT
> POET

Arkansas was terrible. The initial flight was delayed two hours, and when he finally left for Memphis, he was flying in a Beechcraft 1900 Commuter—a very, *very* small plane.

So he was off to Memphis, but the weather, heavy rain and sleet wouldn't break. The little plane just had to stop . . . in Pine Bluff, Arkansas. As the plane approached for landing in Pine Bluff, the gentleman looked out the window. He couldn't see the wingtip through the sheets of precipitation.

> *"Self-doubt is a terrible thing. People who don't believe in themselves . . . you feel like kicking them. You must believe in yourself."*
>
> RAY BRADBURY
> AUTHOR

Trust me: No matter how much flying you do, in situations such as this one you worry a bit. And as the gentleman looked around at the faces of the other passengers, he could see they were afraid, too.

Just then, over the intercom came the pilot's voice, strong and sure:

"Ladies and gentlemen, we will be on the ground in Pine Bluff in just a few minutes. It's raining. It's sleeting. And the visibility is practically zero. . . . So I suggest you be very careful driving home from the airport."

The gentleman's worries immediately went away.

* * *

> *"Confidence is elusive but a great thing for anyone. . . . I see no short-cuts to get it. Hard work plus success equals confidence."*
>
> —Dean Smith, former men's basketball coach at the University of North Carolina

> *"I wouldn't say he's egotistical, but he likes himself, which is great. If you can't be president of your own fan club, who can?"*
>
> MAJOR-LEAGUER JAY BUHNER
> ON TEAMMATE BRET BOONE

The year that he won the National League's Most Valuable Player award, 1949, Jackie Robinson got off to one of the worst starts of his major-league career. He was hitting less than .200 after the Dodgers' first thirteen games that season. Yet when someone asked him about the slump, he said: "The Dodgers will have a great club the day that Robinson joins them."

With that statement, Jackie might as well have been that pilot landing his plane in Pine Bluff. He knew he would hit. He knew he would do his job, no matter how difficult the circumstances. And, of course, he did—hitting .342 that season to win the National League batting title, leading the Dodgers into the World Series.

That sort of confidence is invaluable, in any walk of life. Let me put it this way: When you're sitting on a plane in the middle of a storm, the last thing you should want to hear from the pilot is, "Uh, we're going to try to take off now." I want a pilot who knows he's going to get that plane off the ground and back down again.

"Confidence gives you courage and extends your reach," the former CEO of General Electric, Jack Welch, once said. "It lets you take greater risks and achieve far more than you ever thought possible."

"All the extraordinary men I have ever known were chiefly extraordinary in their own estimation."
PRESIDENT WOODROW WILSON

To survive the unique circumstances around his entrance into Major League Baseball and to sustain a ten-year Hall of Fame career in the face of such bigotry and pressure, Robinson had to have as much confidence as any professional athlete in American history. He had to know that he could play—that he could hit big-league pitching and field his position and understand the nuances of baseball as only the best players can—and he had to know that he was strong enough to focus on playing when hitting, running, fielding and throwing were at their most difficult. When spectators and opponents were taunting him. When the vicious words of racism seemed to be falling from the sky like hailstones.

He couldn't just have confidence in himself, either. He had to have confidence in the people around him. He had to trust that Branch Rickey would fulfill his promise to help Robinson make the majors and would lend him support once he joined the Dodgers. He had to hope his play, determination and competitiveness would win over his teammates

"Without training, they lacked knowledge. Without knowledge, they lacked confidence. Without confidence, they lacked victory."
JULIUS CAESAR

and opponents, especially those who initially didn't believe a black man should play pro baseball. And he had to believe that his family and friends—the people he loved and who loved him—would be there for him throughout his difficult journey. It was because Robinson possessed that deep belief in himself and others that sportswriter Sam Lacy said of him: "Jackie Robinson was not afraid of anything."

"It is no exaggeration to say that a strong, positive self-image is the best possible preparation for success in life."

DR. JOYCE BROTHERS

It would have been impossible for Robinson to put up with all the hate and invective if he hadn't been so sure of his physical ability and mental toughness. For instance, during a game in Syracuse in Robinson's 1946 season in the minors, the spectators and the Syracuse players, according to one baseball historian, "reacted in a manner so raucous, obscene and disgusting that it might have shamed a conclave of the KKK." One player threw a black cat at Robinson and said, "Hey, Jackie, there's your cousin."

Robinson didn't respond until later in the game, after he had doubled and scored.

"I guess my cousin's pretty happy now," he yelled back.

In a way, Robinson's experience, as difficult as it was, is similar to what we encounter every day if we are to find fulfillment in our lives, our jobs and our faith. The trials we experience might not be as harsh as those that Jackie experienced, but the principle is the same: We must have self-confidence if we are to succeed. Our skills will be doubted. Our beliefs will be questioned. Our morals and values will be put to the test. In each of those situations, the only recourse is to be strong enough to stand firm. But self-confidence alone is not enough. We must have confidence and trust in ourselves, but sometimes you have to rely on someone else, like Dodgers pitcher Joe Black had to in 1952, his rookie season.

"Sometimes, I feel discriminated against, but it does not make me angry. It merely astonishes me. How can they deny themselves the pleasure of my company? It's beyond me."

ZORA NEALE HURSTON
AUTHOR

"They called me coon and nigger and old black Joe and all that garbage," Black once said, "And every time I felt like fighting when it came from the stands, Jackie would just put his hand on my shoulder and say, 'You can't fight. Maybe someday, but not now. You can't fight.' It was hard to take.

"Jackie developed this internal defense system, this thick skin, and he just didn't let it bother him. Sure, he was dying inside, but he felt the real answer was just playing well and beating the other guys. . . . Jackie's idea was to win and gain respect. He used that word a lot. He wanted respect as a man as well as an athlete."

One night in 1956, the Milwaukee Braves were playing against the Dodgers at Ebbets Field. Whenever Henry Aaron, still a relatively inexperienced ballplayer then, came to bat, he faked a bunt. But Robinson never inched in closer from his infield position.

"I asked him about it later," Aaron wrote, "and he said that anytime I wanted to bunt in Ebbets Field, that was all right with the Dodgers. I appreciated what he was telling me. He was saying that he respected me at the plate and also that I ought to respect myself a little more. That did a lot for my confidence—especially coming from the man whose judgments I valued more than anybody's."

Jack Lang, formerly of the *Long Island Press,* told me a story that illustrates this same point perfectly. The 1956 baseball season—Robinson's last, that same year he took Aaron aside—was nearing its end, and the Dodgers were struggling. After a Sunday afternoon game in Cincinnati, Lang returned to his hotel room to write his story before catching a midnight train with the team. A knock at his door interrupted him. It was Pee Wee Reese, Rube Walker and Duke Snider. They wanted to talk and hang out a bit.

> *"The difference between cowering and towering is totally a manner of inner posture."*
>
> MALCOLM FORBES
> PUBLISHER

"Walter Alston is now the Dodgers manager," Lang told me, "and he and Jackie are not close. Jackie is at the end, and Alston uses him some at third, some at left and some not at all."

So Lang asked Reese a question.

"What would you do if you were the manager of this club?"

"Do not wish for self-confidence. . . . Get it from within. Nobody can give it to you. It is one of the greatest assets of life. Self-confidence comes to you, every time you are knocked down and get up. A little boy was asked how he learned to skate. 'Oh, by getting up every time I fell down,' he replied. Opportunity is where you are. Weak men wait for opportunities; strong men make them."

RALPH WALDO EMERSON
AUTHOR AND ESSAYIST

Reese said: "I'd put Jackie in there every day and turn him loose."

"That was a tremendous tribute," Lang said in finishing the story, "that in Jackie's final season, Pee Wee wanted him in the lineup every day."

It *was* a tremendous tribute. It was also a tremendous display of Reese's confidence in his teammate and friend—an affirmation of an old Jewish proverb that I love: "The man with confidence in himself gains the confidence of others."

* * *

"Confidence comes with success. Each time you do the job, play a good game, confidence rises."

—Bill Parcells, football coach

"When we were in a huddle with him, it was just like God talking. Nobody ever said a word unless he asked you a question. Because of him, we always knew we could win the game."

FORMER BALTIMORE COLT TOM MATTE
ON QUARTERBACK JOHNNY UNITAS

Before you can put such trust in someone else, however, you must be secure enough to do it. And the only way to become secure in yourself—if you're not already—is to do what I talked about in chapter four. You have to take risks. You have to dare to fail. Only then will you feel the genuine sense of accomplishment and worth that causes self-confidence to grow.

As the father of nineteen children, I can speak from firsthand experience about this growth process. After all, I've watched it take place nineteen times! Here's one example:

My son Michael struggled with baseball, hitting in particular. He just didn't have the confidence to stand in that batter's box and take good rips at pitches, and as a consequence, he hated playing. Finally, in his third year, he started to hit—and he actually started enjoying baseball. I drove him to school one Thursday, and we started talking about the two games he had coming up that weekend.

> *"One must have high confidence in one's purpose, and each step must be so taken as to enhance the confidence of others."*
> JOHN KENNETH GALBRAITH
> ECONOMIST

"Mike," I said, "you're going to get four hits in these two games."

"No, Dad," he said. "You're wrong. I'm going to get six!"

Now, here I am talking about a boy playing Little League baseball, but the process is the same for anyone, even an adult. To Michael, it was a risk to step into that batter's box and swing the bat, but he kept doing it. He kept daring to fail, and at last he began to succeed. Just because we get older doesn't mean we stop grappling with similar insecurities, such as:

> *"Act as if it were impossible to fail."*
> DOROTHEA BRANDE
> WRITER

There's a deadline looming. Can I finish the project on time? Can I make a top-notch presentation at the conference?

I need to be around my kids, to spend some quality time with them. How can I do this without having them regard me as being overprotective or smothering? How can I strengthen our relationship?

> *"When I do a camp for kids, the first thing I tell them is, 'There are two words I never want to hear come out of your mouth: I can't.'"*
> DARRELL ARMSTRONG
> NBA PLAYER

I want to reconnect with my faith and make my belief in God a bigger part of my life. Am I ready to make the necessary sacrifices?

Can I stand in there and hit the pitch?

Or, perhaps, throw it. Robin Roberts, the Hall of Famer for the

Philadelphia Phillies, is one of the greatest right-handed pitchers in baseball history, but he was perhaps most renowned and respected for his ability to pitch well under pressure. Gene Conley, another Phillies pitcher, asked him once how he always was able to "get more on the ball" when he needed to.

"I pitch the same all the time," Roberts said. "The first pitch goes the same way as the last one."

"That can't be true," Conley said, "because I notice when there's a man on third and less than two out, that ball pops a little better."

"Well," Roberts replied, "you can't see what I'm doing. That comes from within."

> *"Calm self-confidence is as far from conceit as the desire to earn a decent living is remote from greed."*
>
> Channing Pollock
> Author

In fact, Roberts once said that only twice in his career did his nerves bother him: his first major-league start and a game he pitched against the New York Giants in 1955, when he nearly threw a no-hitter.

"I think much of the reason nerves never bothered me when I pitched, except for those two occasions, was that I was able to concentrate so well on the mound," he said. "I just stood out there in total isolation, focused on throwing the ball as well as I could. Nothing bothered me, and I was oblivious even to the batter. When I was throwing well, I would only see the bat when he swung, my concentration was so centered on the catcher. As far as I was concerned the ball was going to the catcher, not the batter."

Said another Hall of Fame right-hander, Bob Feller: "Scared? Never. Not in my entire pitching career was I ever scared of any hitter or any situation. That's a luxury you can't afford if you're going to make it as a pitcher. Challenges and crises are what pitching is. If that's a problem for you, then you'd better take up another line of work. . . . You have to have the talent, but if you're out there with any question in your mind at all about your ability to win and your ability to defeat every single hitter who stands up there as a threat against you, then you're going to be a failure."

The following words come from former Dodger Pete Reiser, but Robinson might as well have uttered them himself: "When you get on first, know you are going to second. Know you can beat the pitcher and the catcher and the two of them, combined. You have to have an inner conceit to be a successful base stealer. You have to know you are better than either the pitcher or the catcher."

No matter what the profession is, no matter what the task at hand is, confidence is always a help, never a hindrance, and it was particularly helpful to Robinson, whether on or off the field. When confidence is coupled with determination, as they were in Robinson, it makes for a player or person who will refuse to be intimidated, who will refuse to be defeated.

"If a pitcher ever knocked Jackie down," former pitcher and manager Roger Craig told me, "he would give you 'that look,' which meant, 'Don't do it again.' He would bunt toward the first baseman and then run right over the pitcher covering first. I saw him do that three or four times."

I got to talking with former big-leaguer Calvin Hogue about Jackie once, and he remembered a game in which Robinson hit a single to right field.

"Jackie rounded first a little hard, and the right-fielder threw behind him to first," Hogue said to me. "When Jackie saw this, he took off to second and slid in safely. He was extremely graceful like that."

Athletes call those moments "getting in the zone." The great golfer Nancy Lopez spoke of it when she said, "During my winning streaks, I got to the point where I thought I was never going to lose. Everything was so automatic and so easy. I was so confident. I felt no one could beat me." Confidence and success snowball. Do something well once, you're much more likely to do it well the second time, because now you know you can. All it took for Robinson to become a great ballplayer was for him to know he could be a great ballplayer.

Remember: He was not the Negro Leagues' most talented player in 1945, when Branch Rickey selected him to break the color barrier. Satchel Paige was a dominant pitcher. Cool Papa Bell was as fine an outfielder as there was anywhere. Rickey had selected Robinson because of Jackie's mental and emotional strength, and even Robinson himself knew his baseball-playing abilities—or, more accurately, their limits—would be a large obstacle for him to overcome if he wanted to stay in the major leagues.

"I think I am the right man to pick for the test," Robinson once said. "There is no possible chance that I will flunk it or quit before the end for any other reason than that I am not a good enough ballplayer."

But here's the thing: Robinson may have been a more gifted football player or basketball player or track athlete than he was a baseball player. But, again, he *knew* he was good enough to play for the Dodgers. He just knew. By that, I don't mean to suggest that he knew he would step right into the Dodgers' lineup, having mastered every aspect of the game. I mean he knew that with enough work and practice, he could play in the big leagues—no, *excel* in the big leagues. He had begun the process the season before, in 1946 in Montreal. There, veteran infielder Al Campanis, who went on to become a Dodgers executive, worked with him every day on the fundamentals of playing second base: throwing, pivoting, turning the double play.

"He became better and better and more confident as the season went on," Campanis said.

"Jackie Robinson was *not* the best," former New York Giants outfielder Monte Irvin once said. "He was just the first. And a very fine choice as it turned out. What made Jackie so outstanding was his personal color and his competitive fire. He wasn't a good hitter at the beginning, but he made himself into one. He had great natural speed and quickness and used it to full advantage. He *made* himself into an all-star second baseman, and he developed the knack of stealing bases and particularly stealing home."

The point is, Robinson had enough self-assurance to know that he didn't know everything. That's a hugely important facet of true self-confidence: understanding yourself, knowing your limitations. Author Maury Allen once described him as "an outstanding college football and

> *"I think all champions create that air of expectancy and confidence. Muhammad Ali did it. You expected him to do what he said he would do, and he rarely disappointed. Roger Staubach had that air of expectancy about him, too. So did John Kennedy and Ronald Reagan. There are many other champions I could list who had the same intangible confidence that they would get the job done, regardless of the odds or the obstacles."*
>
> FORMER U.S. REPRESENTATIVE J. C. WATTS

basketball player with some baseball credentials." Allen's description was apt when Robinson broke in with the Dodgers, but soon enough those words became outdated because Jackie worked himself into a true baseball player. And Jackie could do that only by believing in himself.

"Self-confidence," author Samuel Johnson wrote, "is the first requisite to great undertakings."

Dizzy Dean, the great pitcher for the St. Louis Cardinals, made the famous statement: "It ain't braggin' if you can do it." And he's right. You simply have to understand what you can do and what you can't. And

> *"Regardless of how you feel inside, always try to look like a winner. Even if you are behind, a sustained look of control and confidence can give you a mental edge that results in victory."*
>
> ARTHUR ASHE
> PROFESSIONAL TENNIS PLAYER

believe me, once you try, you'll be surprised just how much you can do. You can get six hits in a weekend of Little League. Or land an airplane in a blinding storm.

"Confident people seek responsibility, initiate projects, believe in their purpose, trust their instincts and respect their roles," Dr. Gerald Bell writes. "Therefore they're able to focus on their work, commit to their goals, and work effectively to achieve them. Since they don't feel a need to convince people they're talented, they go about their work and lives by displaying authentic confidence and grace."

Dr. Bell is right. Oftentimes, confident people don't feel the need to convince people how good they are.

But, sometimes, they do.

Jackie Robinson did both.

"Jackie often put us in the position where other teams disliked us," former Dodgers pitcher Clem Labine told me. "He would do a lot of little things to antagonize our opponents. I've seen him get hit by a pitched ball and go limping down to first like he could hardly walk. Then on the first pitch—boom, he's gone. I always thought of it as showboating, and it did make the opposition angry. But I will say this: no matter what Jackie did he was always right there with the bat in his hand ready to face anybody and everybody, and that takes courage. But because of Jackie, a lot of teams

> *"We are all worms, but I do believe I am a glowworm."*
> WINSTON CHURCHILL

played harder against us."

In return, Robinson's opponents often tried to antagonize him. During a 1950 spring-training game against the Yankees, Robinson grounded out, and as he trotted back to the dugout, a rookie infielder started yapping at him from the Yankees' dugout.

"You big busher! It's a good thing you're not in my league. I'd have your job in a week."

> *"Somehow, I can't believe that there are any heights that can't be scaled by a man who knows the secret of making his dreams come true. This special secret, it seems to me, can be summarized in four Cs. They are curiosity, confidence, courage and constancy, and the greatest of these is confidence."*
> WALT DISNEY

That rookie was Billy Martin.

Now, Martin was never the player Robinson was—heck, Robinson was the reigning National League Most Valuable Player when Martin heckled him that day—but Martin needed that cockiness, that edginess, to be at his best. He became a solid infielder for the Yankees during the heydays of their dominance of the American League. He spent eleven seasons in the majors and hit .333 in the six World Series in which he played, and he managed the Yankees to victory in the 1977 Series.

Like I said before, confidence never hurts. It only helps.

* * *

> *"We must have perseverance and, above all, confidence in ourselves. We must believe that we are gifted for something and that this thing, at whatever cost, must be attained."*
> —Marie Curie, physicist

You can always tell confident people, can't you? They look different, feel different when you meet them. Their voices are clearer. Their postures are straighter. Their handshakes are firmer. They make good impressions, and, usually, they have a background, track record or personal history to back up that good first impression.

"Doubt is a thief that often makes us fear to tread where we might have won."

WILLIAM SHAKESPEARE

Once he reached first base, Robinson looked different from every other baseball player who had come before him. No one ran the bases as he did, with such abandon and aggressiveness. Sometimes, he actually would get himself caught in rundowns on purpose, just so he could wow the crowd and infuriate the opposing team by wriggling his way out of them. He would do it, Maury Allen wrote, "almost with a show of arrogant guile. . . .

"Baseball is a game of statistics, but the written evidence of how many times Robinson escaped rundowns to be safe does not exist," Allen continued in his book *Jackie Robinson: A Life Remembered.* "Witnesses will swear it was endless."

We know how many times he stole home: nineteen—a statistic that describes Robinson's daring and confidence as well as one hundred thousand words ever could. Even the most causal baseball fan of today understands how difficult it is to steal home. No major-league base runners these days even try unless they are part of a double-steal in which a runner on first breaks for second, the catcher throws down to second base and the runner on third breaks for home. But Robinson stole home nineteen times, and there wasn't one double-steal among them.

"After I was traded to Boston by the Giants," former Boston Brave Walker Cooper once said, "Robinson was on third base. Warren Spahn was pitching, and I went to the mound. 'Now don't go into your windup with this fellow on third.' Spahn was a pretty headstrong fellow, and he told me I should go back behind the plate, and he would take his chances. Darned if he didn't go into his windup, and Robinson stole home on the first pitch. I don't think Spahnie ever did that again."

Before the 1947 World Series began, Yankees catcher Yogi Berra, who had played against Robinson in the minor leagues when Berra was at Newark and Robinson at Montreal, made a tactical mistake. He said

Robinson had not stolen a base against him in the minors, and he wouldn't steal one on him in the Series. The sportswriters covering the Series, of course, did just what anyone would have expected of them: they told Jackie what Yogi had said.

So Robinson walked in his first at bat of Game One.

Then, he stole second.

"I wish Berra was catching in the National League," he said after the game. "I'd steal sixty bases."

I don't know about you, but when I read that story, I can't help but hear Dizzy Dean's words in my head.

It ain't braggin' if you can do it . . .

"To me," Dodgers broadcaster Vin Scully told me, "the average human being loses some efficiency when he's angry. We all have problems doing our job when we are angry. Jackie's uniqueness lay in the fact that he performed even better when angry. The rest of them figured this out after a while."

They had no choice. Nothing could shake Jackie Robinson. Nothing could shake the immutable belief he had in himself. It was the only way he could survive what he went through and carve out such a marvelous life and career.

"I'm bitter right now," he once said, "but I'm going to hang around long enough to change one letter in that word, the *i* to an *e*."

It was that diligence, that unshakeable belief in himself, that poet Maya Angelou most admires about Robinson. "Jackie demonstrated all the great human virtues," she told me. "However, I think among his most awesome talents was his ability to persevere. He stayed the course. He stuck it out. He held on. He endured. He preserved. He remained. He survived. In fact, he did better than survived. He thrived. And because of that, he is a role model for young women and young men the world over."

> *"It is hard to fight an enemy who has outposts in your head."*
>
> SALLY KEMPTON
> WRITER

Chapter Seven

∼❉∼

A Leader at Heart

I believe in the human race. I believe in the warm heart. I believe in man's integrity. I believe in the goodness of a free society. I believe that society can remain good only as long as we are able to fight for it and fight against whatever imperfections may exist.
—Jackie Robinson

In his own right, Roger Craig was a pretty darned good leader. As the manager of the San Francisco Giants in the late 1980s, he guided the Giants from a last-place finish in 1986 to the National League's Western Division title in 1987—and to within one win of a berth in the World Series. Then, in 1989, the Giants reached the World Series for the first time since 1962. They ended up losing to the Oakland Athletics, who were one of baseball's best teams in a long, long time. But for an organization that had suffered through so much losing, winning the National League pennant was a great achievement in and of itself. After all, it had been twenty-seven years since the Giants had won the pennant. Twenty-seven years!

> *"Managers are people who do things right. Leaders are people who do the right thing."*
> WARREN BENNIS
> BUSINESS EXPERT

But when I called Roger to speak with him for this book and talk to him about leadership, we didn't discuss those Giants teams he managed. We talked about Jackie Robinson, who was Roger's teammate when Roger was a young pitcher with the Brooklyn Dodgers.

"Jackie was the best leader I ever saw on a ball club," he told me. "He would jump on guys right in the dugout and stay on them during the game. He'd say, 'If you are going to play, play as hard as you can. Play like it's your last game.' He talked, and they listened."

Craig himself was one of those who listened. In July 1955, the Dodgers were in the heat of an intense pennant race, and Craig and another pitcher, Don Bessent, were called up from the Montreal Royals. On Saturday, they arrived. On Sunday, the Dodgers swept a doubleheader with the Cincinnati Reds at Ebbets Field, and after the second game, Walter Alston, the Dodgers' manager, called Craig into his office.

There, Alston told him to take a few days to go back to Montreal, gather up his family and personal possessions and come back to Brooklyn for the rest of the season.

"Leaders get out front and stay there by raising the standards by which they judge themselves and by which they are willing to be judged."

FRED SMITH
FOUNDER OF FEDERAL EXPRESS

Craig had one question:
"Where's the airport?"

Just then, Robinson overheard Craig and Alston's conversation.

"Come with me," he said. "I'm going out that way."

Craig was stunned. Here he was, a kid from Durham, North Carolina, in the majors for less than two days, and Jackie Robinson was volunteering to drive him to the airport.

"On the ride," Roger told me, "Jackie told me what I had to do to achieve success in the big leagues. He talked about good work habits. That talk stayed with me my whole career. I never forgot it."

A couple of months later, in September 1955, Roger Craig, the kid who needed a ride to the airport on his second day as a Major-Leaguer, was the winning pitcher in the victory over the Milwaukee Braves that clinched the National League championship for the Dodgers. He hadn't even been with the team long enough to earn the full bonus that each player received for the Dodgers' reaching to the World Series.

But as the players celebrated in the clubhouse, Robinson approached Craig and said: "You have been up since July, but you have won a full Series share already."

"He said it in front of the whole club," Craig told me, "and you could see some heads turn. He told the other twenty-three guys on the team, and that's what happened. I got the full share. That meant about $7,000 to me—and it helped me buy a house."

Robinson's compliment to Craig would have been pretty empty had he not possessed such stature and respect among the Dodgers. The other players knew that when Robinson said something, he meant it.

That's the core of leadership, really. First you say it. Then you do it.

"For the effective leader, doing is always more important than being," author Alan Axelrod says. "The mistake that paralyzes too many would-be leaders is picturing leadership as a throne, instead of what it is: a vehicle. Leadership is not for sitting. It's for moving, for pulling, for pushing. If a decision you make turns the vehicle off course, another decision must be made to straighten it out again—and, if necessary, again and again."

I visited a radio station in Tampa not long ago, and this bulletin was posted there:
"A LEADER:
Takes initiative/Is a decision-maker/Is motivated and a motivator/Inspires/Is a listener/ Has long-term and short-term vision/Is fair/Has foresight/ Knows how to network/ Has dedication/Focuses on common goals/Is knowledgeable/ Is resourceful/Offers respect/ Uses intuition/Is optimistic/ Influences those around him or her/Is positive/ Communicates/Perseveres in all things/Is humble."

"It's not easy when people take their shots, but it's how you react that matters. Are you in control or out of control? A leader, whether it's a quarterback, a CEO or a department head, must always be in control."
MIKE SHANAHAN
HEAD COACH OF THE DENVER BRONCOS

* * *

> *"There are no bad soldiers, only bad officers."*
> NAPOLEON BONAPARTE

"Sure I had to suck it up those first two years. I knew there was a lot riding on me, and I knew the Dodgers had shown faith that I could control my temper until I had established myself and other Negroes were playing at the major-league level. It was very hard, but I knew I had to do it."

—Jackie Robinson

What does it mean to be a leader? It's always a worthy question, but particularly at this time in our society. We're fighting a war against international terrorism that won't end soon. We are about as polarized politically as we've ever been—liberals and conservatives and everyone in between battling among themselves and rarely finding any common ground. We've just been through a rash of corporate scandals that have scarred people's views and understanding of capitalism, the American economy and the term "business ethics."

> *"The one quality that can develop by studious reflection and practice is the leadership of men."*
> PRESIDENT DWIGHT D. EISENHOWER

We need leaders, true leaders, in our government, in our communities, in our businesses, in our schools. Now, I think, more than ever.

So how do we find them? How do we know them when we see them? How can we become these leaders ourselves? We need to recognize and understand certain qualities of leadership.

> *"He was not a born king of men, but a child of the common people who made himself a great persuader—therefore, a leader—by dint of firm resolve, patient effort and dogged perseverance."*
> JOURNALIST HORACE GREELEY ON ABRAHAM LINCOLN

A LEADER IS PERSISTENT AND OPTIMISTIC

During their years in the army, Robinson and Joe Louis were based together at Fort Riley in Kansas, where there were only a half-dozen seats set aside for blacks in the mess hall. They, along with all the other black soldiers, weren't permitted to sit and eat at the white-only tables. They often would have to eat their food while standing, no matter how many white-only tables weren't being used.

Before long, Louis and Robinson joined forces, lobbying for more seats for black soldiers. After a while, the army brass relented.

> *"Don't run with the pack . . . until or unless you can lead it."*
> AL NEUHARTH
> FOUNDER OF *USA TODAY*

It takes a deep belief in people, in their ability to change and their willingness to accept a newer, better way of doing things for someone to maintain the moral commitment that Robinson maintained throughout his life and his career. Otherwise, why bother? If you don't believe your work will have any benefit, why do it? No leader has ever been pessimistic.

Not long ago, we as a country were in the midst of mourning the death of former president Ronald Reagan. The word that Reagan's friends, his political foes and many a media pundit used to describe him was "optimistic," and they were correct to use that word. It's hard to remember all these years later, but when Reagan

> *"Leadership is action, not position."*
> DONALD MCGANNON
> BROADCASTING EXECUTIVE

became president, there was actually something called a "misery index" in the United States—a quantitative way to measure how down the American people were on their country, their economy and themselves. If Reagan did nothing else in his eight years as president, he got us away from feeling sorry for ourselves. In his now famous slogan, it was "morning in America." He infused people with the sense that tomorrow, we will reach higher, run faster, stand taller—that we can and will do better.

Where race and society were concerned, Jackie Robinson felt the same way: we could do better. We had to.

"My fight was against the barriers that kept Negroes out of baseball,"

> *"Great leaders, in my opinion, possess three flexible skills: toughness, tenderness and the ability to know when it is the right time to use one or the other."*
>
> BILL RUSSELL

Robinson once said. "It was the area where I found imperfection and where I was best able to fight. And I fought because I knew it was not going to be a losing fight. It could not be a losing fight because it took place in a free society."

A LEADER CARRIES HIMSELF WITH GRACE

When my college baseball coach, Jack Stallings, graduated from high school in Durham, North Carolina, in 1949, he planned to attend my alma mater, Wake Forest University. Two Brooklyn Dodgers scouts were trying to convince him otherwise, and they took him up to Ebbets Field for a workout.

"We worked out before the starting lineup took the field," Stallings, now retired, told me. "I was at second base taking groundballs and turning double plays. On my last play, I took the ball kind of awkwardly, and I heard this voice: 'Why don't you backhand that ball?'"

> *"The question 'Who ought to be boss' is like asking, 'Who ought to be the tenor in the quartet?' Obviously, the man who can sing tenor."*
>
> HENRY FORD

The voice was Jackie Robinson's.

"For the next five minutes," Stallings said, "the great Jackie Robinson taught me how to make this particular play. I was a perfect stranger—eighteen years old—but I was so impressed he went out of his way to do that for me."

This sort of anecdote is common among former ballplayers who began their careers after Robinson already had started his. When infielder Junior Gilliam came up to the Dodgers from the team's minor-league system, Robinson felt a responsibility to become an adviser to this young black man, to try to calm whatever anxieties Gilliam might have been feeling. "Jackie told Junior what he was supposed to do as a human being, a person, a player," Don Newcombe once said. "It was, 'Act like a champion, carry yourself like a professional.' Jackie nursed Gilliam along so that he overcame his shortcomings and became a star player himself."

Robinson took Dick Williams under his wing in a similar fashion. Williams—who went on to become one of the most successful managers in baseball history, leading the Boston Red Sox and San Diego Padres to the World Series and winning three championships with the Oakland A's—had been a childhood friend of Robinson's brother, Mack, in Pasadena. Jackie remembered him from those days in California, and when Williams joined the Dodgers as an infielder, Robinson did what he could to make the rookie feel comfortable.

> *"Good leaders are like baseball umpires. They go practically unnoticed when doing their jobs right."*
>
> BYRD BAGGETT
> WRITER

"He would show me where to go and what to do, something I needed to learn with every new city," Williams once wrote. "He would constantly remind me to watch my mouth and my wallet. On those dark days when I realized I'd never be accepted into the Dodgers' clique of stars, he would sit beside me in the clubhouse and remind me I was still a Dodger."

That Robinson mentored so many young players was an indication not only of his generosity, but of his understanding of his role as a leader. We form first impressions of the people we meet based on how they dress, how they shake our hands, whether they look us in the eye, how they treat us once we're introduced to them. As a leader on the Dodgers, Robinson made sure he projected an image befitting a leader. He could offer counsel, and he could make demands.

> *"A good team leader is one who takes a little more than his share of the blame and a little less than his share of the credit."*
>
> REGGIE JACKSON
> BASEBALL HALL OF FAMER

He could chew out a teammate for a dumb mistake, and he could throw an arm over the same teammate's shoulder moments later. He could be either commanding or accommodating. He knew how a professional was supposed to act, in any walk of life—whether as a baseball player or as a soldier.

"Jackie was so effective because of the way he presented himself," Rachel Robinson once said. "He went in as an officer and became a lieutenant

> *"Making the right choices is the most important part of leadership. Every other element, from developing and communicating ideas to surrounding oneself with great people, relies on good decisions."*
>
> RUDOLPH GIULIANI
> FORMER MAYOR OF NEW YORK CITY

right off the bat, and he had the ability to mobilize others. Though he didn't call press conferences, he knew those tools were always available to him, and he would not have been reluctant to use them if he couldn't get what he wanted in other ways."

"I have been around a few men in whose presence you feel you are in the presence of royalty," Harry Edwards, a University of California at Berkeley sociology professor and sports historian, told me. "Dr. King was one, and so was Bill Russell. Jackie was also one. When he walked in a room, you saw a magnificent prince in a room full of commoners—even though Jackie didn't treat people like commoners. There was something elevating about him. Every time Jackie spoke, I wanted to grasp each word so I could understand what he meant."

> *"A genuine leader is not a searcher for consensus, but a molder of consensus."*
>
> MARTIN LUTHER KING JR.

A LEADER HAS A VISION—AND NEVER WAVERS FROM IT

When Branch Rickey made the decision to integrate baseball, his wife, Jane, tried to persuade him not to go through with it.

"Why should you be the one to do it?" she said. "Haven't you done enough for baseball? Can't someone else do something for a change?"

At the time, Rickey's son, Branch Jr. ran the Dodgers' farm system. He told his father, "It means we'll be out of scouting in the South."

Rickey's reply: "For a while. Not forever."

No, not forever. No way. America, because of Jackie Robinson and Martin Luther King Jr. and the civil rights movement, would change, and Rickey was a true visionary for recognizing that Robinson's success was a stepping-stone to another American revolution.

During a conversation I was having with him about Jackie Robinson, Andrew Young, the civil-rights leader and a confidant to Dr. King, talked at length about King's leadership skills, about his vision for America and what he was willing to sacrifice to make it a reality. Yes, there would be a revolution, and there would be blood shed in that revolution's name—including, King understood, his own.

"His role as a leader was driven by his faith," Young told me. "He believed that there was a plan of God that he fit into. Dr. King spoke frequently about a 'divine order' and how all of us must find our place in it.

> *"Visions are born in the soul of a man or a woman who is consumed with the tension between what is and what could be. Anyone who is emotionally involved, frustrated, brokenhearted, maybe even angry about the way things are, in light of the way they believe things could be, is a candidate for vision. Visions form in the hearts of those who are dissatisfied with the status quo."*
>
> ANDY STANLEY
> PASTOR AND AUTHOR

"I once heard Dr. King give a sermon on leadership, unity and suffering. He was willing to suffer for what he believed in. He'd laugh and joke with us about who would be the first one killed. He had a comic routine where he'd be preaching at your funeral. He'd act it out and make it very funny. That was the way of dealing with the inevitability of his death."

James Earl Ray assassinated Dr. King in Memphis on April 4, 1968. Had he survived, Dr. King would have been seventy-five years old on the day I conducted my interview with Andrew Young, in September 2004.

"I think he'd be very pleased with the amount of progress we've made," Young told me as we finished the interview. "He always saw the possibility of the future and viewed life with a positive approach—even when things were tough."

A LEADER PREPARES FOR ALMOST ANYTHING

Even though Robinson died at the young age of fifty-three, I'm still stunned that, in the sixteen years he lived after retiring from baseball, no one offered him a managing job. He had such a keen sense of observation, whether noticing a hitch in a pitcher's delivery that might help him steal a base or the manner in which a player reacted in a tense situation. He knew his opponents inside and out. He was a walking, talking example of that cliché so many coaches and athletes use these days: "It's not enough to want to win. You have to prepare to win."

Dodgers pitcher Clyde King was once sitting in the lobby of the Knickerbocker Hotel in Chicago, reading the box scores of the Montreal Royals in *The Sporting News*. Robinson came over and asked to look at the paper. He proceeded to give King a complete breakdown of each player on the Royals' roster—which pitchers were a step away from the bigs, which hitters needed to learn to lay off the curveball in the dirt before they could think about joining the Dodgers. King was amazed at how thorough Robinson's knowledge was, how closely he studied the game.

In one of my interviews with Rachel Robinson, she said to me: "I think Jackie would have been a successful manager. He was a student of the game and would have been a good strategist. He'd have worked with men, and they'd have responded to him. He'd have enjoyed using his knowledge and teaching them. The one thing Jackie had had enough of was the travel, and that might have kept him from managing."

> *"The speed of the leader determines the rate of the pack."*
>
> WAYNE LUCAS
> HORSE TRAINER

Maybe, but one thing's for certain: nothing else would have.

A LEADER HAS INNER STRENGTH

"Athletes, like surgeons and concert violinists, know the dry mouth of pressure. It costs them sleep and shapes their dreams."

—Roger Kahn, author

Solly Hemus, a former Major-Leaguer, was a close friend of Eddie Stanky, the Dodgers' second baseman, when Robinson joined the team. When I talked to Hemus for this book, he told me he had asked Stanky what he thought of Robinson.

"He said Jackie was the leader of the Dodgers," Hemus said. "Everyone looked up to him in a different way because of some of the insults by fans and the hurdles he had to climb. It was not the same for him as it was for his teammates. They admired him because when he went on the field he didn't have to put up with some loudmouth fan.

"Eddie said he saw him a few times when he was frustrated because of unwarranted criticism. He wanted to speak out, but he also knew that some of the things he would say would be misinterpreted. It was more important for him to take the ridicule so other black ballplayers would have the opportunity to play in the majors. Eddie said his teammates realized the sacrifices Jackie was making, and this was one of the reasons they felt he was a leader."

"The only safe ship in a storm is leadership."

FAYE WATTLETON
WRITER

There are so many ways to define "strength." Strength is Henry Aaron playing through the hate mail and the death threats and the pressure of supplanting baseball's greatest player and its greatest record, eclipsing Babe Ruth's 714 home runs with class and pride.

"The best definition of a leader is a man who can make the people who served with or under him do what they don't want to do and like it."

PRESIDENT HARRY S. TRUMAN

Strength is what Marty Stern, who coached Villanova University's women's cross-country team to five national championships, called "playing hurt," meaning that an athlete, or an accountant or a chef gives his best when he least feels like giving his best.

Strength is Jackie Robinson's telling Red Smith in 1946 after injuring his ankle in a game for the Montreal Royals: "I'm not brittle. Football never hurt me. Anybody hitting a bag the way I did the other

"When those disciples were sitting in the boat and the sea was calm, they didn't need Jesus, did they? When the storm hit, that's when they needed leadership."

TYRONE WILLINGHAM
FORMER NOTRE DAME FOOTBALL COACH

night would have hurt his ankle. Anyhow, that ankle always has been bad. It's been broken, but I played six years of football with the ankle taped, and it never bothered me."

Strength is Jackie Robinson's entering the cauldron of racism and emerging a better man for it.

Strength is what Dodgers manager Leo Durocher showed when his team tried to enter the ballpark in Macon, Georgia—in the teeth of a segregated state—for an exhibition game. The game had been sold out. Robinson was in step with the rest of the players, and a police officer stopped him before he could enter the park.

"You can't come in here," the policeman said. "Can't you read?"

He pointed to a sign that said, "WHITES ONLY."

"He can't go in this entrance?" Durocher said.

"No, he can't."

"Well," Durocher replied, "then we're not going in there. You know what that means, don't you?"

The officer did. The sellout crowd might have been a tad upset if the Dodgers didn't play.

He let Robinson in.

> *"The man who wants to lead the orchestra must turn his back on the crowd."*
>
> JAMES CROOK
> AUTHOR

A LEADER UNDERSTANDS ACTIONS SPEAK LOUDER THAN WORDS

Durocher's exchange with the Macon police officer is a good example of this principle, one of the core points of any leader. "Leadership," says fundraising consultant Mary D. Poole, "should be more participative than directive, more enabling than performing."

What does Poole mean? Here's what:

In his autobiography, Buck O'Neil tells the story of an incident in Muskogee, Oklahoma, when he and Robinson were teammates on the Kansas City Monarchs. For years, the team had been buying gas at a service station with one restroom—and blacks weren't permitted to use it. One day, the team bus pulled into the service station, and Robinson got out and started walking toward the restroom. While filling the tank, the owner yelled at him.

"Hey boy!" the owner said. "You know you can't go in there."

Robinson asked why.

"Because we don't allow no colored people in that restroom."

Calmly, Robinson turned to the owner.

"Take the hose out of the tank," he said.

The owner just looked at him.

"Take the hose out of the tank," Robinson repeated.

Robinson then turned to his teammates in the bus—a bus with two fifty-gallon tanks, a bus that meant plenty of business for the owner.

"Let's go," Jackie said. "We don't want this gas."

The bus pulled away. A few weeks later, the Monarchs came back to the service station. The owner stuck the hose in the bus's gas tank and said:

"All right, you boys can use the restroom. But don't stay long."

"From then on," O'Neil wrote, "the Monarchs could use the restroom whenever they passed through. But more importantly, they decided never to patronize any gas station or restaurant where they couldn't use the facilities."

(It's amazing how the lure of losing money—either a sellout crowd or a hefty sale on gas—got people to accept integration back then, isn't it?)

O'Neil's story perfectly illustrates Robinson's leadership qualities—and it is the consummate example of Poole's idea of "participative, enabling" leadership. Instead of "directing" his teammates to boycott the service station, Robinson took action, testing the owner himself, putting himself on the line for the sake of principle. And because he did, he "enabled" his teammates to use the service station restroom in the future. There was no great speech, no grand gesture. There didn't need to be.

"If not for Jackie Robinson's leadership and tenacity, I'm not sure any of us would have made it," Hall of Fame shortstop Ozzie Smith told me. "He

> *"As a leader, one must sometimes take actions that are unpopular or whose results will not be known for years to come. There are victories whose glory lies only in the fact that they are known to those who win them."*
>
> NELSON MANDELA

was a pioneer, the first guy off the tank and right at the front. He had a lot more to deal with than those of us who followed. What we did pales in comparison to Jackie's efforts."

Robinson once told teammate Roy Campanella: "Maybe it's not enough for us to just make out okay. So many people are counting on us—not only Negroes but so many whites, too, who believe in equal opportunity. It's like we're speaking for them by how we play on the field. There are still some guys, you know, who say that Negroes are only a flash in the pan in the majors and that, sooner or later, the color line will be back. Well, we've somehow got to speak up for the people who believe the opposite, and who're rooting for us. We don't do it by speech-making. We've got to do it by playing such outstanding ball that there's no question left in anyone's mind about whether or not Negroes have a contribution to make in big-league ball."

Here's a little story that might contain a lesson for anyone who supervises the work of someone else:
A woman was having the second-floor rooms of her house painted. She thought the painter wasn't making good progress because she couldn't hear a sound.
"Are you working hard?" she called to the painter.
"Yes, ma'am," he said.
"Well," the woman shouted, "I can't hear you!"
"Lady," the painter shot back, "I ain't putting it on with a hammer!"

Not just saying. Doing. As I said earlier, that's what makes a leader. Simply telling someone else what to do—even if you run your own company and have two hundred people working for you—doesn't make you a leader. Words are empty when action isn't filling them. What good is it for a president, a clergyman or a father to tell citizens, parishioners or children how they ought to live their lives if they themselves don't follow through on their own directives? What good is it to say, "I will support you" to someone who needs our assistance, then never lend that helping hand? In 1970, Robinson didn't just pay lip service to Curt Flood's historic legal battle against Major League Baseball's reserve clause—the rule that basically put big-leaguers in indentured servitude to the teams they played for. He testified on Flood's behalf.

"He always knew nobody would care what he said, thought or believed until he had given them a reason to," the late sportswriter Ralph Wiley wrote of Robinson on ESPN.com in 2003, "until he'd shown his skill, talent, tenacity, fearlessness, durability and ability to win and be a team player on the field over time. You don't make an icon over the weekend."

Peter Gammons, one of the preeminent baseball writers in the country when he was with the *Boston Globe* and now a fixture on ESPN as an analyst, was a freshman at the University of North Carolina in 1964 when Martin Luther King Jr. came to Chapel Hill to speak at a civil-rights rally.

"At the end of his speech," Gammons told me, "King said: 'At the end of this century, Jackie Robinson will be one of the ten most important Americans of the twentieth century.' At the time, I thought, 'Wow, baseball is that important!' Then I thought about what a great thing Branch Rickey and Jackie Robinson did together."

Exactly. What they *did*. Not what they said.

> *"Leadership is solving problems, and the day people stop bringing you their problems is the day you stop leading."*
>
> FORMER U.S. SECRETARY OF STATE COLIN POWELL

> *"The winds and the waves are always on the side of the ablest navigators."*
>
> EDWARD GIBBON
> HISTORIAN

A LEADER SETTLES ONLY FOR SUCCESS

Picture it: Jackie Robinson and Robin Roberts, playing golf together. Think there was some competition going on there?

The two played in a threesome one fall while they were in the midst of their baseball careers, and on a par four, Robinson drove his ball into a sand trap near the green. The ball was barely visible, so deeply had Robinson driven it into the sand. The club pro, who was playing with them, started to reach for the ball to pull it out.

"Hey, hey," Robinson objected, "I put it there, and I'll knock it out of there."

The first time Robinson tried to hit out of the trap, the ball caromed backward off the lip of the trap back into the sand. But with a better lie on his third shot, Robinson was able to lift his ball out of the trap to within three feet of the hole. He made the putt to par the hole.

"I thought to myself that there was Jackie Robinson at his best," Roberts remembered. "He was a competitor and did not want anyone to give him anything."

Yet, as badly as he wanted to win—and he would do almost anything to win, in any competitive situation—Jackie also wanted to win honorably. In that moment, on that hole, success for Robinson was knocking that golf ball out of that sand trap, and he took it on himself to do it. He had put himself in a tough spot, and he had to get himself out of it. Even in that little moment, he accepted responsibility, like any decent leader should. When a leader does that, when he accepts responsibility for his or his organization's success or failure, people are much more likely to listen to him and to try to emulate him.

"Leaders are not born. Leaders are made, and they are made by effort and hard work."

VINCE LOMBARDI
FOOTBALL COACH

> 1. *I met a lot of leaders who were never loved. I have never met a great leader who was not respected.*
> 2. *People choose their leaders based on character. Leaders have to lead by example.*
> 3. *Your organization will never get better unless you are willing to admit that there is something wrong with it.*
> 4. *Great leaders do not tell people how to do their jobs. Lousy leaders have no confidence in themselves, so they have no confidence in anyone else.*
> 5. *Failure is contagious; success is infectious.*
> 6. *When placed in command, take charge.*
> 7. *Everyone knows the right thing to do. The challenge is having the guts to do what is right.*
>
> GENERAL NORMAN SCHWARZKOPF
> ON THE ATTRIBUTES OF GREAT LEADERS

Ken Hitchcock, the head coach of the NHL's Philadelphia Flyers, once said: "That's when you grow, when you get into a tough situation. You've got to grow, rather than just hope the problem goes away. You've got to solve it and move on. . . . When you're a coach and you've got natural leaders, they're like gold."

If Hitchcock is right—and I know he is—then the Dodgers had the human equivalent of Fort Knox playing in their infield from 1947 to 1956.

"If a war was going to break out, I wanted to be on Robinson's side," Leo Durocher once said. "He'd win the war, somehow. As you know, we had our spats, but he was a winner, through and through."

"Robbie," said former Dodgers executive Harold Parrott, "was a born leader."

A LEADER INSPIRES OTHERS TO ACHIEVE

All you need to know about Robinson's ability to inspire and motivate his teammates is this:

In their five seasons from 1952 to 1956, the Dodgers won four pennants and one World Series. In 1957, the first season after Robinson retired from pro baseball, they finished in third place, eleven games behind the first-place Milwaukee Braves and three games behind the second-place St. Louis Cardinals.

> *"Even a two-car parade gets fouled up if you don't decide, ahead of time, who's going to lead."*
>
> ZIG ZIGLAR
> MOTIVATIONAL SPEAKER/WRITER

Robinson, according to Leo Durocher, had "magnetism . . . the feeling that this is the man who will carry [a team] to victory." Ruth had it, Durocher said. Dizzy Dean had it. And Robinson did, too. But Robinson didn't serve as an inspiration just to the Dodgers. He inspired an entire generation of ballplayers—and of Americans—to reach beyond themselves. They saw what he had done, what he had overcome, and they asked themselves a simple question:

"If he did that, what can I do?"

"By persevering and prevailing, Jackie Robinson made it possible for those who followed not to be as fearful," Harry Edwards told me. "White owners didn't have to be fearful of signing more black players. Black fans did not have to be fearful of lynching if something went wrong at a ballpark. Jackie is a classic hero of our nation like Abraham Lincoln or Martin Luther King. We still talk about them."

As he closed in on Babe Ruth's record of 714 career home runs, Hank Aaron drew strength from the last time he saw Robinson—in Cincinnati in October 1972, during the World Series. Later that month, Aaron attended Robinson's funeral, and he was stunned to see how few African American players showed up.

"It made me more determined than ever to keep Jackie's dream alive, and the best way I could do that was to become the all-time home run champion in the history of the game that had kept out black people for more than sixty years," Aaron once wrote. "I owed it to Jackie. I just wish he could have seen me do it. God, he would have been proud."

In a speech at Frostburg University, Clyde King said: "Jackie Robinson symbolized for so many Americans in the 1940s and 1950s the struggle for human rights and brotherhood in our country. . . . His accomplishments had a profound impact on millions of Americans, both black and white.

"True leadership is like great art: readily recognized but not easily duplicated."

MARYFRAN JOHNSON
EDITOR

"Jackie Robinson, even though a Dodger in the baseball world, was truly a giant in the world at large. He can never be replaced; we can only attempt to imitate him. My prayer is that what Jackie did for baseball, for his race and for his country will not have been done in vain."

That is my prayer, too. My hope.

"Jackie Robinson was a man who practiced loyalty, hard work, dedication, service to others, tolerance and forgiveness," *Newsday* sports columnist Shawn Powell told me. "His values teach all of us how to live successfully. We could all make this country better if we adopted his life principles."

We could all make this country better. It's a grand goal, and sure, somebody out there, some cynic somewhere, will say that Powell is aiming too high, that he's asking too much of us. But Robinson gave us the model. He showed us the way. All we have to do is remember what he did. All we have to do is follow his example.

Suddenly, it doesn't seem so hard. Does it?

Chapter Eight

❧

Challenges, Choices and Self-Control

Without discipline, there's no life at all.
—Katharine Hepburn, actress

IN THE SPRING OF 2004, right around the time former president Bill Clinton was about to release his autobiography, *My Life,* I was on the telephone, talking with Rachel Robinson.

Now, if you were a living, breathing human being in the 1990s, and if you were old enough to handle the . . . ahem . . . mature content of the Clinton presidency, it was easy to anticipate some of the topics that our esteemed former president covered in his book. No matter what one might have thought of Clinton's politics or policies, this much no one can deny: He hasn't exercised much self-discipline in his life. Just ask Gennifer Flowers. Or Paula Jones. Or Monica Lewinsky. Or . . .

> *"Discipline yourself, and others won't need to."*
>
> JOHN WOODEN
> FORMER BASKETBALL COACH

Anyway, I was talking with Rachel, mining her memories for a few more nuggets for this book, hoping that in getting to know her better, I would get to know Jackie a little better, too.

As we chatted, I told Rachel something I thought would make her quite proud. I had conducted more than eleven hundred interviews for the book, I said to her, and never once had I heard a hint of scandal involving Jackie. I never heard a single anecdote or comment that reflected poorly on his character. In fact, I confessed to Rachel, many people had told me her husband was a man of the utmost integrity.

"There is no such thing as instant genius. Jackie Robinson teaches us about discipline, perseverance and keeping your cool."

ANDREW YOUNG
CIVIL RIGHTS LEADER

"Women were always available to Jack and the other ballplayers," she told me. "Jack turned his head and said, 'No.'"

That was Jackie Robinson, exhibiting self-discipline. And it's not as easy as Rachel made it sound.

STRENGTH IN THE SPOTLIGHT

"He underwent the trauma and the humiliation and the loneliness which comes with being a pilgrim walking the lonesome byways toward the high road of freedom."

—Martin Luther King Jr., speaking about Jackie Robinson

Put simply, no professional athlete has had to endure as much as Jackie Robinson. The racism, the hatred, the strain on his psyche—nothing any other athlete had to withstand comes close. It took a special sort of discipline for Robinson to rise above it all. As Branch Rickey demanded, he did not retaliate during his first two years with the Dodgers, but even as his baseball career progressed, as aggressively as he played, he never raised a hand to another ballplayer. He never started a fistfight, even when he would have been justified in doing so. Jackie never let his guard down and never lost control.

Peter O'Malley, the longtime owner of the Dodgers, talked to me at length about Robinson. "Jackie was the most focused person I've ever met," O'Malley said. "He had a goal, and he wouldn't let anything get him offtrack. You could see his focus and determination everywhere—at bat, on base, in the clubhouse. Along with that was Jackie's discipline in

> *"To act coolly, intelligently and prudently in perilous circumstances is the test of a man."*
>
> GOVERNOR ADLAI STEVENSON

how he took care of himself, his game preparation. He was even a disciplined bridge player. I never played with him, but he knew when to hold 'em and fold 'em."

"He had to be a good player, but he also had to carry himself in the right way," former *Boston Globe* columnist Michael Holley told me. "I'm still awed by the discipline he had. I'm sure there were times when he wanted to knock someone in the head, but he had the restraint not to do it."

Oh, there were plenty of those times, the most infamous being the Dodgers' first series against the Philadelphia Phillies in Robinson's rookie year, in April 1947. Phillies manager Ben Chapman, generously described as a "fiery redneck" by baseball historian John Rossi, bragged to the press before the series began that he would ride Robinson, but no one had any idea of what Chapman would say or do.

Led by Chapman, the Phillies mocked and taunted Robinson in a display of racism worse than anything Robinson endured before or after. But, as I pointed out in chapter one, they couldn't break him. He admitted later to coming close to quitting baseball altogether, but

> *"Do something every day that you don't want to do. This is the golden rule for acquiring the habit of doing your duty without pain."*
>
> MARK TWAIN
> AUTHOR

instead he stood firm, took the punishment and responded only with his performance on the field. In short, Robinson was the embodiment of one of my favorite biblical passages, Proverbs 29:11: "A fool gives full vent to his anger, but a wise man keeps himself under control."

"Branch Rickey realized it was going to take a man of great talent and even greater inner strength to face the challenges that Jackie would face,"

"A bad habit never disappears miraculously. It's an 'undo-it-yourself' project."

ANN LANDERS
NEWSPAPER COLUMNIST

former Dodgers executive Fred Claire told me.

One afternoon, I spoke with Howard Schultz, who the Dodgers had sold to the Phillies because Robinson came up in '47 and took over Schultz's spot at first base, about the Chapman incident. He told me that, during that first series against the Phillies, Robinson reached first base, and standing next to him, Schultz could hear Chapman and other Phillies screaming insults from the dugout.

"I asked Jackie, 'How do you take all this crap?' He replied, 'I'll have my day.' And he did."

"Those who say it is easy to be good, have never tried to be good."

C. S. LEWIS
AUTHOR

The following season, 1948, a pair of future Hall of Famers, outfielder Richie Ashburn and Robin Roberts, made their debuts with the Phillies, and neither had anything but respect for Robinson, mostly because of the restraint he displayed.

"I was on first base one day, and a ground ball was hit to short," Ashburn, who died in 1997, once said. "Robinson covered the bag at second, and I slid into him hard and high on his leg. As I was lying on the ground, Jackie just glared at me intensely. He didn't say anything or go after me. He just glared. I never felt so cheap in my life because Jackie couldn't retaliate. He'd made that commitment to Branch Rickey, and I'd gone after a guy who couldn't fight back."

"Jackie," Roberts told me, "was so under control."

As a native of Delaware, I grew up a Phillies fan, and I was a catcher in their minor-league system for several years. I'm not proud of that ugly history of my favorite baseball team, but at least Ben Chapman did one good thing: He brought out the best in Jackie Robinson. Even now, people who never met Robinson marvel over what he withstood. Here's what some of them told me:

J. A. Adande, sports columnist for the *Los Angeles Times:* "Jackie

Robinson had to have endurance to go through what he had to go through. In the process, he opened the doors for me and an entire race of people. The pressure of being first and what he accomplished for all African Americans . . . well, it still amazes me that one man could achieve that. He teaches us to recognize what is within you. His real triumph was doing his normal job under extraordinarily difficult circumstances. That should inspire us that we can accomplish what we have to do with much less difficult circumstances."

Kevin Blackistone, sports columnist for the *Dallas Morning News:* "He had the ability to put up with so many indignities and didn't give in to his emotional responses. He had the ability to be as rational as possible when his emotions had to be running way out in front of him. His composure remained cool under that wilting spotlight."

> *"He is discipline . . . doing the right thing not some of the time, not most of the time, but all of the time."*
>
> FORMER CHICAGO BULL B. J. ARMSTRONG
> ON MICHAEL JORDAN

Dr. Roger Wilkins, history professor at George Mason University: "Jackie was a rookie in 1947, and all the opponents in other dugouts and some in his own didn't want him there. When he played superbly in his first three years with the Dodgers organization, we didn't know he was under wraps by order of Branch Rickey. Then we realized he was a man who wouldn't back down. We knew the huge price he had to pay to reign himself in."

WORDS FROM THE WITNESSES

"He must have had a turtle shell for skin."

—Donald Gutteridge, former Major-Leaguer, on Jackie Robinson

For a better understanding of what Robinson went through, though, it's still best to rely on those who knew him personally or who witnessed his ordeal firsthand. Again and again in my research interviews, people told remarkable stories of Robinson's fortitude, his unwillingness to be broken by the invective, by the out-and-out hate he knew he had to confront.

Sportswriter Frank Graham Jr.: "In the spring of 1952, the Dodgers stayed at the Fontainebleau Hotel at Miami Beach. One day, I saw Jackie and Pee Wee Reese in the lobby signing autographs. Pee Wee had a big line, and he would send them to Jackie. One guy said, 'Will you sign this for my maid?' Jackie never responded to those slights. He had tremendous self-control."

> *"Discipline is the soul of an army. It makes small numbers formidable, procures success to the weak and esteem to all."*
>
> PRESIDENT GEORGE WASHINGTON

Dick Armstrong, former major-league baseball executive, now a pastor: "In 1946, I was still in college and for several weeks worked out with the Baltimore Orioles of the Triple-A International League. I made a road trip with the team to Montreal, Jackie's first season in baseball. I sat in the dugout during the games and was shocked how brutal the Orioles were to him. I saw and heard what they did to him. Vile obscenities. Racial slurs of the worst kind. And he had to take it. I was ashamed and embarrassed about what took place."

Jack Collum, former St. Louis Cardinals pitcher: "One night, the Dodgers were playing the Cardinals in St. Louis. Jackie was playing third and was only about thirty feet from our dugout. Our players gave it to him, some awful stuff. It was so bad that I told our manager, Fred Hutchinson, that I was going down to the bull pen because I didn't want to hear it anymore. And Jackie just took it."

Dan Colona, Dodgers fan: "I was at Jackie's first game in 1947. I was

> *"Some people regard discipline as a chore. For me, it is a kind of order that sets me free to fly."*
>
> JULIE ANDREWS
> ACTRESS

fourteen at the time. I heard the 'N word' all day, all over the park, from Dodgers fans, and I was upset. I almost got in a fight that day, and I would have if it weren't for my father. I never saw a man take the verbal beating and battering Jackie did. This man just took it."

Vin Scully, Dodgers broadcaster: "Jackie faced more adversity in the big leagues than most people will ever face in their entire lives. It was rather remarkable how he handled all that adversity, his self-discipline. He held it all in, even with all the terrible things he saw and heard."

The following words—from three pitchers, all of whom at one time or another were Robinson's teammates on the Dodgers—were particularly striking to me.

Clyde King: "In one game in 1947, Jackie doubled, and as he went into second base, the second baseman took the ball in his glove and slugged him in the face. He was trying to tag him out, but we knew he wanted to hurt him. You could hear it all the way in our dugout. Jackie didn't say a word. On the next pitch, he stole third. Later, he stole home. And he never said a word the whole time."

Roger Craig: "We will never know what Jackie went through in breaking the color line. He would fight you in a New York minute, but he promised Mr. Rickey he wouldn't, and he honored that commitment."

Carl Erskine: "Jackie was a great man, polished and intelligent. But to me, his most unbelievable quality was his self-control in the face of the indignation he endured. You can search the papers and magazines of that time, and you will not find any reports that Jackie shoved anyone in a parking lot, no reports of any altercations.

> *"There has not been a person in our history who led a life of ease whose name was worth remembering."*
>
> PRESIDENT THEODORE ROOSEVELT

"It's a great lesson for young people: we can't control all that's said and done to us, but we can control how we'll react."

IT DOESN'T HAPPEN OVERNIGHT

"What we do on some great occasion will probably depend on what we already are, and what we are will be the result of previous years of self-discipline."

—H. P. Lidden, theologian

Robinson didn't just suddenly acquire self-discipline once Branch Rickey demanded it of him, of course. He cultivated it within himself over time—

"Excellence," Aristotle said, "is not an act, but a habit"—and in truth, he had to. His father, Jerry, left his mother, Mallie, when Jackie was only six months old. Less than a year later, Mallie packed up her five children and left Georgia for California. "Her great dream for us," Robinson wrote in *I Never Had It Made*, "was that we go to school." While Mallie worked, Jackie's older sister, Willa Mae, all but raised him. "She was dedicated on my behalf," he wrote.

See? He learned self-discipline from his mother and his sister.

For all of Mallie's and Willa Mae's work, it took the influence of a young minister named Reverend Karl Downs to keep young Jackie from falling in with a local gang. Downs, in fact, had a huge impact on Robinson's life, becoming a spiritual counselor and friend for more than a decade.

"Reverend Downs was both stubborn and courageous," Robinson remembered. "He believed in setting up programs and sticking to them, regardless of criticism."

See? He learned self-discipline from his mentor.

At UCLA, Robinson played football, basketball and baseball, ran track—and carried a full academic load.

See? He proved in college he had self-discipline.

When he was stationed at Fort Hood, Texas, Robinson commanded a platoon of the 761st Tank Battalion. Under his leadership, the unit received the highest rating of any platoon at the post.

See? He *taught* self-discipline to others.

> *"Perhaps the most valuable result of all education is the ability to make yourself do the thing you have to do, when it ought to be done, whether you like it or not. It is the first lesson that ought to be learned; and however early a man's training begins, it is probably the last lesson he learns thoroughly."*
>
> THOMAS HENRY HUXLEY
> ZOOLOGIST

Don't think for a second that Branch Rickey didn't see this strength within Robinson. He did. "Jackie had a unique understanding that he was fortunate to be the chosen one, but he knew he had a heavy burden to bear as well," Claire Smith, who covered baseball for the *New York Times* and the *Philadelphia Inquirer*, told me. "Branch Rickey said to Jackie, 'You have to take it.'" In fact, Rickey possessed the same quality himself. In 1905, Rickey joined the Cincinnati Reds, but because of his religious principles, he refused to play games on Sundays. The Reds released him for his personal stand, and all Rickey did in response was this: from that point on, into every baseball contract he ever signed, he included a clause saying he did not have to show up to the park on a Sunday.

So Rickey knew how important it was to find the right man to break baseball's color barrier. He had to find someone who was in control of himself, who understood what was at stake, and had the baseball talent and mental and emotional constitution to do what was necessary to make this great attempt at social justice work. "Our weapons," he told Robinson, "will be base hits and stolen bases and swallowed pride."

"The important thing is this: To be able, at any moment, to sacrifice what we are for what we could become."

CHARLES DU BOS
FRENCH CRITIC

"Jackie wanted the baseball experiment to work," Rachel Robinson told me. "He'd made a two-year commitment to Mr. Rickey not to fight back or retaliate, and that was a pledge he promised to keep. He'd overlook all the abuse and not let himself be provoked into an angry reaction because he always remembered how great the consequences were."

As Dodgers manager Leo Durocher once noted, for Rickey's crusade to succeed, it had to meet six fundamental requirements:

1. The man had to be right off the field.
2. He had to be right on the field.
3. The reaction of his own race had to be right.
4. The reaction of the press and public had to be right.
5. We had to have a place to put him.
6. The reaction of his fellow players had to be right.

Every one of those requirements was a test of Robinson's level of self-discipline, and of someone else's. Consider the third one, for instance. *The reaction of his own race had to be right.* Echoing that spirit, in April 1947,

> "Passions unguided are, for the
> most part, mere madness."
>
> THOMAS HOBBES
> PHILOSOPHER

Walter White, who was then the executive director of the NAACP, wrote the following in the *Chicago Defender:*

It is profoundly to be hoped that baseball fans, especially colored ones, will respect Jackie Robinson's request that he be allowed to pioneer as the first known Negro ballplayer in the big leagues without too much ill-advised interference from the stands. There will be enough pressure on him from prejudiced fellow players and white fans to test the mettle of any human being. . . .

Jackie Robinson may during the coming season be spiked or otherwise injured just as he was during the late days of the training season when Bruce Edwards of the Brooklyn Dodgers ran into him on the base paths and shook him up. . . . Let's be careful about charging that Jackie was deliberately hurt unless it can be clearly proved. . . .

Finally, may I plead with that minority of Negroes who appear to believe a baseball game can be seen only through a haze of alcohol to postpone their drinking until after the games in which they go to see Jackie play. I used to take my family and friends to Yankee Stadium or the Polo Grounds to see colored professional teams play. But for the past few years I have not done so because the drinking and loudmouthed profanity, vulgarity and fighting of some colored fans, female as well as male, so disgusted us.

> "Be gentle to all;
> stern with yourself."
>
> ST. TERESA OF AVILA

These were tenuous times in the United States with respect to race relations, and the right chord had to be struck. Sportswriter Sam Lacy had made the same argument in 1945 that White made two years later: "With us, the first man to break down the bars must be suited in every sense of the word. We can't afford to have any misfits pioneering for us, and for obvious reasons. Unwilling as they are to employ Negro players, they will be quick to draw the old cry: 'We gave 'em a chance and look what we got.'" That's why it was so important that Robinson lived such an upright life, that he didn't drink, didn't smoke and didn't cheat on his wife.

Lacy once warned Robinson about the need for self-discipline by referencing boxer Joe Louis.

"He has NEVER had to deny having made a statement," Lacy said of Louis. "He has NEVER criticized the people who gave him his chance, and he has NEVER blamed someone else for anything that happened."

> *"Haphazard ways of living not only destroy the body, they destroy the talent. Irregular sleep, irregular hours, wasteful habits all must be changed to an orderly way of life, if one is an artist."*
>
> PEARL S. BUCK
> AUTHOR

OUR CHOICE, OUR CHANCE

"He who reigns within himself and rules passions, desires and fears is more than a king."

—John Milton, poet

Once you become a disciplined person, you are better equipped to confront life's challenges. The small choices that comprise who you are as an individual are the preliminary events to the big moments that test your very makeup. There are no undisciplined moral people. The truth of life is, we all have free will, and with certain exceptions, we chart the courses for our lives. Circumstance doesn't. Fate doesn't. Luck doesn't. We do. It is a great gift that God has given us. It is a great power. And we must be guided by the right values when we wield it.

As a high school student, are you going to sit in front of the television all evening? Or are you going to finish your homework (thoroughly) first?

As a college student, are you going to another party tonight? Or are you going to reread the assignment for tomorrow's class, or take in a play or do something more productive with this one night than throw down beers with your buddies?

As someone who made a New Year's resolution to eat better, are you going to stick to it? Or are you going to steal spoonfuls of Rocky Road after your spouse has gone to bed?

> *"Don't dig your grave with your own knife and fork."*
>
> ENGLISH PROVERB

As a spouse, are you going to remain faithful and committed to your marriage vows?

As the coach of your son's baseball team, are you going to allow yourself to become involved in a heated argument with the umpire or the opposing coach? Or are you going to hold your tongue and set a good example for your child?

We all face questions of this sort, and ultimately, how we answer them determines what kind of people we turn out to be. For example, when he was a boy in Mobile, Alabama, Henry Aaron skipped school one day when he heard a rumor that Robinson would be making an appearance in town. Sure enough, Aaron and a group of boys found Robinson, dressed in a suit and tie. Jackie began chatting with them outside a drugstore.

> *"What is the best government? That which teaches us to govern ourselves."*
>
> JOHANN WOLFGANG VON GOETHE
> POET

"Stay in school," he told them. "Stay in school."

These were ironic words for Aaron to hear, considering he had *cut class* that day to see Robinson. Worse, for the next few years Aaron acted as if he didn't hear what Robinson had said, skipping class often and getting expelled from high school.

So at this early point in his life, Aaron had a decision to make. He could continue on the path he was on—failing to take school seriously, jeopardizing his future. Or he could find a new path.

> *"Lost time is never found again."*
>
> THELONIOUS MONK
> JAZZ MUSICIAN

He did. He found baseball. And a year after that meeting with Robinson, Aaron earned his high school diploma at a private school.

Aaron wasn't the only future sports superstar who was touched by Robinson as a boy, of course. In a telephone conversation, Kareem Abdul-Jabbar told me: "I grew up in Manhattan right near the Polo Grounds, but I was a Dodgers fan. Jackie Robinson was my hero. When I was deciding where to go to college, Jackie wrote me and encouraged me to go to UCLA, his alma mater. That meant a lot to me. Jackie was a gifted athlete, but he was a man of integrity. He had a deep desire to see blacks treated better. My mother kept reminding

> "Remember: There is always a limit to self-indulgence, but none to self-restraint."
>
> MAHATMA GHANDI

me how articulate he was. That was motivation to polish myself. I was fascinated with Jackie as a leader. He was baited and spiked on the field, but he never complained. He always gave all that he had no matter the cause."

THE BIG TEST

"You must have principles and discipline. You can't be successful if you don't have discipline."

—Hakeem Olajuwon, former basketball player

"The single most important quality for success is self-discipline," author and motivational speaker Brian Tracy says. "Self-discipline means you have the ability within yourself, based on your strength of character and willpower, to do what you should do when you should do it, whether you feel like it or not."

Late in his playing career, after spending all his years in the big leagues as an infielder, Don Zimmer was called on one day to serve as the Dodgers' emergency catcher. Because he wanted to learn more about how to play the position properly, he spent time in Tampa in an instructional league during the off-season. There, he met a coach named Jim Hegan, a former catcher with the Cleveland Indians, who gave Zimmer some of the best advice he had ever received.

> "The secret of a leader lies in the tests he has faced over the whole course of his life and the habit of action he develops in meeting those tests."
>
> GAIL SHEEHY
> JOURNALIST

"Sometimes," Hegan told him, "the tendency of catchers is to play lazy when there's no one on base.

Because of that, you should approach catching the first pitch of the game as if there's a runner on third base and keep that mental thought in your mind all the time."

In short, a good catcher has to be disciplined. Any good baseball player has to be. But the discipline demanded of Robinson was beyond merely mastering a position. He had to do that four times over, sure—learning first base, second base, third base and left field—but he had to do it while receiving death threats, dodging bottles and rocks from the grandstands, and absorbing verbal and physical abuse just for being black. As Robert W. Cohen wrote in his book *A Team for the Ages,* "We have no way of knowing to what extent this pressure affected Jackie Robinson's performance on the ball field. As it is, he was an exceptional player. But how much better would he have been if he had been allowed to just go out and play the game like everyone else? We'll never know the answer, but one thing is certain: Jackie Robinson was one [terrific] ballplayer."

"To this day," Aaron once said, "I don't know how he withstood the things he did without lashing back. I couldn't have done what Jackie did. I don't think anybody else could have done it."

Ira Berkow, a sports columnist for the *New York Times,* told me: "Jackie Robinson had integrity, faith in himself and incredible heart and will. He teaches us so much about dealing with adversity and not being daunted. Life can be rough, so accept your challenges squarely and don't back down."

"A good leader must be harder on himself than on anyone else. He must be disciplined himself before he can discipline others. A man should not ask others to do things he would not have asked himself to do at one time or another in his life."

VINCE LOMBARDI

In August of Robinson's rookie year, St. Louis Cardinals outfielder Enos Slaughter spiked him at first base—and then blamed Robinson for it, claiming Robinson had kept his foot in the middle of the bag and the collision was accidental. "The base paths belong to the runner," Slaughter said, "and I don't believe I have to apologize for not making an exception . . . for anyone."

None of Robinson's teammates

believed Slaughter's excuse, and pitcher Ralph Branca, working on a no-hitter at the time of the incident, told Robinson, "Don't worry, Jackie. I'll get [him] for you."

"No, Ralph," Robinson replied, "just get him out."

Tony Gwynn, the former San Diego Padres great, told me: "I would never have received an opportunity in baseball if Jackie hadn't played well and handled himself in the proper manner. Without Jackie, there would not be me. I always try to take his way and apply it to what I do. I think about Jackie all the time and ask myself, 'What would he have done?' He proves the value in thinking things through. You can't just react. You must look at both sides of any situation and appreciate the other person's perspective."

> *"Dreams crash daily on the rocks of temptation."*
>
> MIKE MURDOCK
> AUTHOR

During an exhibition game in Alabama, on a day early in Robinson's career with the Dodgers, Robinson ignited both black and white spectators more than any other player on the field. When he fielded a ground ball cleanly or took a pitch for a ball, the blacks cheered wildly. When he fouled off a fastball or flew out to left, the whites cheered. As Roger Kahn remembered it, the crowd regarded the other black players in the game as simply ballplayers, but Robinson was "the threatening, glorious black."

"Does that bother you?" Kahn asked Robinson after the game.

"What?" Robinson said.

"That noise about everything you do and the way fans get pushed around."

"If I let that stuff bother me," Robinson said, "I wouldn't be here."

Really, Robinson had to ignore the taunts and the cheers. He had to ignore everything around him and concentrate on the game, on the next play, on the next pitch. Ultimately, he knew his peers would judge him on his performance on the field, as would his fans, his manager and coaches, and even Branch Rickey—which is really how it is for any of us. In the end, the people who judge you, who evaluate you—your boss, your spouse, your friends and family members—want to be able to count on you. They might be understanding of your faults and failures to a degree, but they also don't want constant excuses for work that isn't finished, responsibilities that aren't fulfilled, promises that aren't kept. Your boss expects you to show up on time. Your spouse is counting on you to help manage the money. Your daughter is counting on you to read a bedtime story to her. Like a CEO of a major corporation, like the fans of any pro sports team, they want *results*.

It's telling, then, to read this short article from *The Sporting News* in 1947, published when the magazine named Robinson the National League's Rookie of the Year:

"That Jackie Roosevelt Robinson might have had more obstacles than any first-year competitors, and that he perhaps had a harder fight to gain even major league recognition, was no concern of the publication. The sociological experiment that Robinson represented, the trailblazing that he did, the barriers he broke down, did not enter into the decision. He was rated and examined solely as a freshman player in the big leagues—on the basis of his hitting, his running, his defensive play, his team value."

> *"No man is free who is not master of himself."*
>
> EPICTETUS
> PHILOSOPHER

In other words, he wasn't judged on the circumstances swirling around him. He was judged on how he played the game. On his results. Just as Rachel judged him as a husband. Just as the citizens of our country judge our former presidents. Just as all of us are judged each day . . . by others, and by ourselves.

So ask yourself: how do I measure up? On those exams—those tests of my self-discipline and, ultimately, my success as a human being—how high are my grades? And how high do I want them to be?

I know this: on those tests, Jackie Robinson would ruin the curve.

Chapter Nine

The Character
Catalog

*I'm not proud just that he performed with excellence on the field.
I'm proud that as a man he had integrity and strength.*
—Rachel Robinson

IT WAS SUCH A SMALL MOMENT, thirteen little words passing from one
man's mouth to another man's ear on an April afternoon in 1947. Lee
Handley, a third baseman for the Philadelphia Phillies, whispered to Jackie
Robinson, and that was all it took—two men encountering each other on
a baseball field and one possessing the decency and depth to acknowledge
the other's humanity.

It was a small moment, but in the context of history, it grows larger as
time passes. It casts a pencil of light on one of the darkest days in
Philadelphia baseball history, and it shows the character and conviction of
a man who otherwise might have been just another ballplayer to play in the
major leagues without further distinction.

The events of April 22, 1947, might be the fulcrum of the Jackie
Robinson story. I've discussed those events and the characters involved in
them—Jackie, his teammates, the Philadelphia Phillies and their manager,
Ben Chapman—at length, and I will continue to discuss them in greater
depth for this reason: that day was a touchstone moment, I believe, in

Jackie's career and in American history. It was the day when people truly began to understand what Jackie Robinson was up against when he started playing Major League Baseball, to understand why it was so important for him to flourish.

Curt Simmons was eighteen years old in 1947. He pitched in only one game for the Phillies that season before winning 114 games over the next ten seasons. He played for Chapman for half a season in 1948, and he faced Robinson who knows how many times before Robinson retired in 1956.

"It was rough," Simmons told me. "They were Southerners. They were nasty. All those guys, everybody. In that era, they called Jackie some bad names. But the more they got on him, the better he played. He was a tough guy. They kept him awake, let's put it that way."

Never was it worse than on April 22. Chapman essentially called Robinson a nigger for nine straight innings. At one point, he shouted, "When did they let you out of the jungle?" Jackie, of course, stayed silent, singling and scoring in the eighth inning for a 1–0 Dodgers win.

"If you call me 'boy,' I want to tear your throat out," Robinson once said. "It's Chapman . . . and I set my face and say, 'I'm supposed to ignore them and play ball.'"

> *"Our character is the result of our conduct."*
>
> ARISTOTLE
> PHILOSOPHER

Everyone knows about Chapman, but few know about what Lee Handley said to Robinson while Chapman embarrassed himself into infamy, about his gesture of goodness toward the man who traveled baseball's loneliest journey.

The moment is documented by author Roger Kahn in his book *The Era*, and so it's better to let Kahn tell it:

Handley "later made it a point to seek out Robinson," Kahn wrote. "He said quietly, 'I'm sorry. I want you to know that stuff doesn't go for me.' Handley was the first opposing player to treat Robinson like a man.

"Robinson remembered Lee Handley, out of Clarion, Iowa, for the rest of his life."

* * *

How do you measure a person's character? There are almost as many ways as there are people. What qualities does a person have to possess to be someone of good character? Can they really be pinpointed and listed? What basis is best to use in determining what the phrase "a person of character" means? Maybe it's just a matter of saying, "I know one when I see one."

Maybe it's just that simple.

It was with Lee Handley.

And with Jackie Robinson.

"Whenever a choice of actions, reactions or just a fork in the road confront today's black athletes," the late Ralph Wiley wrote, "they should all pause, then ask themselves one question: 'What would Jackie Robinson do?'"

Before Wiley died, he speculated what it would be like if Robinson had lived beyond his fifty-three years, if he were alive today. What would he contribute to the various debates concerning race and sports? What would he say about the commercialism and warped values of college athletics, for instance—the permissiveness, the renegade football factories, the grab-all-the-dough-you-can mind-sets of university administrators and major-conference big shots?

"If they were going to budge the university presidents' hearts and minds the way Jackie and Rickey did with American hearts and minds," Wiley wrote, "then that's what it was going to take, someone with the character, the fire, the shoulders, the stomach, the heart of a Jackie Robinson. . . .

> *"When wealth is lost, nothing is lost; when health is lost, something is lost; when character is lost, all is lost."*
>
> GERMAN PROVERB

"The side opposite Jackie Robinson isn't the black or white side. It's the wrong side."

Robinson was unique. He was not beholden to an old boys' club or an interest group or any other allegiance that might lead someone to question his intentions. He was beholden to principles—to independence of thought, to the pursuit of justice, to the belief that things could be changed for the better through small acts of courage, respect and love.

"He saw the world in a larger way," Michael Shapiro, author of *The Last Good Season,* told me. "That's a rare quality that rubs off on everyone. Not many people live like that. It makes your life bigger and better and does the same for everyone around you."

How exactly did he do that? By exhibiting the entire "catalog" of qualities that go into comprising a person of character.

1. HONESTY

During a lengthy conversation one day, Jackie's friend Jack Gordon told me about a clothing store in Harlem that Robinson ran for a while. During the holiday season, Jackie would provide gift packages of food for needy families, and on one Christmas, a woman—dressed in a flashy, expensive outfit—walked into the store. A clerk asked her what he could do for her, and the woman said, "I'm here for my gift package."

"When Jackie heard about that," Gordon said, "he ran her out of the store. He had a basic sense of fairness about him."

"No legacy is so rich as honesty."
WILLIAM SHAKESPEARE

Robinson was never one to keep quiet when he came across an example of injustice or unfairness, and he could be counted on to give an honest appraisal of any situation. Always, he spoke out, even on the smallest issues. Joe Garagiola, the former St. Louis Cardinals catcher and television personality, told me that, when Garagiola was on the television program *Today,* Robinson often called him to discuss the show's topics—usually to challenge the premise behind one of the show's segments.

"To tell the truth, I must know the truth. In matters of fact or principle, only one truth exists. Truth about fact or principles has nothing to do with my feelings, needs or wants. It is what it is—truth."
CHARLES CRISMIER
AUTHOR

"Jackie lived the lessons we all try to learn from books," Garagiola said. "He had the courage of his convictions and was willing to pay the price. He would speak out."

When Robinson did speak out, or speak at all, everyone knew his words had meaning. If he said he would do something, he did it. Always, he kept his word, and he regarded any deviation from that pledge as a lie.

"With Jackie Robinson, it wasn't about baseball; it wasn't the playing part," Giants great Willie Mays told me in an interview. "It was the way he conducted himself and kept his mouth closed during those early years of abuse. That was difficult to do."

What helped Robinson's transition to the majors was that he had people around him who were just as honest and up-front as he was—people such as Rickey and, in Robinson's second year, manager Leo Durocher. Sportswriter Stan Isaacs once said that part of what made Durocher a good manager was that he was honest with all of his players. Whether they were black or white, he treated them the same. "Durocher . . . could rip a black player, and the player would know he was ripping him because he was not good, not because he was black," Isaacs said. "Other managers condescended to them, and the players knew that."

And in Rickey, Robinson had an ally for life, someone who was equally unafraid to stand his ground and "tell it like it is." When Phillies general manager Herb Pennock informed Rickey in 1947 that the Phillies would not take the field

> *"Nothing astonishes man so much as common sense and plain dealing."*
>
> RALPH WALDO EMERSON

against the Dodgers if Robinson was in the lineup, Rickey's reply was short and strong:

"Very well, Herbert. And if we must claim the game nine to nothing, we will do just that, I assure you."

2. OPEN-MINDEDNESS

For all those readers who now assume I'm getting wishy-washy, I think a little explanation is needed here.

By "open-mindedness," I'm referring to the value of having strong morals while using instinct and logic and good sense to evaluate a situation or a person before making a judgment. This was an often-underappreciated aspect of Jackie Robinson's character. Yes, Robinson's antennae were always poised for an example of injustice. But as devoted as he was to advancing racial equality and preserving his dignity, Robinson acknowledged that people aren't perfect. He understood that people with good intentions sometimes were going to make mistakes not because they were racists, but because they were human beings and, as such, inherently flawed.

"Nothing is easier than fault-finding. No talent, no self-denial, no brains, no character is required to set up in the grumbling business."

ROBERT WEST
AUTHOR

In 1954, Glenn Cox was a Dodgers pitching prospect and was with the franchise's Montreal affiliate for spring training at Vero Beach. In a game against the Dodgers, he faced Robinson, who was pinch-hitting.

Cox knocked him down with his first pitch.

"I didn't mean to," Cox told me, "but the pitch got away from me. Jackie ended up flat on his back, and when he got up, he stared at me. Then he said to manager Walter Alston, 'I'm not hitting against that crazy kid.'"

With that, Robinson left the game.

"Later," Cox said, "I apologized to him, and he accepted it and said, 'I know you didn't mean to throw at me.' I got to know Jackie a little bit that spring and always believed him to be an honorable man."

Given the racism that Robinson had encountered throughout his life and particularly since he had joined the Dodgers, it certainly would have been understandable for him to presume that Cox was just another redneck who had thrown at his head on purpose. But Robinson made no such presumption, and he took Cox at his word that he unintentionally had thrown the pitch close to his head. He didn't jump to any conclusions and unfairly paint Cox as an enemy.

"Jackie was the only person without prejudice I ever met," Buck O'Neil told me. "He gave all people a chance. He never prejudged anyone."

"It is not who is right, but what is right. That is of importance."

THOMAS HUXLEY
AUTHOR

Lew Burdette was pitching against the Dodgers one night when Robinson bunted for a base hit. Infuriated, Burdette yelled at Robinson, "You bunting b— —!"

Robinson thought he had said something else.

"After that," Burdette said to me, "Jackie was cold to me, and word got back to me that he was calling me racist."

These rumors so bothered Burdette that, before another game against the Dodgers, Burdette walked to the Brooklyn clubhouse and asked the attendant if he could see Robinson.

"We don't want any trouble around here," the attendant told Burdette.

"I just want to see Jackie Robinson," Burdette said.

Inside the clubhouse, Burdette approached Robinson.

"I didn't call you a black b— —," Burdette said. "I called you a bunting b— —."

"Jackie said, 'I'm really sorry for that misunderstanding,'" Burdette told me. "That resolved it."

As much as Robinson's background formed his strong values and principles, it also cultivated this willingness to see both sides of an issue, to withhold judgment before collecting all the facts. Remember: During his years in the army, at Pasadena Junior College and at UCLA, Robinson often had interacted with whites—

> *"You can tell a big person by the way he treats little people."*
>
> THOMAS CARLYLE
> AUTHOR

some of whom treated him poorly, some of whom treated him as their equal. The stories of Robinson's defiance in the face of discrimination and bigotry are so numerous and powerful that they overshadow how different his background was from other black ballplayers of his era, and how that difference shaped him and those around him.

"We never had any doubt about Jackie's ability, but we wondered whether or not he could take the stuff that he had to take in the majors," Negro Leaguer Othello "Gangster" Renfroe once said. "We never thought he could take it. A couple of times, we would pull up to service stations in Mississippi where drinking fountains said 'white' and 'black,' and we'd have to leave without our change. Jackie'd get so mad. If Mr. Rickey had known about Jackie's temperament, I don't think he would have signed him."

That's just it, though: Rickey did know about Robinson's temperament, but he knew, too, that Robinson's education and life experience would counterbalance that fiery temperament. Those who were close to Robinson—sportswriter Sam Lacy, for instance—also saw the same balance in him that Rickey saw.

"Having played football with an otherwise all-white team at UCLA, the Kansas City shortstop would be well versed in diplomacy," Lacy wrote in August 1945, when Robinson was still playing in the Negro Leagues with the Kansas City Monarchs. "He would have neither the inferiority complex we must avoid nor the cocky bulldozing attitude we likewise should abandon. All his life has been spent in an interracial setting, a fact that is bound to be a distinct help as a trailblazer."

In fact, as Lacy pointed out in another column two months later, Robinson's "open-mindedness" was diametrically opposed to the ignorant attitudes Major League Baseball's men of power had held for so many years.

> "Sneaky behavior is always a confession of weakness."
>
> JOHN KENNETH GALBRAITH
> ECONOMIST

"Baseball, in its time, has possessed its full share of men from every other racial strain except Robinson's," Lacy wrote in October 1945. "It has given employment to known epileptics, kleptomaniacs and a generous scattering of saints and sinners. A man who is totally lacking in character has often turned up to be a star in baseball. A man whose skin is white or red or yellow has been acceptable. But a man whose character may be of the highest or whose ability may be Ruthian has been barred completely from sport because he is colored."

It was Robinson who was most responsible for changing those attitudes. Through his mere presence in the Dodgers' clubhouse, he forced his peers either to change their perceptions of blacks or to express their support for racial equality more forcefully than they ever had before. Consider this small story involving Dodgers center fielder Pete Reiser and the petition his teammate Dixie Walker wanted him to sign after word got out that Robinson had been called up to the big leagues.

Just after the army had transferred Reiser to Richmond, Virginia, his daughter became ill. Unfamiliar with the city, Reiser opened the Richmond phone book and called the first doctor he found. The doctor told Reiser to bring the girl to his office. When Reiser arrived at the office with his daughter, he realized that he was in a black neighborhood, that he had telephoned a black doctor.

"I didn't think anything of it," he once said. "What was the difference?"

The doctor cured Reiser's daughter with a shot of penicillin.

Later, before the 1947 baseball season, when Walker approached Reiser and asked him to sign that petition, Reiser told Walker the story about his daughter and the Richmond doctor.

> *"Your life is made up of a series of experiences. Each one will make you stronger, even though it may be hard for you to realize it."*
>
> JACK ERWOOD
> AUTHOR

"What would you have done?" Reiser asked him.

"I would have turned around," Walker said, "and walked away from that neighborhood."

"I told him I thought he was a damned fool," Reiser said years later, "and then I told him what he could do with his petition."

3. TOUGHNESS

It's one thing to know what the right thing to do is. It's another thing to have the courage to do it. That's the kind of toughness I'm talking about here. Being able to throw a punch doesn't necessarily make you tough. Being able to take one does.

No one took more punches than Jackie Robinson.

"He was the right man at the right moment in American history," David Robinson, Jackie's son, told me. "He handled his task with talent, grace and perseverance. He was a remarkable individual with a unique mix of human qualities: inner strength, fire, patience. He was a simple and righteous soul."

The most important decisions we make in our lives rarely are the easiest ones. When you have to make such a choice, when you have to chart a course for yourself, you fear the answers to some basic questions: *What if I fail? What if I'm wrong? How will other people respond to my decision? What are the ramifications of my decision?*

"A lot of people run a race to see who is the fastest. I run the race to see who has the most guts, who can punish themselves into an exhausting pace and, then, punish themselves even more at the end. If I lose, forcing the pace all the way, well . . . at least I can live with myself."

STEVE PREFONTAINE
TRACK STAR

At these moments, it is vital to have a set of principles and priorities to call on—an index in your mind, in your heart and in your soul of what's really important. And when you summon those values and invoke those principles, you have to be "tough enough" to stand firm in the face of those who don't understand or don't share them. You might have to accept ridicule or abuse, but above all else, don't compromise your independence, your conscience or the goals you have set for yourself.

As my boss, Rich DeVos, the founder of Amway and the owner of the Orlando Magic, puts it: "The only thing that stands between a man and what he wants from life is often merely the will to try it and the faith to believe that it is possible." That will and faith can only come from within ourselves, from rising to meet internal and external challenges with the same stalwart strength Jackie Robinson so often showed.

"Looking back, I realize that one of the things I admired most about my father was how he stayed in the game until the end," Sharon Robinson, Jackie's daughter, wrote in her book, *Promises to Keep*. "He stood firm even when his opinion wasn't popular. Whether questioning an umpire or an American president, Dad used his celebrity to challenge an unjust system and support a movement organized to correct the wrongs."

"Knowing what's the right thing to do is usually easy, but consistently doing the right thing, in the face of adversity, is something else. That is the true test of character."

JUDITH MOLLOY
AUTHOR

Sportswriter Maury Allen told me: "Jackie was a very combative personality in every area. He became a Rockefeller Republican, which was most unlikely, but that was typical of him. He enjoyed the give and take of intellectual competition. Jackie and Pee Wee Reese argued about everything—the weather, players, all kinds of things. Once Jackie got to know you, he'd engage you."

Again, there's that "open-mindedness" I wrote of just a few pages ago, and it's not incompatible with "toughness." Robinson was willing to get to know someone, to give him the benefit of the doubt, before he evaluated the person on an intellectual or emotional level. What's remarkable is that his patience in dealing with people and his core beliefs didn't crumble under the deluge of racism and hatred directed at him.

> *"Strength does not come from physical capacity. It comes from indomitable will."*
>
> MAHATMA GHANDI

"Jackie should have gotten into the Hall of Fame without ever swinging a bat because of what he had to put up with," Joe Garagiola told me. "Guys on the Cardinals would yell, 'You'll be back pickin' cotton soon.' 'Pick up my bag, boy.' 'When's the watermelon truck comin'?' One day, the Dodgers were in town. Don Newcombe was pitching. Campy was catching. Jackie came over to the mound for a conference, and one of the guys yelled, 'No wonder you can't get a decent shoe shine in town. They're all on the mound.'"

And still, Robinson excelled on the field for the Dodgers. Newcombe once pointed out that after Robinson debuted with the Dodgers, other blacks came up to the majors in 1947. Larry Doby joined the Cleveland Indians. The St. Louis Browns called up Hank Thompson and Willard Brown from the minors. Later that same season, the Dodgers added another black player, Dan Bankhead. "All these men were talented," Newcombe said, "but it says something that only Jackie Robinson had a good year in 1947. Jackie alone in the National League received letters full of threats and insults and suffered abuse from players,

> *"One of the most destructive cultural changes of the last twenty years has been this country's slide into moral relativism. Too many people, especially our young people, are uncomfortable acknowledging that there is right and wrong, good and evil, in this world."*
>
> FORMER U.S. REPRESENTATIVE
> J. C. WATTS

*"Supreme Court Justice Clarence
Thomas's presentation of his life
often includes . . . a faded yellow
statuette of St. Jude, patron saint
of hopeless causes. 'That's what
they called me,' Thomas has said
in public speeches, 'a lost cause.'
Thomas won the statuette nearly
forty years ago in a Latin bee at St.
John Vianney Minor Seminary, the
high school run by the Diocese of
Savannah for young men
considering the priesthood.
He loves to tell visitors his St. Jude
story: Someone among his white
fellow seminarians broke the head
off his statuette in the open
dormitory, leaving the head next
to the body on the bureau. . . . He
glued [it] back together. And when
they broke it again, he used
thicker glue. They got the
message—he, Clarence Thomas,
could not be broken."*

THE WASHINGTON POST
OCTOBER 10, 2004

managers and fans."

"He was a good ballplayer, but he wasn't the best ballplayer we had," Jesse Williams, a shortstop on the Kansas City Monarchs, said of Robinson. "But he was the best for that particular role that he played, being the first . . . to go up there and take the abuse he took. I wouldn't have taken it. If they had picked me, you possibly wouldn't have heard of Mays and Campanella and all those other fellows cause I would possibly have gotten in a lot of trouble."

It took Robinson playing through that abuse, never relenting in his commitment to Rickey's grand experiment, to persuade people of the truth in a wonderful little line from *New York Times* sports columnist Arthur Daley: "Character and performance, you see, know no color lines."

"I think there is only one word that describes Jackie Robinson— unconquerable," the famed sportscaster Howard Cosell wrote. "He was the most unconquerable human being I have ever known."

4. INTEGRITY

"He was a role model to me because he was a great leader and a man of great integrity."

—New York Mets owner Fred Wilpon, on Jackie Robinson

Historian Bill Kashatus said that when he thinks of Jackie Robinson, he thinks of Stephen Carter's definition of "integrity." Carter, a law professor at Yale University, writes that the word conveys a "sense of wholeness" that can be found in the "serenity of a person who is confident in the knowledge that he or she is living rightly." In his book—appropriately titled *Integrity*—Carter cites three essential steps to achieving integrity:

1. Discerning what is right and what is wrong, which "captures the idea of integrity as requiring a degree of moral reflectiveness."
2. Acting on what you have discerned, even at a personal cost. This criterion acknowledges that a person with integrity is "steadfast, which includes the sense of keeping commitments."
3. Saying openly that you are acting on your understanding of right from wrong. "A person of integrity," Carter writes, "is unashamed of doing right."

"As a human being, Jackie Robinson was among the most giving people our society has ever known," Kashatus told me. "Ultimately, he gave his life for civil rights because he was a person of such great integrity. When he saw something that he felt was ethically wrong, he spoke out against it. He criticized the militancy of the Black Panthers because he didn't believe that the civil rights

> *"Integrity is actually a combination of the words* integritas *and* integer, *which were both used by Roman soldiers to describe their readiness for challenges.* Integritas *was the word to signify that their armor was in sound condition. In Latin, the term meant material wholeness and completeness. The word* integer *indicated that the soldier wearing that armor was of sound character. His standards and morals were high.*
>
> Robin Grugal
> Author

"When a company has integrity, consumers see it, workers know it, alliances respect it. It becomes the reason to trust the company, to honor commitments to the company, and to stay with the company."

MARJORIE KELLY
PUBLISHER

movement could achieve its goals through militancy. At the same time, he had a very public disagreement with Dr. King's attempt to link the war in Vietnam with the struggle against racism at home because he believed that all men—black and white—had an obligation to serve their country. While these views were extremely unpopular among African Americans, they reflected Robinson's fundamental belief that segregation was destructive for both blacks and whites.

"Jackie Robinson's example mirrored all those things," Kashatus continued. "And because of that, he was, in my estimation, the ultimate example of integrity."

"In 1925, the great golfer, Bobby Jones, lost the U.S. Open in a play-off. He would not have been in the play-off had he not penalized himself one stroke for accidentally moving his ball a fraction of an inch in an incident that no one else saw. Commended for the honesty of his actions, Jones demurred, 'There is only one way to play the game. You might as well praise a man for not robbing a bank.'"

BYRON YORK
JOURNALIST

Boiled down, integrity is the essence of character, a combination of intellectual honesty, emotional empathy and decisive action. People of integrity are consistent in their thoughts and beliefs, applying their core principles in the same way in every situation.

I look around these days, and I see example after example of public people demonstrating how little integrity they really have. Within the last year, the governors of Connecticut and New Jersey have resigned in disgrace. You can't open the business section of a newspaper nowadays without reading about another corporate scandal, and you won't find any refuge in the sports pages, either, because so many pro athletes are in trouble with the law. Doesn't anyone know the difference between right and wrong anymore? And if they do, why don't they act accordingly—the way Jackie Robinson did?

Or as former MLB Commissioner Happy Chandler did. Chandler succeeded Kennesaw Mountain Landis as the commissioner of Major League Baseball in 1945. "Chandler had known Satchel Paige, Josh Gibson and Buck Leonard, and he had a strong sense of justice," Peter Golenbock wrote in *Bums*. "Chandler saw that America's black soldiers had given their lives fighting against the Axis in World War II. If they could die for freedom, he reasoned, why couldn't they have an equal opportunity to play Major League Baseball? Though Chandler hadn't the power to change society as governor, as it turned out, he had that power as baseball commissioner."

Soon, two black journalists, Wendell Smith and Rick Roberts of the *Pittsburgh Courier*, approached Chandler and asked him if blacks might someday play Major League Baseball. "I am for the Four Freedoms," Chandler said, "and if a black boy can make it in Okinawa and go to Guadalcanal, he can make it in baseball."

> *"Integrity is thinking of the bigger picture, finding a purpose that is bigger than yourself."*
>
> MILLARD FULLER
> FOUNDER OF HABITAT FOR HUMANITY

Two years later, of course, Jackie Robinson was a Brooklyn Dodger, and Happy Chandler, who supported Branch Rickey's plan and allowed him to implement it despite the opposition of the owners, was part of the reason. Like Rickey, Chandler recognized the social ramifications if Rickey's plan were to work. He recognized the good that could come from the right man—a man of integrity—breaking baseball's color barrier. Even through the blurry prism of the passage of time, Robinson's integrity, as a man and a ballplayer, was easy to see, as several people pointed out to me.

Dr. David Colburn, provost of the University of Florida: "From Jackie Robinson, we can all learn about integrity. He had a quiet dignity that allowed him to endure the racial epithets, the harassment from white teammates, the black housing in spring training. He was a model to the rest of the nation for carrying himself the way he did."

Dr. Elliott Gorn, history professor at Brown University: "I can describe

> *"Somebody once said that, in looking for people to hire, you look for three qualities: integrity, intelligence and energy. If you don't have the first, the other two will kill you. You think about it, it's true. If you hire somebody without the first, you really want them to be dumb and lazy."*
>
> WARREN BUFFETT
> ENTREPRENEUR

Jackie Robinson in one word: guts. He was a man who had the courage of his convictions, and they were thought-out. He valued certain things and never veered from those values. Jackie never backed off from taking a stand in society, even though it could cost him plenty. Very few athletes have been willing to do that."

Bill Mardo, sportswriter for the *Daily Worker:* "Jackie was a man with a fierce, strong devotion to sports and his fight against racism. Many athletes stay clear of controversy, but Jackie teaches us you don't compromise your ideals. Stand up and be counted. Use your influence to make things better for others. Make your life stand for something beyond batting averages and stolen bases.

"With all his athletic accomplishments, he never forsook his social ideals. Yes, he wanted to succeed on the diamond, but above all, he wanted to make life better for his people."

Dr. Steven Wisensale, a history professor at the University of Connecticut, gave me an interesting explanation for why Robinson remained so resolute during his early years in baseball, why he could maintain such a firm code of conduct when others surely would have suc-

> *"Integrity first. Service before self. Excellence in all we do."*
>
> SLOGAN OF THE UNITED STATES AIR FORCE

cumbed to the pressures he faced.

"He had a strong inner core that was partly due to his religious faith and also due to the parenting of his mother," Wisensale told me. "But beyond that, I think his move from Georgia to California was an extremely significant event in his life. Although there were some signs of racism and segregation in California, it was little in comparison to what he would have experienced had he remained in Georgia. By going to California, he played integrated sports at a young age at Pasadena College and UCLA. So when he joined the Dodgers organization, playing with whites was not such a shock to him.

"I doubt if Willie Mays and Henry Aaron, both of whom lived their youth in the Deep South and were subjected to the worst kind of racism, would have made the same kind of transition that Jackie did. Perhaps they would have had less self-confidence and lower expectations. They would have made it, I'm sure. But Jackie was the right guy at the right time, and his religion, his mother's parenting and his experience playing integrated baseball in California early on gave him both confidence and high expectations."

Baseball author and editor Richard Peterson told me that he and his wife met Rachel Robinson a few years ago at a book signing in Cooperstown, New York, at the Baseball Hall of Fame. Rachel, Peterson said, was more interested in talking about her grandchildren than she was in talking about her book.

"We could see very quickly where the heart of this gracious lady really lay," Peterson told me. And through Rachel, Peterson could see it in Jackie, too.

"His outstanding character set him apart. Branch Rickey saw something in him that gave him a sense of comfort, strength of character, courage and determination."

"All of Jack's life," Rachel Robinson told me, "he had these major goals to achieve. He had strong convictions about things and wanted to bring about change. Even when he was suffering from diabetes and was going blind, he still had work to do. Jack's life had meaning to him right to the end. Through all his ups and downs, he never became cynical."

> *"Integrity is a moral value, which means that a person is the same on the inside as he claims to be on the outside. A man of integrity can be trusted."*
> REVEREND BILLY GRAHAM

5. UNSELFISHNESS

I'm a Delaware native, so this story has special meaning for me. It comes courtesy of George Frick, a longtime Delaware sportscaster.

Jackie Robinson stopped in Wilmington, Delaware, once in the 1950s with a barnstorming team. Frick was there, and in a newspaper article he described what he saw from Robinson:

"He was working out, and the kids were leaning over the fence, trying to get autographs. He'd go over and sign an occasional one. I was talking to Jackie, and I said, 'Could you take time out for five or ten minutes, and we could do a little Q&A with these kids?' He said, 'Yeah, sure.' We went over to the fence, and the kids were asking him questions while he was autographing. He was just tremendous. He answered all their questions."

> "You can become a better leader by frequently reevaluating plans to make certain that all of the ambition existing in your strategy is for the cause and none is for yourself."
>
> JIM COLLINS
> AUTHOR

Maybe all anyone needs to know about what kind of man Jackie Robinson was, about the way he placed others before himself, is this:

For all his fame, for all the spoils he could have reaped from his life in baseball, for all the doting he did on his wife and children, he only ever owned one car.

"He knew," Rachel told me, "that things don't make the man."

6. LOYALTY

On August 19, 1999, Bill Madden, the longtime baseball columnist for the *New York Daily News,* sat in a church in Louisville. He had come to Kentucky for a funeral. Pee Wee Reese had died from cancer at age eighty-one.

In the church, too, were Carl Erskine, Don Zimmer, Ralph Branca and Clyde King—Dodgers one and all. Sandy Koufax had been on a cruise in the Caribbean, and upon learning of Reese's death, he had the ship make a special stop so he could fly in for the funeral. "He was my captain for four years and my friend for forty-five," Koufax told Madden. "What else can I say?" Duke Snider had caught a red-eye flight from California to be there.

So had Rachel Robinson. Reese, of course, made that now-famous gesture to Jackie Robinson during the 1947 season, putting his arm around Robinson while the two were on the field in a show of support, of understanding what Robinson was going through. The moment grew into legend, even if no one could quite remember where it had taken place. Was it Chicago? Was it Boston? Does it matter?

"I prefer a loyal staff officer to a brilliant one."

GENERAL GEORGE S. PATTON

"I wanted to hug him when I heard about it," Rachel told Madden. "That's why there was no way I wasn't going to be here today. It took twelve hours, but Pee Wee was a major person in my life, and this is my last tribute to him.

"What it did was change the dynamics of the whole team, showing them they had something dramatic to deal with. The dissidents were traded, and those who were left had to adjust. Jack felt very close to Pee Wee the rest of his life. Each of them had a strong sense of their impact on social change."

What's more, they had a strong sense of loyalty. Reese once said that Robinson "didn't need no . . . protector," but when he was a rookie with the Dodgers, he did need a friend. Reese became one, and remained one for the rest of their lives.

When the Dodgers played an exhibition game in Atlanta and the Ku Klux Klan threatened to shoot Robinson if he played, it was Reese who made Jackie smile for a moment during warm-ups by quipping, "Jack, don't stand so close to me today. Move away, will ya?" When Dodgers outfielder Al Gionfriddo started a game of hearts in the clubhouse and someone asked how anyone could play alongside Robinson, it was Reese who said, "What the hell's wrong with playing with a guy on your own team?" It was Reese who was the nucleus, the beating heart of those Dodgers teams that were so close-knit they were like family, from Branch Rickey on down. You didn't cross the Dodgers, and in 1947, Jackie had joined the family, and he never would leave it.

Joan Hodges, Gil's widow, told me

"Please keep these words in your heart, as long as you live. How great a player you are or how smart you are will not determine your ultimate success on your job. Your trust and your loyalty will be the measures that people remember you by."

MEL HANKINSON
COLLEGE BASKETBALL COACH

> *"Lots of people want to ride with you in the limo, but what you want is someone who will take the bus with you when the limo breaks down."*
>
> OPRAH WINFREY

a pair of stories that illustrate that closeness. In March 1949, Joan was twenty-one years old, and she and Gil, the Dodgers' first baseman, had recently married. In West Palm Beach, the Dodgers played a spring-training game against the Philadelphia A's.

"I was sitting behind the A's bench with Nancy Ramazzoti, another player's wife, and it was just a bench, no dugout," Joan said. "Jackie came to the plate, and I was rooting for him. An A's player who didn't know who I was turned around and said to me, 'How would you like to sleep with him tonight?' Connie Mack, the A's manager, was there in his black suit and straw hat, and you could see him look very uncomfortable. Nancy Ramazzoti really laced into that player for saying that."

The second story is even more powerful.

"Gil died in April 1972," she said. "Jackie was quite ill at the time but attended the funeral in Brooklyn. Howard Cosell was at the service. After

> *"Love is absolute loyalty. People fade. Looks fade. But loyalty never fades."*
>
> SYLVESTER STALLONE
> ACTOR

the service a couple of friends assisted Jackie into a limo outside the church. Howard stopped Jackie and put a microphone in front of him and asked, 'Jackie, what a sad moment. How would you sum up what Gilly meant to you?'

"'It hurts almost as much as when I lost Jackie Junior,' he said.

"That's all I need to say. That's my most precious memory of Jackie."

Ben Chapman crossed the Dodgers family, and made the family stronger in doing so. "He did more than anybody to unite the Dodgers," Rickey once said. "When he poured out that string of unconscionable abuse, he solidified and unified thirty men, not one of whom was willing to sit by and see someone kick around a man who had his hands tied behind his back. Chapman made Jackie a real member of the Dodgers."

Even after that ugly day at Ebbets Field, Chapman wouldn't stop attacking Robinson in private. And the Dodgers wouldn't stop defending him. In Philadelphia one day, Chapman pulled aside Dodgers executive Harold Parrott under the stands. The two had known each other since Chapman was a player for the Dodgers in 1944 and 1945.

"We had played a lot of bridge on the long Dodger road trips," Parrott wrote in his book, *Lords of Baseball*. "And he had far-out bidding ideas, which he called the 'Winslow System.' I always called him 'Winslow' after that."

> *"Loyalty is the vital virtue."*
>
> RUDOLPH GIULIANI
> FORMER MAYOR OF NEW YORK CITY

Under the stands, Chapman began chiding Parrott—not only about Robinson, but about Brooklyn's right fielder, Carl Furillo, who was Italian.

"Poor Parrott," he said. "Know how you're going to end up? You'll be the nursemaid to a team of twenty-four niggers and one dago."

"If I was short a hotel room," Parrott said in return, "and had the choice of bunking with you or with Number 42, know what I'd do? I'd room with Robinson, Winslow."

The examples of the camaraderie, the allegiance Robinson's teammates felt toward him and each other go on and on:

- Former New York Giant Rudy Rufer talked to me about the intensity of the rivalry between the Giants and the Dodgers, and he made clear the level of loyalty Robinson possessed. "One time, we were playing the Dodgers at Ebbets Field, and Carl Furillo had killed us in the past couple of series. Leo Durocher, our manager, yelled at the pitcher, Sheldon Jones, to hit Furillo behind the ear or he would never pitch again. Jones nailed him and knocked him unconscious.

  "Jackie saw this and ran right at Durocher, charging him. Jackie had to be restrained from killing Durocher. He stuck up for his teammates, white or black. I always appreciated that about him."

  And remember: Durocher had been Robinson's manager in Brooklyn!

> *"Lip-loyalty is not loyalty at all.*
> *The only homage that counts is the*
> *homage of deeds, not words."*
>
> PRESIDENT THEODORE ROOSEVELT

- Red Barber, the great broadcaster for the Dodgers and New York Giants, wrote of the day Robinson reported to the Montreal Royals, who at the time were managed by Clay Hopper. Hopper hailed from Mississippi and, Barber wrote, was not all that happy with the prospect of managing a black ballplayer. So Rickey told him: "You can manage correctly, or you can be unemployed. You manage this fellow the way I want him managed, and you figure out how I want him managed." In response, Hopper said the only thing he could.

"Yes, Mr. Rickey."

"Looking back, I can see how the conviction of Jackie and Mr. Rickey to bring a black man into baseball was fortified by the fact that they were alike in so many ways," Rachel once said. "Jackie had the good influence of older men in his life, and he was deeply spiritual, with a strong belief in God. Both were religious, and both said 'we' rather than 'I.' We could always call Mr. Rickey on the phone; he was always available to us. It wasn't as if he had just thrust Jack into a situation and left him to fend for himself. He took responsibility.

> *"To be true to ourselves,*
> *we must be true to others."*
>
> PRESIDENT JIMMY CARTER

"Nor were we ever distrustful of Mr. Rickey's motives. He was a man of integrity, and we could trust him. Whatever his mixed motives may have been, he became a lifelong friend, someone we admired tremendously."

- Clyde King: "One day, in a game I was pitching, someone threw at Jackie. I told him that I'd take care of it, and he said that I didn't need to do that, but I did anyway. In those days, the pitchers had to bat. Well, when that pitcher came to the plate I knew what pitch I was going to throw. He got set in his stance, and I went into my windup and threw a ball inside under his chin. His bat went one way. His helmet went the other way. He hit the ground. I took care of things for my friend and teammate."

• Don Zimmer, in his autobiography, *Zim:* "I'll never forget that first day I set foot inside Yankee Stadium and saw Jackie Robinson at first base for the Dodgers. I think of that every time I walk into Yankee Stadium. That was Jackie's rookie season, and little did I know a few years later I'd be calling him a teammate and, even more importantly, a friend. . . .

"On December 13, 1956, the Dodgers announced they had traded Jackie to the Giants for a journeyman pitcher named Dick Littlefield and $30,000 cash. But a couple of days later, he pulled the plug on them by announcing he was retiring to accept an executive position with the Chock Full o'Nuts coffee company. The following winter, I got a call from him at my home in Treasure Island. He said he was coming to Tampa on business and asked me if I could get a golf game together. That was about as big a thrill as I ever had—Jackie Robinson thinking enough of me to want to play golf with me. He was a great friend, and I still miss him."

There are so many of these stories, and truth be told, when a team is at its best, such stories are plenty. And by "team," I don't mean just the twenty-five men who make up a Major League Baseball roster or the twelve men on an NBA roster. I mean the police precinct. I mean the newsroom of the local paper. I mean the accountants at the firm or the women in the sorority or the parishioners in the church. I mean your family and friends.

> *"No more duty can be urged upon those who are entering the great theater of life than simple loyalty to their best convictions."*
> EDWIN HUBBEL CHAPIN
> CLERGYMAN

These relationships are the core of our society, and we cultivate them only through a willingness to be loyal, to say yes and to assume that yes lasts forever. Just as Jackie Robinson and his Dodgers family did.

* * *

I started this chapter with Lee Handley, that third baseman for the Phillies who gave us a glimpse into his character though an act of kindness

> *"Your character eventually outdistances your life's accomplishments. They will remember what you were more than what you did."*
>
> DR. HAROLD SALA
> AUTHOR/PASTOR

toward Jackie Robinson, a moment of grace given to baseball's bravest soul. So it's fitting that I finish this chapter with him as well.

That 1947 season was Handley's tenth in the majors, and his last. He had played for the Pittsburgh Pirates from 1937 to 1946, and after retiring from baseball, he moved back to Pittsburgh. He was fifty-six years old when he died of a heart attack there on April 8, 1970—two years before Jackie Robinson, ravaged by diabetes and heart disease, died on October 24, 1972, at age fifty-three.

They say the good die young. They had that right.

Chapter Ten

❧

Moments of Grace

The most luxurious possession, the richest treasure anybody has, is his personal dignity.

—Jackie Robinson

HE WAS A SIXTEEN-YEAR-OLD kid riding the elevated train to Ebbets Field, and suddenly Frank O'Reilly realized: *The man sitting across from me is the one who's going to change baseball forever.*

Frank worked as an usher at Dodgers games, and that day's game was a big one. Granted, it was merely a preseason exhibition game, but it was big, nonetheless. The Dodgers were playing the Yankees, and Jackie Robinson would be playing in his first game in Brooklyn. And here was Jackie, right in front of Frank, riding the train to the park, not another soul around.

"I thought to myself, 'That can't be Jackie,'" O'Reilly told me. "But it

> *"Class is an aura of confidence that is sure without being cocky. Class has nothing to do with money. Class never runs scared. It is self-discipline and self-knowledge. It's the sure-footedness that comes with having proved you can meet life."*
>
> ANN LANDERS
> ADVICE COLUMNIST

was. He was all by himself, and that amazed me. There were no reporters or Dodger officials with him on this important day."

When the train arrived at the station, the kid worked up the nerve to ask a question.

"Are you Jackie Robinson?"

"He said, 'Yes,' and we walked to the ballpark together and had a nice chat," O'Reilly said. "His high-pitched voice kind of amazed me. I guess I was the first fan to extend a Brooklyn welcome to him."

So on the day he was making his Brooklyn debut, when anyone would have excused him had he been agitated or nervous or unwilling to talk to anyone, Jackie Robinson chatted with a sixteen-year-old usher as he walked to the ballpark. And this episode was no anomaly. Jackie did his best to live by the "Golden Rule," expressed in Matthew 7:12: "Whatever you wish that men would do to you, do so to them."

> *"A person with class is an individual of integrity, someone you would love to have as a parent or child, a friend or neighbor, a mentor or advisor."*
>
> ZIG ZIGLAR
> AUTHOR AND MOTIVATIONAL SPEAKER

When Jackie retired from the Dodgers, North Carolina sportswriter Mary Garber wrote a column in appreciation of him. The thrust of the column was that, because of his promise to Rickey to turn the other cheek, Robinson never had the chance to be himself during his career with the Dodgers. In her article, Garber asked: "How could he and his career be judged fairly? He had always been a symbol."

As it turned out, one of Garber's readers mailed Robinson a copy of the column. A few weeks later, Garber received a handwritten note from Jackie thanking her. "That impressed me so much," Garber told me, "that I donated the letter to the North Carolina Sports Hall of Fame in Raleigh."

> *"Class is an intangible quality that commands, rather than demands, the respect of others."*
>
> JOHN WOODEN
> COLLEGE BASKETBALL COACH

According to renowned newspaper columnist and author Jimmy Breslin, after games at Ebbets Field

Rachel Robinson would park the family's car at a gas station on Bedford Avenue, across the street from the park. She'd roll the car window down a bit and wait there, and neighborhood kids would drop postcards into the window. Jackie would sign all of them, and mail them back.

Tommy Ferguson was the visiting clubhouse attendant for the Milwaukee Braves in the 1950s, and when the Dodgers would come to town, Robinson, Pee Wee Reese and several other players would arrive at the park early in the afternoon to play bridge.

"The Dodgers were so first class, and Jackie was always a gentleman with me," Ferguson told me. "Whenever he wanted a sandwich, he would have the money in hand. Pee Wee would tell his teammates, 'You are in the big leagues now. Treat the clubhouse guys first class.' It was standard for each player to pay me five dollars a series. Jackie would give me five dollars a day and the bat boys a dollar a day. Whenever I would see Jackie later, he would holler, 'There's Milwaukee man!'"

"When I was with the Phillies, I would see Connie Mack on occasion. He was always a gentleman, a regular guy who didn't act like an owner or manager. He called me 'Mr. Seminick.' I totally enjoyed being around him. He seemed so appreciative of everything."

ANDY SEMINCK
FORMER MAJOR-LEAGUE CATCHER AND
MINOR-LEAGUE MANAGER

Considering Reese's background and the position in which Robinson's presence placed him, one might assume their relationship should have been rather contentious. Growing up in Louisville, Reese had little exposure to blacks, and Robinson, a black man on the Dodgers, was talented and tenacious enough to take Reese's job from him. Robinson, remember, had played shortstop in the Negro Leagues, and shortstop was Reese's position. In fact, Bill Williams, a former executive with Louisville Slugger told me an interesting story: at the company's headquarters, there is an exhibit of all the contracts Louisville Slugger has signed with players. On Jackie Robinson's 1947 contract, his name is typed in with the position listed as "SS." But someone else had crossed out the "SS" and scribbled "2B" in its place.

"I guess," Williams said, "someone didn't want Pee Wee to lose his position."

Yet, Reese's attitude was, *If he's man enough to take my job, he deserves it.* Because of his attitude toward Robinson's presence, "Reese established his reputation as a man of dignity and integrity," Peter Golenbock once wrote, "and . . . Reese and Robinson became Dodger symbols of integration and harmony."

> *"The gentleman does not needlessly or unnecessarily remind an offender of a wrong he may have committed against him. He cannot only forgive, he can forget. And he strives for that nobleness of self and mildness of character that impart sufficient strength to let the past be the past."*
>
> GENERAL ROBERT E. LEE

Billy Williams, the great outfielder for the Chicago Cubs, told me that each year, at the Baseball Hall of Fame induction ceremony in Cooperstown, he made a point of finding Reese, putting his arm around him and saying, "Thanks."

"He always seemed pleased," Williams said. "One year he said to me, 'It just seemed like the right thing to do at the time.'"

Pee Wee's son Mark told me: "Dad always said Jackie did a lot more for him than he ever did for Jackie."

HAVING CLASS MEANS YOU ACT WITH GRACE AND MATURITY

"He was one of my favorite ballplayers because he treated everybody the same—black or white, superstar or scrub."

—Henry Aaron, on St. Louis Cardinals great Stan Musial

In comic book terms, Ben Chapman was Lex Luthor to Jackie Robinson's Superman. Chapman was Jackie's ultimate nemesis, the consummate test of Robinson's ability to stand up to and defeat the bigotry he was bound to encounter. Every time he had to deal with Chapman's overt racism, Jackie proved how much class and grace he possessed.

During the Dodgers' final series in Philadelphia in Robinson's rookie year, Chapman approached Harold Parrott, the Dodgers' traveling secretary, with a request.

"Will you do me a big favor?" Chapman asked. "Ask Robinson if he'll agree to have a picture taken shaking hands with me?"

If you ask me, Chapman had some nerve, considering his treatment of Jackie. Likewise, Parrott was stunned by the request.

"A picture like this in the newspapers may save my job," Chapman said. "I'll come over to your dugout this evening to have it taken, if he'll agree."

When Parrott told him of Chapman's request, Jackie said, "Tell Ben he doesn't have to come over to our dugout. I'll meet him halfway, behind the plate during batting practice."

"I'll go with you," Parrott said.

"No," Robinson said. "This is something I should do alone, not as if I'm being urged."

Chapman and Robinson couldn't have been more different in terms of their values and their behavior. "Jackie couldn't stand anti-Semitism and was against intolerance of any kind," Roger Kahn told me. "You didn't tell an ethnic joke when he was around." It had to gall Jackie to stand there and smile for the camera, but he did it anyway, and who could say? Maybe his gesture of goodwill would spark a change in Chapman. Nobody knew then what baseball scout Al Goldis would make clear to me years later: that Chapman would never change, that his hatred of blacks ran into the deepest regions of his soul.

The Six Basic Principles of Maturity:

1. *Accept yourself.*
2. *Accept others.*
3. *Keep your sense of humor.*
4. *Appreciate simple pleasures.*
5. *Enjoy the present.*
6. *Welcome work.*

FROM WHY SMART PEOPLE DO DUMB THINGS
BY MORTIMER R. FEINBERG
AND JOHN J. TARRANT

"Maturity—doing what you're supposed to do, when you're supposed to do it, regardless of how you feel."

DOM CAPERS
PRO FOOTBALL COACH

"You can only be young once, but you can be immature forever."

LARRY ANDERSEN
FORMER MAJOR-LEAGUER

"A mature person is one who does not think only in absolutes, who is able to be objective even when deeply stirred emotionally, who has learned that there is both good and bad in all people and in all things, and who walked humbly and deals charitably with the circumstances of life, knowing that, in this world, no one is all-knowing and, therefore, all of us need love and charity."

ELEANOR ROOSEVELT

"In 1961, I was playing in the Reds Instructional League with Lee May, then a young player, and Billy Chapman, the son of Ben," Goldis told me. "Both players lived in Birmingham. Lee had a car and invited Billy to drive back to Birmingham with him. Billy thanked Lee but declined: 'If my daddy ever found out I drove into the city of Birmingham with a black man driving, he would kill me.'"

So the men met face-to-face, with the photographer nearby, that day in 1947. Chapman smiled and extended his hand, and Robinson took it, and the photographer clicked away.

"Having my picture taken with this man," Robinson said later in his life, "was one of the most difficult things I had to make myself do."

At Ebbets Field one day early the following season, 1948, Chapman and Robinson ran into each other in a common runway between the park's two dugouts. The Dodgers had swept the Phillies in a doubleheader the day before, and Robinson was the primary catalyst, picking up seven hits. As Jackie walked past, Chapman said, "Robinson, you're one hell of a ballplayer, but you're still a nigger." Phillies pitchers Robin Roberts and Curt Simmons heard what Chapman said, and Roberts thought a physical confrontation might ensue. But Robinson said nothing and continued walking.

"Jackie Robinson was a class guy," Russ Meyer, who pitched for the Phillies and the Dodgers, once said. "He was a guinea pig, and he took a lot of stuff that a common, ordinary white guy would never have taken."

Incidentally, the photo didn't accomplish what Chapman had hoped it would. The Phillies fired him in the middle of the 1948 season.

* * *

People with class have strong senses of empathy; they are willing, as the cliché goes, to put themselves in others' shoes. That way, they're better able to understand and sympathize with them. Maybe the best example from Robinson's career of this empathy was an exchange he had with Hall of Fame first baseman Hank Greenberg in 1947. Greenberg was playing for the Pittsburgh Pirates that season after spending his previous eleven big-league seasons with the Detroit Tigers, where he had encountered prejudice because of his Jewish heritage.

Robinson's first season would be Greenberg's final one, and during a Pirates-Dodgers game, Robinson singled and stood on the bag next to Greenberg, who said to him, "Don't let them get you down. You're doing fine. Keep it up."

"Class tells," Robinson once said in remembering that moment. "It sticks out all over Mr. Greenberg."

Usually, it sticks out in what seem to be small ways. A word of encouragement. A quiet exit. There are rarely great, giant displays of class because being classy is about moving the focus, the spotlight, away from yourself. Robinson did this too many times to count.

> *"Maturity begins when we're content to feel we're right about something without feeling the necessity to prove someone else is wrong."*
>
> SYDNEY J. HARRIS
> SYNDICATED COLUMNIST

In 1949, during his ninth game in the majors, Pirates left fielder Dino Restelli hit a first-inning home run off Dodgers pitcher Rex Barney. The following inning, Robinson lined a hit into the left-center field gap and barely beat Restelli's throw into second base. In the third inning, Restelli walked and, on an infield ground ball, slid hard into Robinson, trying to break up a potential double play.

"When we both got up," Restelli told me, "he smiled and said, 'Nice hustling, rookie. And that was a great home run.' The irony of it all was that in the fourth inning, the game was called because of rain. Neither my home run nor his double counted in the stats."

Jim Greengrass, an outfielder for the Reds and the Phillies during the 1950s, tried to stretch a single into a double during a game against the Dodgers in 1952, but Brooklyn right fielder Carl Furillo made a laser-beam throw to second, where Jackie was waiting. "Jackie put a nice, easy tag on me and said, 'Nice try, Jim,'" Greengrass told me. "I went back to the dugout and thought, 'What is all the criticism about? He's a nice guy.'"

Wayne Terwilliger, a former infielder with the Dodgers and a teammate of Robinson, still remembers a small compliment he received from Jackie more than fifty years after Jackie gave it to him. "I played second base one game that he took off," Terwilliger told me. "I made a good backhanded play behind second base in the game, and afterward Jackie came up to me and said, 'I never would have gotten that one.' Well, he would have and he knew it, but I'm sure that he realized I could use the pat on the back. He was a fierce competitor, but he had class, too."

> *"Do they know that you had all the tools: talent, smarts and skill, well blended with civility plus an unmistakable ironclad will?"*
>
> TOMMY HAWKINS
> FORMER NBA PLAYER AND DODGERS
> EXECUTIVE, ON JACKIE ROBINSON

"He was such a gentleman, one who was filled with compassion and competition," former Major-Leaguer Art Fowler told me. "Definitely a man of class. He had so many obstacles to overcome, and he did it with honor, humility and great pride."

Perhaps because Greenberg showed him understanding in 1947, Robinson was particularly gracious with rookies and younger players. During an exhibition game against the Boston Braves in 1948, when Robinson made an error at second base behind rookie pitcher Elmer Sexauer, he came to the mound and apologized to Sexauer. "I had a lot of respect for him for doing that," Sexauer told me.

Pitching against the Dodgers one day during his first season in the majors, John "Red" Murff snared a sharply hit ball by Robinson and threw him out at first. On his way back to the dugout, Robinson said to Murff, "Nice play, rook."

"He was quite a gentleman," Murff told me. "It was an honor to pitch against him."

My favorite Robinson "rookie" anecdote came from former Dodger Ron

Negray, who was called up to Brooklyn from the minors in St. Paul, Minnesota, in July 1952. The Dodgers went on to win the National League pennant, and as a reward, every player was given a wristwatch—every player except Negray, who hadn't been with the team for the full season.

"Jackie noticed that and came over to me and said, 'Here, take mine. I'll get another one,'" Negray told me. "My dad wore that watch for years, and after he died, I got it back. That was Jackie for you—always thinking about someone else."

Even after the most difficult defeats of his baseball life, Robinson did as Negray said: he thought of someone else. Legendary football coach Vince Lombardi once said, "Show me a good loser, and I'll show you a loser." Now, I admire Lombardi for his success as a coach and his ability to push his players to great heights, but giving everything you have in pursuit of victory and acting with graciousness after defeat are not mutually exclusive qualities. Each is a virtue, and a person of class possesses both. After the Phillies defeated the Dodgers on the final day of the 1950 regular season to win the National League pennant, for instance, Robinson entered the visitors' clubhouse at Ebbets Field and went from locker to locker, shaking the hand of every Phillie.

> *"You must be the change you want to see in the world."*
>
> MAHATMA GHANDI

"It was an exceptional act by an exceptional individual," Robin Roberts once wrote, "particularly given the Phillies' inexcusable treatment of him in 1947. . . . I'm not sure I would have thought to do the same at that time if the roles had been reversed and the Dodgers had won the pennant on the last day of the season."

Robinson's entering an opposing clubhouse to offer congratulations wasn't an unusual occurrence. After the deciding game of the 1952 World Series, after his Dodgers had lost to the Yankees, Robinson found Mickey Mantle amid the Yanks' celebration and told him, "You're a heckuva ballplayer." Years later, Mantle said of that moment, "What a classy guy. I never could have done that, not in a million years. . . . That meant a lot, especially after the year I'd been through, with my father dying that May and all that. I can't tell you how thrilled he would have been to hear Jackie Robinson say that about his son."

> *"I always want my players to show class, knock 'em down, pat them on the back, and run back to the huddle."*
>
> PAUL "BEAR" BRYANT
> COLLEGE FOOTBALL COACH

Back in chapter three, as an example of how competitive Jackie was, I mentioned that he made sure Bobby Thomson touched every base after Thomson hit "The Shot Heard 'Round the World," the 1951 home run that beat the Dodgers and won the New York Giants the National League pennant. After that game ended, Robinson entered the Giants' clubhouse to shake hands with his former manager, Leo Durocher—a man with whom Robinson had a contentious relationship.

"I knew he'd rather have been congratulating anybody in the world but me," Durocher wrote in his autobiography, *Nice Guys Finish Last*. "And still Jackie had come in smiling."

Once he had finished congratulating Durocher, Robinson went back into the Dodgers clubhouse, where he found Ralph Branca, the pitcher who surrendered Thomson's home run. Branca has had to live with giving up the most famous home run in baseball history for more than fifty years now, but he once said he has never forgotten what Robinson said to him after that game.

"Don't be too hard on yourself," Jackie said. "Do you think they brought in our worst pitcher in that situation? No, they brought in our best."

HAVING CLASS MEANS YOU ACCEPT RESPONSIBILITY

"Jackie had class. . . . He wasn't perfect. He made his share of mistakes. But Jackie would never knowingly demean himself or shame himself, his family or his team."

—Rachel Robinson

There were no black players in the National Basketball Association until 1950, three years after Robinson integrated Major League Baseball, but that first group in the NBA faced similar prejudices and hardships to those Jackie faced. Bob Wilson, of the old Milwaukee Hawks, was one of those NBA pioneers. One morning in Baltimore, Robinson, who was in town with the Dodgers for an exhibition game, joined Wilson and two other NBA pioneers—Don Barksdale and Nat "Sweetwater" Clifton—for breakfast.

"He counseled us about the new beginning in the NBA," Wilson told me. "He said, 'Attitude is everything. Stay focused on your mission. Your talent is your agent, and that has to carry you. Be a gentleman at all times.' It was very positive."

It's Robinson's reminder to "be a gentleman at all times" that I treasure from his talk with Wilson, Barksdale and Clifton. Essentially, Jackie was reiterating to the three men their need to take responsibility for their own actions. The burden of their triumph as players and as men ultimately was on them, and that burden included taking responsibility for their characters and others' perceptions of them. Robinson knew better than anyone the harm that could come from prejudging someone. He had been an obvious victim of such ignorance.

"I am still determined to be cheerful and to be happy, in whatever situation I may be, for I have also learned, from experience, that the greater part of our happiness . . . depends on our dispositions and not upon our circumstances."

MARTHA WASHINGTON

But Robinson also knew that he could control, or at least influence, how people perceived him. If he was accommodating to a young fan who wanted an autograph, if he didn't embarrass himself or those around him, if he didn't give people a reason to judge him negatively, they would be less likely to do so, and he would earn their respect. His mind-set was no different than that of Michael Jordan, who made sure he wore a suit and tie in public whenever he wasn't playing basketball so that the paying

"Joe DiMaggio was very inspirational to all of us; not by what he said, but just by how he'd carry himself. He'd always run out to the outfield, and he always ran back. He never came to the ballpark without a shirt and tie and a dark blue suit. He was always very well dressed. Everything he did, he did right."

YOGI BERRA

public saw a man who respected himself and respected his image. Jackie couldn't be caught in a compromising position, start a fight in a bar, spit on an umpire or do anything that would damage the way people viewed him. His reputation, his character and the importance of his quest were all at stake.

> *"There is only one corner of the universe you can be certain of improving, and that's your own self."*
>
> ALDOUS HUXLEY
> AUTHOR

"Jackie Robinson's success was due to two qualities," historian Doris Kearns Goodwin told me. "He had the courage to make the decision to break the color line knowing of the uproar and violence that could ensue. He also had the confidence and dignity to handle the uproar and defuse any activities that would trigger violence. That is a rare combination of character qualities, and Jackie had them."

He maintained that confidence and dignity throughout his life, and those qualities were of vital importance as his role in the civil-rights movement grew. "Robinson," wrote author Arnold Rampersad, "became a forceful, respected part of the civil-rights debate, able to hold his own on programs such as *Meet the Press* or to field bristling questions from the journalist Mike Wallace about housing discrimination." Contrary to much of the lowest-common-denominator television we see nowadays—including many "roundtable" programs that seem to consist of people screaming at

> *"The price of greatness is responsibility."*
>
> WINSTON CHURCHILL

each other—Jackie didn't have to shriek or foam at the mouth to make his point. And he wasn't above giving credit to someone else when credit was deserved.

When Arkansas Governor Orval Faubus called in the National Guard to stop the integration of a school in Little Rock, Robinson wired a message to the White House that was critical of President Dwight Eisenhower's call for patience. "We are wondering to whom you are referring," he wrote, "when you say we must be patient." But as soon as Eisenhower sent one thousand paratroopers from the 101st

Airborne Division to protect the nine black students while they attended school, Jackie quickly expressed his gratitude to the president. "I should have known you would do the right thing at the crucial time," he said in a wired message to Eisenhower. "May God continue giving you the wisdom to lead us in this struggle."

Jackie remembered his responsibilities—to his principles, to his family, to his job, to himself—in every situation, big or small. In everything he did, he was a professional. Julius Erving, one of my dear friends and a man who I watched walk on air during our years together with the Philadelphia 76ers, once said, "Being a professional is doing the things you love to do on the days when you don't feel like doing them." That was Jackie.

> *"Nobody owes anybody anything. It's up to each individual to set high standards for himself or herself, and to set about working hard and creating a solid future."*
>
> KATHARINE HEPBURN
> ACTRESS

Merle Harmon worked with Robinson when Jackie began his brief career in broadcasting, and he spoke with me about the manner in which Jackie approached his new job. "He never demanded any special treatment on the set," Harmon said. "He wanted to be a team player. His attitude was, 'Help me. This is a new adventure for me.' He was a marvelous human being. And at the time, he was under a lot of strain because his son, Jackie Jr., was serving in Vietnam. Jackie was a worried father when I worked with him."

HAVING CLASS MEANS YOU TAKE PRIDE IN YOURSELF AND OTHERS

"Jackie had so many battles to fight, but he had the ability to keep hold of the situation. He had the support of the front office and the players. He won us over with his play. For me, it was a pleasure just to go to the park and watch him."

—Clem Labine, Dodgers pitcher and Robinson teammate

After the Minneapolis Lakers selected him in the 1959 NBA draft,

Tommy Hawkins, fresh out of Notre Dame University, got a telephone call from Carl Rowan, a columnist for the *Minneapolis Star-Tribune*. At that time, Rowan had recently collaborated with Robinson on the book *Wait Till Next Year*, and he had a question for Hawkins:

"Would you like to spend a day with Jackie Robinson?"

Rowan invited Hawkins to go to a department store with him for a book signing. The two of them picked up Robinson at the airport, and off they went.

"It's still one of the most incredible days of my life," Hawkins told me. "In Jackie Robinson, I saw a man of tremendous presence and personal dignity. He was still a fiery competitor, but friendly and warm. I had one hundred questions for him, and he must have felt like he was getting a personal bombardment from this kid basketball player."

> *"When a man loses his pride,*
> *he isn't worth a darn."*
>
> EDDIE ROBINSON
> COLLEGE FOOTBALL COACH

There was a good reason Hawkins had so many questions for Robinson.

"In 1955," Hawkins said, "when I enrolled as a freshman at Notre Dame, I was the only black in my class and one of only ten blacks in a university of eight thousand students. Jackie taught us the importance of self-respect. If you don't respect yourself, no one else will. Like Jackie, you have to insist on this."

Robinson's 1944 army court-martial and the events that led to it provide a prism into the pride he had in himself. Robinson had earned notoriety and acclaim throughout the country for his athletic exploits at UCLA, but in an army still tarnished by Jim Crow, he was denied the chance to play for his camp's baseball team and, in light of that insult, refused to play football. With his pride already pricked, Jackie simply could not tolerate a driver ordering him to the back of an army bus just because he was black. His self-respect compelled him to take the chance that a court-martial would vindicate him—no small gamble in those days. In hindsight, he put his entire baseball career and Branch Rickey's plan to integrate baseball at risk by defending himself so vigorously. The army, in those days, might have tried to make an example of a black man who was considered too "uppity." As historian Jules Tygiel has pointed out, had Robinson been dishonorably discharged, Rickey might never have chosen him.

"In the climate of postwar America, a black man banished from the army would have had little popular support," Tygiel once wrote. "It is not unreasonable to suppose that Robinson . . . might never have made it to the major leagues had he been forced to wait for another man to act as trailblazer. Fortunately, his defiance had the opposite effect. His army experiences, which graphically illustrated the black man's lot in America, also demonstrated Jackie Robinson's courage and pride. Those were the very qualities that would prove essential in making the assault on baseball's color line."

Several of the people I interviewed for this book pointed to Robinson's self-respect as the quality they most admired in him.

NBC anchorman Tom Brokaw: "Jackie Robinson was a man of enormous resolve and dignity. He was not a patsy, and his competitive fire was never put out. Through all his trials, he always maintained his dignity."

Palm Beach Post sportswriter Chris Perkins: "Jackie Robinson has been a real inspiration to me. It was not easy to take what he took and not lash out in an ugly fashion. I admire him for his diplomacy and the gentlemanly way in which he carried himself."

Gerald Early, director of humanities at the University of Washington: "Because Robinson was unable to respond to any of the insults he had to endure, it made his competitive spirit seem that much more intense, but it also served as a kind of protective armor. I think Robinson made the American public think about competitive drive in a humane, almost poetic way for a certain period of time in his career. He had both a certain grace and a profoundly informed sense of dignity. I don't think any other athlete has done that—make hard-driving competition seem so dignified and ethical."

> *"In the history of the world, no one ever washed a rented car."*
>
> LAWRENCE SUMMERS
> PRESIDENT OF HARVARD UNIVERSITY

Fred Claire, who was an executive with the Dodgers for more than thirty years, cherishes his memory of June 4, 1972, the day the Dodgers retired Jackie's No. 42—twenty-five years after he broke the color barrier. By then, because of retinal bleeding, Robinson's vision had deteriorated to the point that he could barely see anything at all. He was standing near the Dodgers dugout when a fan, who didn't know about Robinson's blindness, yelled, "Jackie, Jackie, please sign this ball."

The man tossed the ball toward Jackie, and it glanced off Jackie's shoulder and hit him in the head. Everyone around Jackie went wild, screaming at the fan. But Jackie spoke in a soft voice.

"Give me the ball," he said. "Calm down and give me the ball. He doesn't know."

He signed the ball and gave it back to the fan.

"I have never had a problem answering the question of my proudest moment as a Dodger," Claire told me. "It was to be in the company of Jackie and Rachel Robinson and to know I was a part of an organization that had a role in giving Jackie Robinson an opportunity to establish himself as a true leader."

A rather classy thing to say, don't you think?

HAVING CLASS MEANS YOU
SHOW POISE UNDER PRESSURE

During World War II, before he became a Hall of Fame center and linebacker for the Philadelphia Eagles, before he became the last sixty-minute man in the National Football League, Chuck Bednarik flew thirty combat missions over Germany . . . all when he was nineteen years old.

"Nothing gives one person so much advantage over another as to remain cool and unruffled under all circumstances."

PRESIDENT THOMAS JEFFERSON

"That was pressure," Bednarik once said. "That gave me some toughness. So when I survived the war and came home and went out on a football field, I figured, 'Shoot, this is easy.'"

I can't help but think that Jackie Robinson, when he went out on a baseball field, felt the same way. As it was for Bednarik, the game was Jackie's refuge, the place where showing poise in the face of pressure suddenly didn't seem so difficult because he already had been through so much.

"We can't fathom what Jackie went through and the pressure he must have felt," NBC's Greg Gumbel told me. "The way he played under that pressure made him exceptional. All professional athletes have talent, but the question is, 'Can you do it when it counts?' That's the measure of athletic greatness, and that's what made Jackie unique."

Jackie could do it when it counted. And he didn't dance afterward. When he homered in the fourteenth inning to beat the Philadelphia Phillies 9–8 and force a three-game play-off with the New York Giants for the National League pennant in 1951, he didn't point to the sky or

> *"Pressure is something you feel when you don't know what you're doing."*
>
> CHUCK NOLL
> PRO FOOTBALL COACH

gesture to the Phillies' bench. After scoring any of his touchdowns for the UCLA football team, he didn't pull a pen from his sock and sign the football. He didn't show anyone up, he didn't lose control of his emotions and he never allowed anyone to distract him from what he had to do—whether it was hit a curveball or, later in his life, deliver a speech on civil rights.

"Baseball is a sport that requires intense concentration and a relaxed attitude," Dick Crepeau, a University of Central Florida history professor, told me. "In the middle of all that's required to play Major League Baseball, Jackie is being harassed by opponents and fans, and he's getting death threats. It's almost beyond belief that he could perform at the level required of him with all the pressure mounted on his shoulders."

Ask yourself: How do I handle the pressure situations I must deal with in my life? Can I maintain a professional demeanor around the office when I'm having a disagreement with a coworker? Do I lose it when the baby needs his diaper changed and the five-year-old wants another cookie? Can I control my impulse to go bananas, refocus and perform the task at hand? And if I am able to handle these situations and I earn praise for it, how do I react to that recognition? Do I brag about it? Do I go on and on about the wonderfulness of myself?

Robinson didn't. At any time in any game, no matter how tense the situation was or who was harassing Jackie from the opposing dugout or how many eyes were watching him, a fan or an aspiring pro athlete could look at him as a model for how a professional carries himself.

"Nobody can lead men if he cannot keep his head in a crisis."
ADMIRAL WILLIAM F. HALSEY

"What often goes unrecognized about Jackie Robinson's impact on sports is not what he did, but what his character kept him from doing," *Philadelphia Daily News* sportswriter Marcus Hayes told me. "Robinson embodied the superior athlete whose ego was recognized but not flaunted.

"Even in surgery, it's often not just a question of skills, but of professional style, as well. While still in school, I used to get a scalpel and practice just, say, cutting a piece of meat or something like that. You sort of learn how you want to hold your fingers and . . . try to become graceful when you operate, because it's that gracefulness and poise at the operating table that inspires others."
DR. DENTON COOLEY
HEART SURGEON

"Pioneers are always special, but Jackie Robinson handled his situation with grace and dignity," Greg Gumbel told me. "The suffering he went through, he internalized more than most could have done."

His comportment as a black athlete laid a template for the rest to follow.

"He could have acted like Terrell Owens or Allen Iverson or Barry Bonds, players whose feats are diminished by their self-celebratory and standoffish attitudes that they justify because of the pressure they experience. The best learned from Robinson, who experienced pressures they could not imagine. Witness Michael Jordan. Witness Tiger Woods. See how the class of Donovan McNabb helps his marketability outstrip his accomplishments, how the maturity of LeBron James made him a brand in high school. Thankfully, some black athletes learned that elegance on the field means little without grace off it."

GRACIOUS, EVEN IN HIS FINAL DAYS

I began this chapter with a story about the beginning of Jackie's career, and I end it now with a story about the end of Jackie's life. It gives me chills whenever I think of it.

The date was October 15, 1972. At Riverfront Stadium in Cincinnati, before Game Two of the World Series, Robinson stood before a microphone and, to the crowd he could hear but could not see, expressed his deep hope that someday, a Major League Baseball franchise would hire a black man as its manager. This was the same day that Robinson, as I mentioned earlier, was shunned by several black players on the Oakland A's. But three years later, he got his wish: Frank Robinson took over the Cleveland Indians and became baseball's first black manager.

Down on the field, Robinson came face-to-face with *Los Angeles Times* columnist Jim Murray. The two had engaged in several verbal battles over the years because of the content of Murray's columns. But now, Robinson extended his hand and said, "I'm sorry, Jim. I can't see you anymore."

Jackie Robinson died nine days later. Murray's column the next day was an obituary for Jackie, and he closed it with these words:

"I'm sorry, Jackie, *I* can't see *you* anymore."

Chapter Eleven

❧

The Unbroken Promise

In 1947, Jackie Robinson not only symbolized all of black America on trial in the eyes of white America and the expansion of the ideals of democracy, he also represented the best of a traditional black quest for dignity, excellence and integrity. . . . When Jackie Robinson states that he 'never had it made,' he means, in part, that he had to fight in a variety of ways and on a number of fronts to preserve both his sense of dignity and his integrity; and in part that he was able to fight primarily because of the love and support of those fighters who came before him and those who . . . stood by his side.

—Dr. Cornel West, Princeton University

A FAN HAD THROWN a bottle onto the baseball field, and it had landed not far from where he was standing. So he picked up the bottle. He walked over to the stands. He found the fan who had thrown it. He began shouting at the fan, then screaming at the fan. He scowled. He threw the bottle forcefully down into the stands, as if he were spiking a football in anger.

Soon, the umpires and his teammates ran out to right field, where he was putting on this display, and pulled him away from the stands. As he stalked off the field, he ripped off his uniform shirt—a jersey virtually identical to the one Jackie Robinson had worn for the Brooklyn Dodgers years before.

"The fans," Los Angeles Dodgers outfielder Milton Bradley later said, "disrespected me."

As I watched this scene unfold in late September 2004—Bradley, a talented player, completely losing his cool because some delinquent had chucked a plastic beer bottle at him—I couldn't help but think of Jackie Robinson. What would his reaction have been to the same situation? How would he have handled himself? I know this: there is no way he would have approached the fan. There is no way he would have thrown the bottle back into the stands. There is no way he would have embarrassed himself, his teammates and the Dodgers franchise. No way.

> *"He who resolves upon doing a thing, by that very resolution often scales the barriers to it and secures its achievement."*
>
> SAMUEL SMILES
> AUTHOR

Whatever distress Bradley suffered that night in Los Angeles, Robinson endured a hundred times more. Maybe a thousand. And I know that Jackie Robinson never, ever, would have reacted the way Bradley did. First, he had too much pride in his self-image to do something so undignified. As Ray Bartlett, Jackie's teammate on the Pasadena Junior College and UCLA football teams, told me: "Jackie was strong on conduct in public. He would not have liked baggy pants, rap music or tattoos." If Robinson had ever been involved in an incident similar to this one, he would have embarrassed himself, his family and the Dodgers. He would never have put himself in such a position.

> *"One person with belief is equal to a force of ninety-nine who have only interests."*
>
> JOHN STUART MILL
> PHILOSOPHER

Second, Jackie Robinson never would have jeopardized his credibility as a man sincerely seeking to improve society. No matter how often he may have wanted, deep in his heart, to lash out at those who were against him, he wouldn't compromise his values, his cause or his own standards by allowing himself to lose control. His commitment—to racial equality and justice, to his values of service and humility, and to the people whom he loved and who loved him—simply couldn't be broken. He had—in the words of his daughter, Sharon—"promises to keep."

During one of my interviews with her, Rachel Robinson spoke with reverence about her husband's commitment and core beliefs. "All of Jack's life, he had these major goals to achieve," she said. "He had strong convictions about things and wanted to bring about change. Even when he was suffering with diabetes and was going blind, he still had work to do. Jack's life had meaning to him right to the end."

HIS COMMITMENT TO HIS RACE

Sunday, April 16

"My thoughts are on Jackie Robinson today, my birthday. I was born in Harlem the day after Jackie's first major-league game across the river in Brooklyn's Ebbets Field. It was forty-two years ago that I was born and that Jackie Robinson, in 1947, at age twenty-eight, crossed baseball's color line. I have always considered it a gift that I slipped into the world just at that moment.

"All the courage and competitiveness of Jackie Robinson affects me to this day. If I patterned my life after anyone, it was him."

—From the diary of Kareem Abdul-Jabbar, 1989

In early 1997, Rich Hofmann, a sports columnist for the *Philadelphia Daily News*, sat in a room at the Schomburg Center for Research in Black Culture, a division of the New York Public Library. The center is located at 135th Street and Malcolm X Boulevard in Harlem, and Hofmann was there to research Jackie Robinson's life. Soon, Hofmann would have to write about Robinson for the special section the *Daily News* planned to publish to commemorate the fiftieth anniversary of Jackie's debut with the Dodgers.

"Most people skate through life avoiding commitment and involvement. A cherished few touch others along the way and, in touching them, leave them better and blessed."

CHARLIE STUART
ORLANDO BUSINESSMAN

In the course of his research, Hofmann came across some revealing material. He found, for instance, a letter Malcolm X once wrote to Robinson.

"You became a great baseball player after your white boss lifted you to the major leagues," the letter said. "You proved that your white boss had chosen the 'right' Negro by getting plenty of hits, stealing plenty of bases, winning many games and bringing much money through the gates and into the pockets of your white boss. . . . You stay as far away from the Negro community as you can get, and you never take an interest in anything in the Negro community until the white man himself takes an interest in it. You, yourself, would never shake my hand until you saw some of your white friends shaking it."

Then Hofmann read an excerpt from *I Never Had It Made,* Robinson's autobiography, in which Jackie recounted a conversation with New York sportswriter Dick Young. Young had compared Robinson to Roy Campanella by saying, "Personally, Jackie, when I talk to Campy, I almost never think of him as a Negro. Anytime I talk to you, I'm acutely aware of the fact that you're a Negro."

> *"Do what you can with what you have where you are."*
> PRESIDENT THEODORE ROOSEVELT

In response, Robinson had said: "If you think of me as the kind of Negro who's come to the conclusion that he isn't going to beg for anything, that he will be reasonable but he damned well is tired of being patient . . . I want to be thought of as that kind of Negro."

When he finally sat down to write, Hofmann, using those two anecdotes as his fulcrum, described Robinson like this:

"Too accommodating to some. Too outspoken to others. Attacked by all sides."

It was a perfect description of the man. By dedicating himself to the goals of equality for blacks and their integration and assimilation into American society, Robinson placed himself in a strange spot: he never compromised his values, yet he was constantly being accused of compromising his values. That said, I'm not sure how much such criticism really bothered him. So long as Jackie was honest with himself and others, as long as he stayed true to his principles, I suspect he could sleep well at night.

"Whenever racism reared its ugly head, Jackie Robinson would get angry," *Daily Worker* sportswriter Bill Mardo told me. "When Dick Young complained by saying his conversations with Roy Campanella were pleasant, but with Jackie they were always about racial issues, Jackie confronted Young and said, 'Never forget, I'm black.' That summarizes Jackie's life. He was consumed with the struggles of his people, and he'd never compromise on that."

Had Robinson, once he retired from baseball, spent the rest of his life growing flowers in his garden or spending every moment with Rachel and his children, he still would have been a great catalyst to advance race relations and inspire blacks to find their full potential in America. "Jackie was a breakthrough character and an important symbol in the civil-rights struggle," Patrick Miller, a professor at Northeastern Illinois University, told me. "His courage and sacrifice left the most important legacy before the *Brown* decision in 1954. What Jackie did was the single most positive civil-rights image in America and around the world."

"A champion is someone who proves themselves in every environment. No matter what level you are playing, you still play to be your best. It's all about hard work. That's where a champion comes in. You can either stick to your goals, or you can just go through the motions and rest on your status."

KRISTINE LILLY
U.S. WOMEN'S SOCCER PLAYER

Still the president of the National Council of Negro Women, still working in Washington, D.C., Dr. Dorothy Height, ninety-two, is a living history of the civil-rights movement. She talked with me for a few moments about Robinson's impact on African Americans.

"As my parents used to tell me, you make a way out of no way," she said softly into the telephone. "If you know what it is you want, keep pursuing it. Jackie went beyond anyone's expectation because he had the energy, ambition and capacity to do what was needed in any situation. When Jackie came to Brooklyn in 1947, it was a pivotal moment in history, and he stood up for his people with every hit, every stolen base. The black race identified with Jackie."

Jesse Jackson, the famed civil-rights activist, told me in an interview: "Jackie became the epitome of emancipation. Keep in mind that he came before integration of the military, before *Brown v. the Board of Education*, before Rosa Parks, before Dr. King. If Jackie had failed, the critics could point and say a black man can't do it. The fact is, Jackie excelled against all cultural, legal and athletic odds. That's why he is an American hero and arguably the most significant American of the twentieth century. The black race never had a talent difference. We had an opportunity difference. Jackie changed that and created an even playing field. He broke the first link in the chain, and once he broke it, all others came behind him. And once he was inside the door, Jackie never compromised his dignity of being a black man. He knew his public conduct and private behavior would affect the entire culture.

"When Jackie arrived in Brooklyn, baseball was king, so he was taking on the culture as well as the game. Many black players could have taken on the game, but only Jackie could handle both. He was a minority with a majority vision. He was capable of absorbing punishment for the sake of cultural change. That's an awful lot to put on one man. He took all the blows for the black race and paid a steep price for that."

> *"Life's most persistent and urgent question is: What are you doing for others?"*
> MARTIN LUTHER KING JR.

In any discussion of race in America, context is vital. Our attitudes toward diversity and equality have matured and changed so much over the last century that we must remind ourselves that we weren't so enlightened years ago. "Every American should have a sense of pride in the progress we have made in civil rights in the last fifty years and a sense of shame of where we were," baseball historian David Shiner told me. "Jackie Robinson is a great symbol of that. In the 1940s and '50s, baseball was the national sport. Jackie played a larger-than-life role, and he handled it in a larger-than-life way."

> *"Nothing of worth or weight can be achieved with half a mind, with a faint heart and with a lame endeavor."*
> ISAAC BURROW
> AUTHOR

Consider a few examples of what

Shiner means when he talks about the progress we've made:

- The great sportswriter Grantland Rice wrote of Joe Louis: His skills "are a matter of instinct with him, as with most of the great Negro fighters. . . . The great Negro boxer is rarely a matter of manufacture, like many white boxers. He is born that way." He wrote that Olympic champion Jesse Owens was "like a wild Zulu running amuck," and according to author Charles Fountain, Rice often referred to Louis, Owens or even Robinson in conversation as "the nigger."
- Jake Powell, who hit .455 for the Yankees in the 1936 Series against the Giants, once was on a radio show in Chicago. In those days, baseball players weren't multimillionaires; they worked other jobs during the off-season. When the interviewer, Bob Elson, asked Powell what work he did when he wasn't playing baseball, Powell said he was a police officer in Dayton, Ohio. The interviewer then asked if Powell liked the job. "Oh, yeah," Powell said. "What I like to do is go around beating those niggers on the head."
- Jackie had a few Japanese friends as a boy in Pasadena—though it was difficult to grow close to someone of another race in those days of segregation. One of his Japanese friends was Yoshi Hasegawa. "When we ate lunch" at school, Hasegawa once said, "the blacks sat on one side of the table, and the Japanese sat on the other side, and we monopolized the whole area. We were friendly, but we each knew our place."

These examples might appear antiquated now, but they were very much the norm in America when Robinson broke the color barrier. They are indicative of the attitudes that he tried to change. "Jackie rec-

"Commit to the Lord whatever you do, and your plans will succeed."
PROVERBS 16:3

ognized the context that history placed him in, and it was far beyond baseball," history professor Bill Simons told me. "The whole effort was about more than him. It was about segregation and racism in the United States. He was always aware of the historical significance of what he was doing."

So, in the context of his time, Jackie's ten seasons with the Dodgers were truly the most pressurized ten years any ballplayer ever spent in the big leagues. On his shoulders rested an entire people's hope for a real chance, for a better life. "How many people are asked to carry an entire race?" the *Philadelphia Inquirer's* Claire Smith asked me rhetorically. "It was an amazing feat that he was asked to carry all that."

Frank Robinson broke in with the Cincinnati Reds in 1956, Jackie's final season with the Dodgers. "He spoke to me before a game one day in Cincinnati," Frank told me. "He said, 'Watch how you conduct yourself on and off the field. You will be judged in both areas, and if you step out of line, it will make it tougher for the next black guys.'"

"He had to deliver not just for himself but for an entire race, an entire nation, and he came through," *New York Daily News* sports columnist Vic Siegel told me. "There is no higher praise."

Former Major-Leaguer Ed Charles spoke with me about how important Robinson was to the black community in the 1940s and '50s. "He brought a lot of hope to those of us in the South who were living under the shadow of Jim Crow," Charles said. "After Jackie joined the Dodgers, we felt we had a shot. When I first got into pro ball, I played in Southern cities, and it was really tough for me and other black ballplayers. A lot of times, I felt like quitting, but then I thought of Jackie and what he went through. I thought of the boys back home and what they would say: 'I told you that you didn't have what it takes.' Jackie helped me hang in there, no matter what."

Hall of Fame pitcher Ferguson Jenkins told me, "If it wasn't for Jackie Robinson, I would never have been signed out of Canada in 1962."

And Robinson's impact spread beyond blacks to other minorities who faced similar struggles. In Robinson, they could see the potential that they themselves possessed. "Jackie is one of the most important figures in U.S. history," ESPN baseball analyst and former Major-Leaguer Harold Reynolds told me. "We wouldn't have the sports world of today as we know it without him. All the roots for blacks, women, Asians and Latinos go back to him."

Minnie Minoso, one of the pioneers in the Latin American revolution in Major League Baseball, expressed the same sentiment to me. "Every baseball player, every athlete for that matter, owes Jackie Robinson a genuine debt of gratitude," Minoso said.

But no discussion of Robinson's dedication to his race is complete without detailing what he did apart from baseball. Always, he acted and

spoke out for integration, not separation. "Unless we're able to prove that
blacks and whites can work together
as we did in baseball," Robinson told
the *New York Times'* Dave Anderson
in 1971, "the breach that's here now
will get wider." His was a philosophy
of inclusion, not exclusion. He
believed deeply that every man and
woman, black or white, should be
treated as an individual, worthy of
dignity and respect.

"Rosa Parks was not the first person denied a seat on a bus, and she
was not the first person who refused
to do it," *Washington Post* columnist
William Raspberry told me. "Rosa
had a combination of dark skin and
the character to parlay these things
into a movement. It was the quality
of Rosa's character, and it was the
same with Jackie. For African
Americans, Jackie represents a commitment and choice that was not

*"Then one day we got the news
about Jackie Robinson. I remember
all the folks in the black
neighborhoods sitting around
playing their card games and
saying, 'Did you hear? Branch
Rickey's going to bring Jackie up
to the majors.' Everywhere you
went, people had their newspapers
out and they were talking about
it. It was the talk of the black
community because it gave spirit
and hope to the downtrodden.
Once Jackie broke the color
barrier, I guess the thinking was
that if you could break it in
baseball, anything else in the
world was possible."*

SHARPE JAMES
MAYOR OF NEWARK, NEW JERSEY

always obvious. Here was the question: does one reasonably expect we will
join the mainstream of American society like the Italian Americans or the
Greek Americans, or will we be that indigestible lump that never gets
digested? Jackie's choice came out right. He represents not just a sports first,
but a political and social watershed. He gave a lot of people a lot of hope."

Jackie really was a revolutionary, and his record as a public servant in the
name of his ideals was truly staggering.

In 1949, Robinson testified before the House Un-American Activities
Committee against Paul Robeson, the movie star, civil-rights activist and
radical socialist. Robinson, a soldier, had been subpoenaed to refute
Robeson's statement that blacks "would never go to war on behalf of those

who had oppressed us for generations." Robinson understood the sensitive nature of his testimony and the long-term effect it might have. Under oath, he said blacks would "do their best to help their country stay out of war; if unsuccessful, they'd do their best to help their country win the war." Years later, he all but apologized for testifying: "I do have an increased respect for Paul Robeson who . . . sacrificed himself, his career, and the wealth and comfort he enjoyed because, I believe, he was sincerely trying to help his people."

> *"Who do you think stayed in family homes and segregated hotels with Jackie Robinson when he entered the big leagues and had to play in places such as Cincinnati and St. Louis, not to mention spring-training stops in Florida?"*
>
> WASHINGTON POST SPORTS COLUMNIST MICHAEL WILBON ON SPORTSWRITER AND ROBINSON CONFIDANT SAM LACY

I bring up the Robeson situation only to show how uncomfortable Jackie was in taking ramrod-straight political positions. Politically, he could not be labeled. He attacked Adam Clayton Powell for urging blacks to abandon the NAACP for the Black Muslims. He supported Republican Richard Nixon for the presidency in 1960 and resigned from the NAACP in 1967, in part because it opposed his connection with New York Governor Nelson Rockefeller, also a Republican. Yet he threw his support behind Minnesota Senator Hubert Humphrey, a Democrat, in the 1968 presidential campaign, and formed a close bond with the liberal Jesse Jackson, who delivered the eulogy at Jackie's funeral.

"Jackie was uninterested in adhering to any inflexible political perspective," Whitman College professor Patrick Henry once wrote. "His sole commitment was to integration and improved social conditions for black Americans."

As the chairman of the NAACP's Freedom Fund drive, Jackie raised $1 million in 1957 alone. That year, he gave a speech in Chicago in which he said: "We have waited almost one hundred years for these rights. In my view, now is the time for Negroes to ask for all of the rights which are theirs."

On February 16, 1958, with a hostile white crowd outside the building, Robinson delivered a speech in Jackson, Mississippi, imploring blacks to "press on peacefully for rights." In 1962, Martin Luther King Jr. selected Robinson to lead a fund-raising drive to rebuild black churches in the South.

"Jackie was to sports what Martin Luther King was to civil rights," civil-rights leader Andrew Young told me. "I have never forgotten that when they started burning churches in the South in the early '60s, Jackie came to Albany, Georgia. That elevated the whole thing nationally and internationally."

"I used to have talks with Jackie Robinson not long before he died, and he impressed upon me that I should never allow myself to be satisfied with the way things are. I can't let Jackie down—or my people, or myself. The day I become content is the day I cease to be anything more than a man who hit home runs."

HENRY AARON

He went, too, to Birmingham, Alabama, in May 1963, speaking to a packed church there with King at his side—not long after King's hotel had been bombed.

"I don't think you realize down here in Birmingham what you mean to us up there in New York," Jackie said that day. "And I don't think white Americans understand what Birmingham means to all of us throughout the country."

According to author Taylor Branch, Robinson could barely get his words out, explaining that the only thing he could think to tell the crowd was that "when he left New York his three children had wanted to come with him to go to jail, too, because they had seen Birmingham children going to jail for what they believed in . . . I can't help getting emotional about this thing. . . . And I wish that this same kind of enthusiasm that was shown right here in this church tonight could be shown to Negroes throughout America."

Until the day he died, Robinson pointed out time after time the need for a greater minority presence in the managerial offices and the boardrooms of professional sports. In a speech in Detroit, he once said, "For some reason, there are no Negro players on the fields of Detroit. Detroit is a great sports town. But you can't help but wonder about the absence of Negro players in both football and baseball."

For years, Marty Appel, the longtime publicist for the Yankees, was in

"When I was a kid in Indianapolis, we'd drive down to Cincinnati to see the Dodgers when they played the Reds. It gave me such a sense of pride to see Jackie Robinson play."

OSCAR ROBERTSON
NBA HALL OF FAMER

charge of planning the team's annual Old Timers' Game at Yankee Stadium. It was a huge event—the likes of Mickey Mantle and Joe DiMaggio returning to the field where they had shined. During the late 1960s and into the early 1970s, Appel would telephone Jackie Robinson each year and invite him to the celebration, and each year, Jackie would respond to Appel by returning the call and answering in the same way.

"Mr. Appel, when the Yankees have a black man managing or coaching them, then I will consider attending your event. But in the meantime, I must respectfully decline."

Appel told me: "Every time Jackie would say that, I'd thank him, hang up the phone, pump my fist and say, 'Way to go, Jackie.'"

Robinson's was a strong voice denouncing anti-Semitism among blacks. In 1962, Sol Singer, the owner of a national chain of steakhouses, bought a property in Harlem and leased it to Frank Schiffman, the owner of the Apollo Theater. Chants of "Jew, go away. Black man, stay" greeted the men's new business; the chants were led by Lewis H. Michaux, a local bookstore owner and the president of a black nationalist group called the Harlem Consumers Committee.

On July 14, Robinson wrote a column in *The Amsterdam News* that read in part: "Anti-Semitism is as rotten as anti-Negroism. It is a shame that, so far, none of the Negroes of Harlem have yet had the guts to say so in tones which could be heard throughout the city."

Eventually, the controversy cooled, and Singer and Schiffman opened their restaurant without incident.

Clem Labine was enjoying his first summer of retirement in 1963 after pitching for four big-league teams, including the Dodgers, for thirteen years when a telegram arrived at his home. It was from his friend and former teammate, Jackie Robinson. "He invited me to participate in the March on Washington," Labine told me. "I didn't go, and I wish I had. I regret it to this day."

Had Labine been there, in our nation's capital on August 28, 1963, he would have watched history play out. I was twenty-three years old at the time, and I attended the march with my mother and my sister. None of us will ever forget it. What a sight to see: an official count of a quarter million people— though Congressman John Lewis, who marched that day, wrote in his autobiography *Walking with the Wind,* "I swear there were more." There was King, making his timeless "I Have a Dream" speech. There were people of all religions, races and backgrounds coming together, in Lewis's words, "in hope and harmony." And there was Jackie Robinson, telling a reporter: "We cannot be turned back."

He never was turned back. But it's always good to remember that Jackie's work on mending the wounds among the races is not finished.

> *"If the leader is committed, there will be a greater chance for the followers to be committed."*
>
> MIKE KRZYZEWSKI
> COLLEGE BASKETBALL COACH

"Jackie Robinson teaches us that if you have a goal, pursue it at all costs, but count the cost in advance," Michael Eric Dyson, a religion professor at the University of Pennsylvania, said to me. "He understood what it would entail for him. Racism is a poison that pollutes the waters of life, but Jackie refused to drink from that pollution. He always had in mind the value of his fellow human beings.

"Jackie used baseball as a springboard to affect the larger concerns of society. He lived in a broader world and understood it was not a matter of black vs. white. It was right vs. wrong. We still haven't solved the race issues in America. There are a bunch of problems left. We have a nostalgia for Jackie's time when the racial issues were clearer. You knew what you were up against. Today the racial matters are murkier."

> *"The name Jackie Robinson soon became a euphemism for anyone becoming the first black person in his field. When my father, LeRoy Mitchell Jr. was named the superintendent of labor relations at Inland Steel Company in 1963, he privately called himself 'the Jackie Robinson' of his department."*
>
> FRED MITCHELL
> SPORTSWRITER, *CHICAGO TRIBUNE*

ESPN and ABC broadcaster John Saunders told me, "Race relations are still in disarray in our country, and some of the same problems Jackie Robinson faced still exist. If Branch Rickey had picked the wrong guy, the 'great experiment' would have been set back twenty years. We haven't gotten to the point where race doesn't matter in America. Jackie set us on the road, but we're still not there. Sports is the only place in this country where we have true equality. It's still not there in everyday walks of life."

HIS COMMITMENT TO SERVICE

"Life owes me nothing. Baseball owes me nothing. But I cannot as an individual rejoice in the good things I have been permitted to work for and learn while the humblest of my brothers is down in the deep hole hollering for help and not being heard."

—Jackie Robinson

In the early 1970s, broadcaster Dick Enberg, who has called hundreds of NFL games, college basketball games and pro tennis matches for NBC and CBS, hosted a television sports-quiz show called "Sports Challenge," in which athletes from the past competed against each other. About a year before his death, Jackie appeared on the show with some of his former Dodger teammates.

"I remember Jackie still had an elegance about him," Enberg told me. "But he was very tired. He seemed exhausted, like a great fighter who had gone ten rounds but had very little left for round eleven. I felt Jackie had lived twice the years of his real age in carrying such a heavy load of responsibility for all those years. He died at fifty-three, but he probably was 106. His role in society had been so significant, but in the process it helped send him to an early grave."

Enberg was not the only person I interviewed who made this bittersweet suggestion: the very thing that made Jackie great—his belief that service was an obligation that required every ounce of his being—was also the thing that ended his life so soon. By the time he died, he had nothing left to give.

"Jackie Robinson's life was built around service to an idea, an ideal or a cause," the late sportswriter Ralph Wiley told me before his death. "He was always at the service of someone or something: UCLA, the U.S. Army, the Dodgers, the Republican Party, Branch Rickey, the NAACP. He was a champion that way to all people, not just blacks. He was a combination of the times he lived in and the fire that burned inside him. There has never been anyone quite like him. He burned with such intensity and needed a cause to direct it into. He was perfect for a cause. He needed to impact society through his efforts.

"Service to others is the rent I pay for my room here on Earth."

MUHAMMAD ALI

"He was addicted to competition and service, and I think it cost him his health. He was so driven to perform at a certain level to be a champion for his people. The lesson is that the brightest star often has the shortest life."

ESPN anchor Stuart Scott told me that if he could interview only one person, it would be Jackie Robinson. "And if I could ask him one question," Scott said, "it would be, 'How did you endure what you did without losing your cool when the whole world was against you?' I think he would answer, 'Because I wasn't doing it for me. I had a responsibility to everybody else. My journey was much larger than myself.'"

To embark on such a journey, a man must be humble. He must be willing to put his self-interest aside, to sacrifice his time and energy so that others might benefit in the future.

"A lifetime of service was my father's commitment to America and his challenge to you."

SHARON ROBINSON

Branch Rickey, for example, was the baseball coach at Ohio Wesleyan University in 1904 when he saw the team's catcher, Charlie Thomas, sitting on a cot, crying, clawing and scratching as his hands. "Black skin, black skin," Thomas said. "If only I could make them white." That scene stayed with Rickey, and it compelled him, once he had the power, to try to end segregation in baseball—to lift blacks up to an equal plane with whites in at least one aspect of society.

Robinson was supremely confident in his athletic ability, and he certainly was unafraid about expressing that confidence in the heat of the game. But like Rickey, at his core Jackie acknowledged and understood that selfishness had no place in his crusade. He had to be strong and confident, yes, but he also had to remember that the common good, not his ego, came first.

"Jack was a man who had the courage to be himself in the face of great opposition," Rachel told me. "He was never afraid to take on issues and face them directly. He was persistent and determined because he wanted to achieve results. He always had a strong sense of identity. You could tell him he was inferior, but he didn't believe it. He had great confidence in his identity. In fact, that was one of the qualities I so admired in him when we met on the UCLA campus. Through all of this, though, Jack remained a man of great humility."

When Chicago Cubs manager Dusty Baker was a teenager playing American Legion baseball in Riverside, California, his coach was former Dodgers third baseman Spider Jorgensen, who had spent five years in Brooklyn and actually made his major-league debut on the same day that Jackie did: April 15, 1947.

"In all the time he coached us, I never knew Spider played for the Dodgers," Baker told me. "I knew he was a terrific coach, but he never once mentioned he was a former ballplayer."

> *"I think my father understood that he helped to change a nation. But you can't believe how humble he was."*
>
> SHARON ROBINSON

Years later, after Baker had been traded to the Los Angeles Dodgers, he was walking down a hallway at the Dodgers' spring-training complex in Vero Beach, Florida, looking at the photographs on the walls.

"I saw one picture and said, 'That's Spider Jorgensen, my old coach!'" he told me.

Jorgensen was so humble that it took Dusty Baker's becoming a big-leaguer himself before he discovered his old coach, a man who was now serving his community by working with youngsters, had been Jackie Robinson's teammate. I'm willing to bet Spider learned some of that humility from Jackie, too.

When author David Zang was ten years old, his father took him to

Williamsport, Pennsylvania, to watch the Little League World Series. There, standing alone behind one of the dugouts, was Jackie Robinson, signing autographs.

"I ran up to him and he got his pen ready, but I went right past him to the Japanese team," Zang told me. "Jackie was not offended. His reaction was, 'I understand. He's a kid, and he wants those Japanese signatures on his program.' Jackie had been through fierce fights on the field, but he did not appear to carry that over to the kids who idolized him."

After Bob Wilson, one of the NBA's first black players, retired from pro basketball, he became the director of a YMCA in one of the most poverty-stricken areas of Milwaukee. In 1953, the Boston Braves relocated to Milwaukee, and the Dodgers came to town for a series of games.

"I was in contact with Jackie," Wilson told me, "and I invited him to come to the 'Y' and speak to my kids. He did. He spoke to fifty or sixty young people about studying hard. 'You can make it,' he told them. Jackie always felt a sense of responsibility to his people and the world in general."

Rachel has that same sense of responsibility, and she ensured that Jackie's legacy would continue by

"Despite his nonchampionship season, Dhani Jones, twenty-five, a Giants linebacker, is nonetheless ever vigilant against the swelling of his own head.

To guard against creeping egotism, he said, at a Muscular Dystrophy Association benefit at Chelsea Piers, he retreats to the subway and plays a makeshift musical instrument for spare change.

'A lot of times when you play in New York, people put you on a pedestal, you hear the cheers,' said Mr. Jones, dressed in a gray pin-striped suit and a purple and black bow tie. 'You start to think that you are important.'

Down in the subway, usually somewhere along the D line, Mr. Jones said, he dresses in blue jeans with paint stains and plays a washboard bass. The most he made was $4.85. 'It's a dose of reality for me,' he said. 'It helps my ego.'"

NEW YORK TIMES
JANUARY 8, 2004

"If I can be the world's most humble man, I can be its highest instrument."

LAO-TZU
PHILOSOPHER

"Humility is like underwear. Everybody needs it, but don't let it show."

JIM HENRY
PASTOR, FIRST BAPTIST CHURCH IN ORLANDO

creating the Jackie Robinson Foundation in 1973. The foundation, which now has more than one thousand graduates, provides educational and leadership opportunities to youths from low-income and troubled backgrounds.

"She is a remarkable person," Ray Isum, Rachel's younger brother, told me. "I have seen her with the president of the United States and the trashman, and she treats them the same. She doesn't ignore people. And she is great with all the students in college through the Jackie Robinson Foundation. She is in touch with them even after they have finished school. She will have students over to her house for visits. Her house is never locked."

HIS COMMITMENT TO HIS FAMILY

"When they try to destroy me, it's Rachel who keeps me sane."

—Jackie Robinson

In 1952, Jackie Robinson wrote a letter to his wife.

"I'll be very glad when this baseball is over and we settle down as a family," he said in the letter. "I would rather not be away so much."

Five years would pass before Jackie finally retired from baseball, before he and his family could settle in the suburbs of Connecticut and begin the life he longed for. If you think about it, his letter demonstrates how much he loved and treasured his family; after all, he was expressing these thoughts at the midpoint of his career. Truth be told, one of the more controversial moments of Jackie's career was its end. He announced his decision to retire in an article in *Look* magazine—after the Dodgers had traded him to the New York Giants. Buzzie Bavasi, then a vice president with the Dodgers, speculated publicly that Jackie would accept a contract offer from the Giants after *Look* had paid him for his story. But even in that article, which stunned the Dodgers and created some bitterness between Robinson and the only baseball organization he had known, he said he was leaving baseball to be a family man. "I know I'll miss the excitement of baseball, but I'm looking forward to new kinds of satisfaction," he said. "I'll be able to spend more time with my family. . . . They won't have to look for me on TV."

Spend more time with his family? How? You might assume that, given all the time he spent away from his family, given the ten years of playing baseball and the traveling and the speeches and the public life he led, Jackie had little time for his family.

> *"The security and elevation of the family and of family life are the prime objects of civilization, the ultimate end of all industries."*
> CHARLES W. ELIOT
> EDUCATOR

And you might assume Rachel and their children—Jackie Jr., David and Sharon—resented him for it.

And if you made such assumptions, you would be wrong.

"Family was important to Dad," Sharon Robinson told me. "He was a good father. He was able to forge a special bond with each of us. He was away a lot, but we bought into his mission, and we all felt part of it. He had a way of making us feel special. It was hard to get his attention at home, but once you got it, you had it. He shared with us why the civil-rights movement was important, and then we shared it as a family."

"Can you imagine having Jackie and Rachel Robinson as your parents?" David, who owns and operates a 120-acre coffee farm in Tanzania, Africa, told me. "What a blessing. I remember my dad for his stoic quietness. He was not a great talker but made an effort to be with his kids. He fished with us, and I caddied for him. I seldom saw him angry, which was remarkable considering all he'd been through."

Jackie's devotion to family grew out of his childhood, Rachel told me. His mother, Mallie, was his model.

"Mallie was so strong, and that definitely rubbed off on Jack," Rachel said. "Think about it. She left Georgia with five children. She had no help, no job. She settled in Pasadena and somehow purchased a home. She

> *"Jack was the sweetest man in the world. He was very family-oriented, just intense about family. If he loved you, there were no boundaries."*
>
> BRENDA WILLIAMS
> JACKIE'S SISTER-IN-LAW

worked as a housekeeper to earn a living. She'd take in people who needed help. Her son Mack had a mentally handicapped boy, and she took him in and cared for him completely. She had strong faith in God. She kept on going."

This upbringing had a profound effect on Jackie, on the importance he attached later in his life to creating the right environment to raise his children and on the value a strong family life could have for any young person.

"I did a feature on him in the early 1970s," *Houston Chronicle* sportswriter Mickey Herskowitz told me. "He mentioned that he drove by Ebbets Field regularly, so I asked if he had any sentimental feelings about the park. He said, 'None.' I asked again, and he said, 'No feelings. The apartments there are needed more than Ebbets Field.' Jackie had strong feelings about

> *"Commit yourself to whatever it is you love to do, and don't forget to appreciate the people who help you along the way."*
>
> JACK NICKLAUS
> GOLFER

the needs of young blacks. He said, 'The education doesn't matter if a youngster doesn't have a decent home to come home to after school. It's hard to do anything in life if you don't have a decent place to live and a family to take care of you.'"

As strong an individual as Jackie was, he also needed and relished the feeling that comes with knowing you can count on those who are close to you. In that way, his family extended beyond the boundaries of his own flesh and blood. Pee Wee Reese was family. The Reverend Karl Downs, Jackie's childhood mentor, was family. Branch Rickey was family. When Rickey died on December 9, 1965, at age eighty-four, Jackie said it was "almost as if I had lost my own father."

His partner in life

Roland Hardin was a basketball player at Samuel Houston College in Austin, Texas, in 1944 and 1945—just after Robinson had left Fort Hood in Temple, Texas. At that time, the college's president was the Reverend Karl Downs, Jackie's childhood mentor. Before Jackie left to play for the Kansas City Monarchs in '45, Downs hired him as an assistant basketball coach at Sam Houston. Hardin scrimmaged with and against Jackie during practices and, in a conversation with me, remembered being impressed with Jackie's athletic ability. But he was more impressed with something else.

"He wrote Rachel every day," Hardin told me. "They weren't married yet, but he was so devoted to her."

They married on February 10, 1946, after a courtship that had lasted almost six years. They had met while Jackie was at UCLA, and they took their time in their relationship to make sure they were right for each other. And they were. They were married for almost twenty-seven years.

"Mom and Dad were true partners," Sharon told me. "We all need other people. Mom was totally behind him. She was up front with him, and she listened to him. She is a director, and, to this day, she directs all of us. She is an optimist and a perfectionist. Dad listened to her and was very dependent on her. He was deeply in love with her his whole life."

Of course, the Robinsons' life was not always easy. Then again, what family's is? Love requires work, but Rachel and Jackie had more work thrust upon them in the first five years of their marriage than most couples ever

> *"As a youngster with a voracious appetite for the written word, I developed a passion for Ernest Hemingway. . . . Years later, my father revealed that when the Dodgers were in Cuba in the late forties, he and Jackie Robinson were the only Dodgers not invited by Hemingway to the author's home. An oversight? Papa Hemingway specifically requested that the Dodgers not bring any black ballplayers. As my father explained, he had not spoken of this encounter when I was a teenager because he didn't want to discourage me from reading Hemingway or any other authors."*
>
> ROY CAMPANELLA JR.
> SON OF DODGERS GREAT ROY CAMPANELLA

encounter. When an opposing pitcher fired a fastball toward Jackie's head, Rachel practically dropped to the ground with him. When a base runner charged toward Jackie and crashed into him with spikes high, it was as if Rachel herself were bleeding, too. She felt the pain of every insult that Jackie heard during his early days with the Dodgers, every moment of doubt, every night when he told her he wasn't sure if he could take it anymore.

"The few times I met Jackie, I could tell he was a family man," former Negro Leaguer Ernest Burke told me. "If Rachel had broken down one time, I think Jackie would have quit. That's how important she was. She doesn't get enough credit for what Jackie did."

"Rachel is a wonderful woman," Sam Lacy told me before his death. "One time, I was with Jackie on a road trip in 1947. He was so frustrated and discouraged that he wanted to quit. I said, 'Rachel told you from the beginning what to expect. If you quit now, you've violated your pledge to Rachel.'"

I guess that was all Jackie needed to hear.

Jackie's teammates on the Dodgers certainly knew how much Rachel meant to him, to his career and to his cause. To a man, when I talked to them, they couldn't say enough wonderful things about her.

> *"I frequently hear people say that marriage is a 50/50 proposition. I disagree. It is a 100/100 proposition. Each spouse has to put the other spouse's interests first, 100 percent of the time. The same is true of being a parent."*
>
> DAN PATRICK
> AUTHOR

Gene Hermanski: "Rachel was such an encouragement to Jackie. She'd tell him not to get down, to stay with it."

Dick Williams: "Rachel was a guiding light to Jackie."

Carmen Mauro: "Rachel was a soothing factor in Jackie's life. When he'd go home upset and agitated, she was always there to calm him down. You can't begin to estimate how important that was to his success."

Carl Erskine: "Rachel was Jackie's off-the-field support. When Branch Rickey first met her, his thought had to be, 'My, my, for a man to marry a woman this impressive, he's got to be the real deal.'"

Clem Labine: "Rachel gave Jackie balance in so many ways. Once he and

Rachel committed to break the color line, they both went headfirst into it. She and Jackie remained gracious even when things were difficult."

And what is Rachel's response to this warmth, to this recognition of her love and devotion to Jackie?

"We had a wonderful marriage," she told me. "A lot has been said about how much I helped Jack and how much he needed me. I needed him just as much."

But for all they endured as Jackie was beginning his baseball career, nothing matched the tragedy of June 17, 1971, when Jackie Robinson Jr. after years of battling a drug addiction, drove David's yellow MG off the Merritt Parkway. The car crushed four wooden guard posts, and Jackie Jr. was killed. He was twenty-four.

Nothing tested their love like the loss of their eldest child.

"The formula for a happy marriage? It's the same as the one for living in California: When you find a fault, don't dwell on it."

JAY TRACHMAN
AUTHOR

"A man would have no pleasure in discovering all the beauties of the universe, even in heaven itself, unless he has a partner to whom he might communicate his joys."

CICERO
PHILOSOPHER

"She was always there for Dad," David told me. "She was his savior in many ways."

Jackie, in her words

"It is interesting to me that Rachel never remarried," Susan Rayl, a history professor at SUNY-Courtland, said to me. "I am sure she could have had many suitors, but there was only one person for her."

I realized how right Rayl was during a lengthy conversation I had with Rachel in early 2004. Though Jackie had been gone for twenty-two years, Rachel's memories of him were still so fresh, flowing like a bubbling stream of crisp, clean water. She knew him so well, it was as if she still talked to him every day.

"Most writers dwell on the troubles Jack endured and the troubling times in which he lived," she told me. "They like to peg him as a martyr. This is a mistake. Jack had many positive things in his life. First was his religion. He knew God was with him and wanted Jack to do great things. Second was his great family life. Our love and deep bond were incredible, and they sustained both of us. Jack wanted a family, and we had both the joys and troubles that all parents do.

"Jack had fun. He was always happy on the golf course. He had a putting green in his living room at home, and he would practice putting at night. Our family vacations were fun. Jack had a sense of humor and was able to laugh at our difficulties. In the early years, we would be in a hotel in the South. We would go back to the room after a rough day, and we would look at each other and just laugh. Jack would say, 'Can you believe this?'"

When Rachel was talking about Jackie's sense of humor, I couldn't help but think of a little story I had heard about the first day of his major-league career. As he was heading out the door, Jackie kissed Rachel good-bye and said, "If you come to the ballpark today, you won't have any trouble recognizing me."

He paused for comedic effect, then said: "My number is forty-two."

"I don't let football define who I am. I'm a man. I'm a husband. I'm a father."

TROY VINCENT
NFL CORNERBACK

"He loved being home in the evening," Rachel told me. "In fact, he would race home and time himself. He would call and say, 'I'll be home by six.' Then he would try to beat it. Home was a haven for him because the real richness of his life was at home. He had a favorite easy chair. He loved to do crossword puzzles because he wanted to extend his language skills. Jack read mainly newspapers and magazines. This is part of his life that's not talked about. Jack was a tender and loving man."

Really, that's what Jackie Robinson's life was. It was a story about a man dedicated to his wife and his children, to his country and so many of its citizens and to ideals and values that were at once uniquely his and universal among decent people. A man who stood before the world's injustices and snarled in defiance, who accepted the responsibility for shaping the generations who would come after him, who held true to the vows he had made to those who counted on him.

His life was a love story, maybe the best one I know.

Epilogue: The Legacy He Leaves

The way I figured it, I was even with baseball and baseball with me.
The game had done much for me, and I had done much for it.
—Jackie Robinson

DURING THE COURSE OF MY WRITING THIS BOOK, *Total Baseball,* one of the essential encyclopedias of the sport, published its list of the top one hundred people in baseball history.

Jackie Robinson was ranked second. To Babe Ruth.

Now, it's difficult to argue that any player had a greater impact on the sport of baseball than Ruth had. He changed the way the game was played, taking it from a sport based on speed to one built on power. He gave those fans who had turned away from baseball in the wake of the 1919 Black Sox scandal reason to love the game again. He remains the sport's greatest icon, perhaps the greatest icon in all of American sport.

But Robinson—as the editors of *Total Baseball* acknowledged in explaining their rankings—changed more than baseball. He changed America. True, he would have been a Hall of Fame inductee on his statistics alone: a .311 career average, six postseason appearances in ten seasons, six seasons of 100 runs or more, an MVP award and a Rookie of the Year award. But as marvelous a player as Jackie was, he becomes more important in baseball history and American history as time passes—not because of what he did on the diamond, but because of who he was and what he withstood and achieved apart from the game. He was, as George Mason University history professor David Wiggins told me, "more than an athlete."

I wrote this book in the hope of inspiring people. In describing the qualities that comprised this great man, I wanted to show people how they, too, can be courageous. Or be a true leader. Or carry themselves with class and dignity. In a way, this book is an oral biography of Jackie Robinson, an exploration of his life. But in writing it, I was merely a conduit, allowing those who knew him, loved him, played with or against him, and studied him to share their insights and memories of an American hero.

So, to me, it was only right to close by sharing with you a few more of those insights and memories, with words that make clear why Jackie Robinson was so special then, why he is important and relevant now, and why his life will remain a touchstone for generations to come.

A CHARACTER THAT COULDN'T BE QUESTIONED

Clifford Reid, professor, Colby College:

"We remember Jackie Robinson because of the example he provided us. He could have been a bitter person, but he always came out to do his best. He was a wonderful teammate who helped to bridge the racial gap."

Claire Smith, journalist, the *Philadelphia Inquirer*:

"Jackie makes you stop and think before you utter the words, 'Life isn't fair.' Life is not fair in many ways. Jackie was held down for much of his life, but he fought through it. He wouldn't allow himself to fall into the trap of 'I am a victim.'"

Fred Claire, former Dodgers executive:

"First and foremost, he showed that what was really important in life was helping others. Jackie is remembered today not for his records on the baseball field but for his contributions to mankind. He was a great athlete, but he used his athletic skills for far more than personal achievement and fame."

Michael Wilbon, sports columnist, the *Washington Post*:

"People look at what Jackie Robinson did and know they couldn't have done it. We couldn't make it through all that, endure it and prosper. Jackie changed the world, but who would want to take that on? The further we get away from the Robinson era, the harder it seems to us."

Michael Lomax, professor, University of Iowa:

"He was always his own man. He was consistent in all that he did and was never afraid to criticize the baseball industry if he felt it deserved it. I've always felt that Jackie's heart was in the right place."

Roy Campanella Jr., son of Dodgers great Roy Campanella:

"Jackie had a commitment to excellence and also a commitment to citizenship. He was a great American citizen. He was always accountable for his actions and was a man of very high ethical standards. He had a great intellect, and once an athlete learns to focus on that, it can be a great benefit to him. Jackie Robinson was truly a renaissance man."

Daniel Okrent, journalist, the *New York Times*:

"The ability to turn the other cheek can be as powerful a weapon as fists or guns. Not only was Jackie a pioneer, there was nothing in his public life that was anything but noble and admirable. He was one of the last true heroes."

Eddie Miksis, former Dodgers teammate:

"He never gave up. He showed so much determination under constant strain. I saw it firsthand. No human being could go through what he went through. He was a great man to endure all that."

Elijah Anderson, professor, University of Pennsylvania:

"Jackie Robinson understood the context that he lived in. He knew that you can't trust everyone, but you can't distrust either. Jackie was sensitive to friendship and fellowship and was not just concerned with his own kind. He understood this and prevailed because he did."

Todd Parrott, son of former Dodgers executive Harold Parrott and former Dodgers batboy:

"I was ten years old when Jackie came to spring training in 1947. Then I was with the Dodgers when they barnstormed up north. I saw the pain Jackie went through. I heard what was being yelled at him. Any normal person would have punched those people out, but Jackie accepted it and played winning baseball. Do you know how hard that is to do? Jackie has received much credit for what he did for this country and for so many people, but it's not enough. You can't possibly give him enough credit."

AN ATHLETE FOR THE AGES

Larry Gitler, former UCLA basketball player:

"Jackie was a great all-around athlete. He was a star in football, track and basketball. We couldn't run a fast break because he was so fast. The two men on the wings couldn't keep up with him and were so far behind, the only way the break would work was if Jackie did it alone. His weakest sport at UCLA was baseball."

Joe Garagiola, former Cardinals catcher and television personality:

"He was so strong, so athletic. I've never seen a player get out of a run-down like he could. He'd have everyone in on the play, including the vendors, and somehow escape."

Peter Williams, author:

"I most remember Jackie Robinson's base running and that lateral movement as he was skittering off the bag. I think that came from his football days; those were the moves a good football player makes. Watching Jackie steal a base was so exciting. He'd get a walk, and everyone would cheer because they knew what was coming next."

Sharon Robinson:

"If Dad were coming out of college today with all his athletic talent, I think he would go into the NFL as a running back. Football was really his best sport."

John McHale, former baseball player and executive:

"He had the fastest feet I ever saw, and thick, powerful legs. When he slid into a base, he would almost tear it apart. Yet he was so athletic, like a gymnast around second base. Guys would go after him, but he would jump in the air to avoid them."

Furman Bisher, sports columnist, the *Atlanta Journal-Constitution*:

"He was a magnificent athletic specimen with a personal flair—a total athlete."

HIS PLACE IN HISTORY

David Shiner, baseball historian:

"Jackie was a key part of American history, and all of us can be justly proud of that. Jackie changed the way all of us, black or white, think about race relations."

Larry Hogan, professor, Union College:

"What Jackie Robinson did was as important to this country as *Brown v. the Board of Education.*"

Steve Kraly, former Major-Leaguer:

"Jackie Robinson made a great contribution to the game. The hurdles that he had to defeat to allow other black ballplayers to play were great. His memory will live forever. He is an immortal in the same class as Ted Williams, Mickey Mantle and Babe Ruth. What he did for the game will live on forever."

James McPherson, history professor, Princeton University:

"America is obsessed with sports, and what Jackie Robinson did in 1947 is the pivotal intersection between sports and cultural development in United States history. Jackie set the model for desegregation of other areas of American life and gave momentum to those other areas. He was a revolutionary and led a powerful breakthrough in Major League Baseball. More important was the way he did it. Ernest Hemmingway describes courage as 'grace under pressure,' and Jackie demonstrated that better than almost anyone in history."

David Falkner, sports historian:

"He was essentially the path-maker and mold-breaker for the entire civil-rights movement. It began with him. Jackie's career made it possible for others to follow, Martin Luther King included. He has become a myth because he embodied that entire era. The walls of segregation came tumbling down, and he did it."

Doris Kearns Goodwin, historian:

"At the time Jackie Robinson joined the Dodgers, we didn't realize the significance of what was happening. We soon learned what a great player he was, but his efforts were a monumental step in the civil-rights revolution in America. And it happened in baseball, a sport beloved by millions. Jackie's accomplishments allowed black and white Americans to be more respectful and open to one another and more appreciative of everyone's abilities."

Bill Deane, baseball historian:

"Jackie Robinson shattered the long-standing barrier in American culture by opening people's eyes that blacks were not inferior athletically or intellectually. We can't overstate what Jackie endured to make this possible. America has always been fascinated with pioneers and trendsetters in all areas of life. Jackie is probably the last American pioneer of note."

Branson Wright, sportswriter, the Cleveland *Plain Dealer*:

"Jackie Robinson is an all-American hero. He was a four-sport star at UCLA, a soldier, a ballplayer, a human rights leader. He transcends the sport of baseball. Jackie was all alone on the island, but he stood tall because he knew it was not about himself. His was a much bigger story than that."

A SYMBOL FOR SOMETHING
GREATER THAN OURSELVES

David Shiner, baseball historian:

"Jesse Jackson said, 'You can't have a resurrection without a crucifixion.' Jackie's trials made him a greater player."

Marc Spears, sportswriter, the *Denver Post*:

"Jackie had some Jesus-like qualities. They beat up Jesus, and he took the pain for future gain. Jackie took the pain of vile words and death threats— all because he knew what he was doing was bigger than just baseball. Jackie refused to retaliate because he saw the big picture of his actions. The average man would not have turned the other cheek; he would have thrown a punch. Jackie was a role model for all of us."

Mike Warren, former UCLA basketball player:

"Jackie Robinson was almost like Job. He went through so much and must have asked, 'Why?' He could have given up at any time, and you couldn't have blamed him. Because of what Jackie did, I was able to play at UCLA and not have to face what he did. How did he do it? He was a fighter. He wouldn't give up because he saw a bigger picture."

Len Elmore, New York attorney and former NBA player:

"Given the setting and the backdrop of the 1940s, we have never seen anyone like Jackie Robinson before or since. That fascinates us. He knew why he was chosen, and he understood the impact of what he was doing."

Clarence "Bighouse" Gaines, former college basketball coach:

"What Jackie teaches is that if you are a good person and associate with good people, good things will happen to you. I believe that Jackie realized that part of God's plan was to have him do this. It's as if God said, 'This is your chore, young man.' And Jackie went along with it."

Stedman Graham, speaker and author:

"Jackie represents what so many of us are longing for—the courage to step outside the boundaries of being an average person. The world puts us in a box, so we are fascinated by people who decide to step outside the box like Jackie."

LESSONS THAT LAST A LIFETIME

Bill Simons, history professor, SUNY-Oneonta:

"Jackie Robinson's life teaches us about the need for an America that is defined by its inclusiveness. We all need to reach out and recognize those untapped sources of talent. Don't discard people's potential because of physical defects, different accents or different cultures. Jackie's life says to us, 'Look for that talented person who is different and give him a fair chance.'"

Vida Blue, former major-league pitcher:

"My grandfather loved Jackie Robinson, and I can still remember sitting on his lap as a little boy in Louisiana listening to Dodgers games. Jackie

Robinson was a true pioneer and had to be a unique person to go through what he did. His life teaches us that when given a fair chance in life, you must take advantage of it because it may not come around again."

Bob Watson, Major League Baseball executive and former player:

"Jackie Robinson shows us that given the opportunity, you have a chance to succeed regardless of gender, skin color or religion. He also teaches us the importance of being patient and never giving up."

Dwain Price, sportswriter, the Fort Worth *Star-Telegram*:

"Jackie shows us that we can endure all and overcome all with God in our lives. Jackie's attitude was, 'OK, I am going to do this, and no one will stop me.' I may not be sitting at my computer today were it not for Jackie and what he did."

David Wiggins, George Mason University history professor:

"Jackie teaches us to exercise independence. I tell the athletes I teach that it is better to establish a nonsports identity than just play ball and have nothing. Jackie teaches us to take a broader and larger view of life, to recognize that there are lots of important things in life to accomplish outside of sports."

Willie Davis, former Green Bay Packers great:

"Jackie Robinson was the great example of how to handle a difficult situation. He never let things defeat him. He set out to climb the mountain, and then he climbed it. He is one of the first bigger-than-life black Americans. I saw a little bit of myself in everything he did. He gives us an example of demanding more from yourself and fighting for what you believe in. And Jackie did it at a time when there were not very many victories being won by African Americans."

Roger Rosenblatt, author and essayist:

"Jackie teaches us to always push the wheel forward in life. Those moments come when we must decide if we are going to let our fears force us to back up or if we are going to go forward. Jackie never went backward. He was always heading toward home."

Andrew Zimbalist, Smith College professor and author:

"He taught us how to succeed under extreme adversity, and because of this what he did was about as significant a human feat as we witnessed in the twentieth century."

AN EFFECT THAT STILL RESONATES

David Stern, NBA commissioner:

"I grew up in New York and was a big Giants fan. By the 1950s, Jackie was just another hated Dodger to me. But it was not a racial issue at all. In every era, a pathfinder has to be willing to take the risks and face a lot of uncertainties. You are blessed if the right guy comes along. In baseball, Jackie was the right man. What a big moment it must have been for young black children. Jackie is a hero for all of us."

Marian Wright Edelman, founder and president of the Children's Defense Fund:

"I was a child when Jackie Robinson began playing for the Brooklyn Dodgers, and like so many other people, Jackie Robinson was one of my great heroes and the Dodgers became a passion. As the first black player in the major leagues, Jackie Robinson was a trailblazer who very literally stepped up to the plate to do what had to be done—and he did it with great grace, dignity, courage and, above all, talent. He made us proud in every way and changed the image of what black folks can do. Jackie Robinson inspired all of us who went on to participate in the civil-rights movement and continues to be an example today for everyone still working to make America live up to its creed by giving every young person an equal chance to use their gifts and follow their dreams. His courage, grit and determination transformed sports, which transformed America's culture. His career was a grand slam against American racism."

John Thorn, baseball historian:

"As the years go on, Jackie will continue to grow in stature. All of us are shaped by our surroundings, but Jackie is the exception. He was an individual who shaped the crowd. Today in America, we have such diminished expectations for heroism. Jackie blazed the trail for himself and widened it for others. What he did is without parallel in living memory."

Claude Lewis, columnist, the *Philadelphia Inquirer*:

"Jackie Robinson died from the effects of diabetes. I am battling diabetes right now, but I continue to teach at Villanova University twice a week and write my weekly column. It's not easy, but I think of Jackie often. He inspires me as I face the same battle he did."

Richard Peterson, baseball editor:

"We are still fascinated with Jackie Robinson because what he started in 1947 is not over. Racial relations in America have improved, but equality of the races is still just a hope and a dream. Jackie's battle continues in baseball and beyond."

J. A. Adande, sports columnist, the *Los Angeles Times*:

"We remember Jackie Robinson to this day because his legacy continues to be seen so widely in all of sports. Today, we can't imagine baseball, football or basketball without African Americans. Before Jackie, there were none, but today, anytime you watch a game you see Jackie Robinson's descendants. He didn't accomplish what he did and then see it all disappear."

Ivan Hemetz, Long Island attorney:

"All human beings need heroes. Jackie Robinson had been my hero since I was ten years old. He is still my hero. He taught me how I should go through life. He taught me how to be a man."

Ed Charles, former Major-Leaguer:

"Jackie was about democracy. He picked us up and moved us in that direction. That is something we can't forget because it validates being a true democracy for everybody. We honor our heroes, and Jackie was a true American hero with George Washington, Abraham Lincoln and the rest. He improved our way of life."

Rachel Robinson:

"I think that if more people could join the fight, and if more people could struggle with the issues that are facing us today—and we are faced with major issues—then I think Jackie Robinson's life will mean more."

THE CHALLENGE FOR ALL OF US

Mike Freeman, sports columnist, the *Florida Times-Union*:

"What he did was historic, and it sets him apart. Jackie stands as a symbol of great triumph over racial prejudice, but also as a measuring stick of how much progress we have made in terms of race relations in this society, both inside and outside of sports. It is like looking at the Wright brothers and the first time they flew a plane. You look at that moment and then compare things to where we are now: supersonic jets, men walking on the moon.

"With Jackie, we look at that moment and measure what has gone both right and wrong since he made history. How many black coaches and managers have we had since Jackie? How many black quarterbacks? How many black team owners? He helps us measure how far we have come, and how much further we have to go."

Elliot Gorn, history professor, Brown University:

"The job Jackie Robinson started is not finished. We are way down the road from 1947, but there still is a lot of work to do."

Doug Battema, media scholar, Western New England College:

"Jackie Robinson's life forces all of us to answer the question, 'What will your legacy be?'"

Jim "Mudcat" Grant, former major-league pitcher:

"Jackie Robinson was put on this earth for a special reason, and it was more than just about playing baseball. He taught us that we all can overcome tremendous obstacles in life with perseverance, confidence and a humanitarian spirit. We all have a survival kit within ourselves, and we must use it. Jackie came. He played. He conquered. And in the process, he taught America that we can live together and survive together."

Acknowledgments

❦

With deep appreciation I acknowledge the support and guidance of the following people who helped make this book possible:

Special thanks to Bob Vander Weide and John Weisbrod of the Orlando Magic.

I'm grateful to my assistant, Diana Basch, who managed so many of the details that made this book possible.

Many thanks to Doug Grassian for all of his hard work in helping to coordinate the research for this book.

Hats off to four dependable associates—Andrew Herdliska, my adviser Ken Hussar, Vince Pileggi of the Orlando Magic mail/copy room, and my ace typist, Fran Thomas.

Special thanks to Dick Crepeau for making significant contributions to this book.

Hearty thanks are also due to Peter Vegso and his fine staff at Health Communications Inc. and to my partner in writing this book, Mike Sielski. Thank you all for believing that I had something important to share and for providing the support and the forum to say it.

And finally, special thanks and appreciation go to my wife, Ruth, and to my wonderful and supportive family. They are truly the backbone of my life.

—Pat Williams

Thank you to my parents, Ann and Chuck Sielski; to my sister, Jessica; and to all my family members for their love and patience.

Thank you to those dear friends who contributed their ideas and support for this book, especially to Domenick Cosentino, Jeff Beideman, Kevin Cooney, Tom Moore and all my colleagues at Calkins Media Inc.; to

Gabriel Fagan, Brian and Andrea Parks, Tom and Rannette Schurtz, Jason and Rachel Darnell, Mark Prybutok, Seth Oltman, Oshrat Carmiel, John McGrath, and Rich Hofmann.

A deep thank you to Bill Lyon, who has been everything a young writer could ask for in a mentor and a friend, and without whom I never would have become part of this project.

Thank you to Health Communications Inc. and to Amy Hughes in particular.

And, of course, thank you to Pat Williams, a model of enthusiasm and vigor, for his friendship and his faith in me.

—Mike Sielski

Bibliography

❖

Aaron, Hank. *I Had a Hammer*. New York: HarperCollins, 1991.

Abdul-Jabbar, Kareem. *Brothers in Arms*. New York: Broadway Books, 2004.

Alexander, Charles C. *Our Game: An American Baseball History*. New York: Henry Holt, 1991.

Allen, Lee. *The Giants and Dodgers*. New York: G.P. Putnam's Sons, 1964.

——. *100 Years of Baseball*. New York: Bartholomew House, 1950.

Allen, Lee and Tom Meang. *King of the Diamond*. New York: G.P. Putnam's Sons, 1965.

Allen, Maury. *Jackie Robinson: A Life Remembered*. New York: Franklin Watts, 1987.

Allen, Mel. *You Can't Beat the Hours*. New York: Harper & Row, 1964.

Alston, Walter and S. Burick. *Alston and the Dodgers*. Garden City, NJ: Doubleday, 1966.

Alvarez, Mark. *The Perfect Game*. Dallas, TX: Taylor Publishing, 1993.

Anderson, Dave. *1955 in Sport*. New York: Sport Classic Books, 2004.

——. *Pennant Races: Baseball at its Best*. New York: Doubleday, 1994.

Attiyeh, Mike. *Who Was Traded for Lefty Grove?* Baltimore: Johns Hopkins University Press, 2002.

Baldassaro, Lawrence and Richard. *The American Game*. Carbondale: Southern Illinois University Press, 2002.

Barber, Lylah. *Lylah*. Chapel Hill, NC: Algonquin Books, 1985.

Barber, Red. *The Rhubarb Pitch*. New York: Simon & Schuster, 1954.

——. *1947: When All Hell Broke Loose in Baseball*. New York: Da Capo, 1982.

Bavasi, Buzzie. *Off the Record*. Chicago, IL: Contemporary Books, 1987.

Berkow, Ira. *Hank Greenberg: The Story of My Life*. New York: Times Books, 1989.

Berra, Yogi. *Ten Rings*. New York: HarperCollins, 2003.

Bloomfield, Gary. *Duty, Honor, Victory*. Guilford, CT: Lyons Press, 2003.

Boxerman, Burton and Benita Boxerman. *Ebbets to Veeck to Busch*. Jefferson, NC: McFarland, 2003.

Branch, Taylor. *Parting the Waters*. New York: Simon & Schuster, 1988.

——. *Pillar of Fire*. New York: Simon & Schuster, 1998.

Broeg, Bob. *Stan Musial: The Man's Own Story*. Garden City, NJ: Doubleday, 1964.

Bruce, Janet. *The Kansas City Monarchs*. Lawrence: University Press of Kansas, 1985.

Bryant, Howard. *Shut Out*. New York: Routledge, 2002.

Burk, Robert F. *Much More Than a Game*. Chapel Hill: University of North Carolina Press, 2001.

Burns, Stewart. *To the Mountain Top*. New York: HarperCollins, 2004.

Cannon, Jack and Tom Cannon. *Nobody Asked Me, but. . . . The World of Jimmy Cannon*. New York: Holt, Rinehart & Winston, 1978.

Carey, Mike. *High Above Courtside*. Champaign, IL: Sports Publishing LLC, 2003.

Carrieri, Joe. *Searching for Heroes: The Quest of a Yankee Batboy*. Minneola, NY: Carlyn Publications, 1995.

Castro, Tony. *Mickey Mantle: America's Prodigal Son*. Washington, D.C.: Brassey's, 2002.

Cataneo, David. *Casey Stengel: Baseball's "Old Professor."* Nashville, TN: Cumberland House, 2003.

Chandler, Happy. *Heroes, Plain Folks and Skunks*. Chicago: Bonus Books, 1989.

Claire, Fred and Steve Springer. *Fred Claire: My 30 Years in Dodger Blue*. Champaign, IL: Sports Publishing LLC, 2004.

Cohen, Robert W. *A Team for the Ages*. Guilford, CT: Lyons Press, 2004.

Conlan, Jocko. *Jocko*. Philadelphia: J.B. Lippincott, 1967.

Connor, Anthony. *Voices From Cooperstown*. New York: Callahan Books, 1982.

Cook, Marshall and Jack Walsh. *Baseball's Good Guys: The Real Heroes of the Game*. Champaign, IL: Sports Publishing LLC, 2004.

Cook, William A. *Pete Rose*. Jefferson, NC: McFarland, 2004.

Cosell, Howard. *Cosell*. Chicago, IL: Playboy Press, 1973.

Daley, Arthur. *Times At Bat: A Half Century of Baseball*. New York: Random House, 1950.

Dark, Alvin and John Underwood. *When in Doubt, Fire the Manager*. New York: E.P. Dutton, 1980.

Dorinson, Joseph. *Jackie Robinson: Race, Sports and the American Dream*. New York: M.E. Sharpe, 1998.

Dravecky, Dave. *Called Up*. Grand Rapids, MI: Zondervan, 2004.

Drysdale, Don and Bob Verdi. *Once a Bum Always a Dodger*. New York: St. Martin's Press, 1990.

Duckett, Alfred, with Jackie Robinson. *I Never Had It Made*. Hopewell, NJ: Ecco Press, 1995.

Durocher, Leo. *The Dodgers and Me: The Inside Story.* Chicago: Ziff Davis Publishing, 1948.

———. *Nice Guy's Finish Last.* New York: Simon & Schuster, 1975.

Durso, Joseph. DiMaggio: *The Last American Knight.* Boston, MA: Little, Brown & Company, 1995.

Dyson, Michael Eric. *The Michael Eric Dyson Reader.* New York: Basic Civitas Books, 2004.

Edwards, Bob. *Fridays with Red.* New York: Rocket Books, 1993.

Einstein, Charles. *The Baseball Reader.* New York: Lippincott and Crowell Publishing, 1956.

———. *The Second Fireside Book of Baseball.* New York: Simon & Schuster, 1958.

———. *Willie's Time: Baseball's Golden Age.* Carbondale: Southern Illinois University Press, 1979.

Erskine, Carl. *Tales from the Dodger Dugout.* Champaign, IL: Sports Publishing LLC, 2000.

Erskine, Carl and Burton Rocks. *What I learned from Jackie Robinson.* New York: McGraw-Hill, 2005.

Falkner, David. *Great Time Coming.* New York: Simon & Schuster, 1995.

Feller, Bob. *Strikeout Story.* New York: A.S. Barnes, 1947.

Fountain, Charles. *Sportswriter: The Life and Times of Grantland Rice.* New York: Oxford University Press, 1993.

Gaines, Clarence E. *They Call Me Big House.* Winston-Salem, NC: John F. Blair Publishing, 2004.

Gates, Henry Louis, Jr. *African American Lives.* New York: Oxford University Press, 2004.

Gentile, Derek. *Baseball's Best 1000.* New York: Black Dog and Leventhal Publishers, 2004.

Giglio, James. *Musial: From Stash to Stan the Man.* Columbia: University of Missouri Press, 2001.

Gilbert, Bill. *Now Pitching Bob Feller.* New York: Birch Lane Press, 1990.

Golenbock, Peter. *Amazing.* New York: St. Martin's Press, 2002.

———. *Bums.* New York: G.P. Putnam's Sons, 1984.

———. *Dynasty.* Englewoods Cliffs, NJ: Prentice-Hall, 1975.

———. *The Spirit of St. Louis.* New York: Avon Books, 2000.

———. *Wrigleyville.* New York: St. Martin's Press, 1996.

Gould, Stephen *Jay. Triumph and Tragedy in Mudville.* New York: W.W. Norton, 2003.

Halberstam, David. *Summer of '49.* New York: William Morrow, 1989.

Hall, Alvin. *The Cooperstown Symposium on Baseball and American Culture.* Jefferson, NC: McFarland, 2000.

Harwell, Ernie. *My 60 Years in Baseball.* Chicago: Triumph Books, 2002.

Helyar, John. *Lords of the Realm.* New York: Villard Books, 1994.

Henrich, Tommy and Bill Gilbert. *Five O'Clock Lightning.* New York: Birch Lane Press, 1992.

Holmes, Tommy. *Dodger Daze and Knights.* New York: David McKay, 1953.

Holtzman, Jerome. *The Commissioners: Baseball's Midlife Crisis.* New York: Total Sports, 1998.

Holtzman, Jerome. *The Jerome Holtzman Baseball Reader.* Chicago, IL: Triumph Books, 2003.

Honig, David. *Baseball America.* North Carolina: Macmillan, 1985.

——. *A Donald Honig Reader.* New York: Simon & Schuster, 1975.

Jennings, Peter. *The Century.* New York: Doubleday, 1998.

Kahn, Roger. *The Boys of Summer.* New York: Harper & Row, 1971.

——. *The Era.* New York: Ticknor & Fields, 1993.

——. *Games We Used to Play.* New York: Ticknor & Fields, 1992.

——. *Memories of Summer.* New York: Hyperion, 1997.

——. *October Men.* Orlando, FL: Harcourt, 2003.

Kahn, Roger and Al Helfer. *The Mutual Baseball Almanac.* Garden City, NY: Doubleday, 1954.

Kashatus, William C. *September Swoon.* University Park: Pennsylvania State Press, 2004.

Keene, Kerry. 1951: *When Giants Played the Game.* Champaign, IL: Sports Publishing LLC, 2001.

Kiner, Ralph. *Baseball Forever.* Chicago: Triumph Books, 2004.

Kiner, Ralph and Joe Gergen. *Kiner's Korner.* New York: Arbor House, 1987.

King, Clyde. *A King's Legacy.* Chicago, IL: Masters Press, 1999.

King, Larry. *Why I Love Baseball.* Beverly Hills, CA: New Millennium Press, 2004.

Koufax, Sandy. *Koufax.* New York: Viking Press, 1966.

Kuhn, Bowie. *Hardball.* Lincoln: University of Nebraska Press, 1987.

Lamb, Chris. *Blackout.* Lincoln: University of Nebraska Press, 2004.

Lanetot, Neil. *Negro League Baseball.* Philadelphia: University of Pennsylvania Press, 2004.

Lasorda, Tommy and David Fisher. *The Artful Dodger.* New York: Arbor House, 1985.

Leavy, Jane. *Sandy Koufax*. New York: HarperCollins, 2002.

Lewis, John. *Walking with the Wind*. New York: Harcourt Brace, 1998.

Mac, Toby and Michael Tait. *Under God*. Minneapolis: Bethany House, 2004.

Madden, Bill. *Bill Madden Presents*. Champaign, IL: Sports Publishing LLC, 2004.

———. *Pride of October*. New York: Warner Books, 2003.

Mandelbaum, Michael. *The Meaning of Sports*. New York: Perseus Books, 2004.

Mann, Arthur. *Branch Rickey: America in Action*. Cambridge, MA: Riverside Press, 1957.

Mantle, Mickey. *The Quality of Courage*. Garden City, NY: Doubleday, 1964.

Marsh, Irving T. *Best Sports Stories 1956*. New York: Dutton, 1956.

Marshall, William. *Baseball's Pivotal Era, 1945-1951*. Lexington, KY: University Press, 1999.

McCarthy, Kevin. *Baseball in Florida*. Sarasota, FL: Pineapple Press, 1996.

McKelvey, G. Richard. *The MacPhails*. Jefferson, NC: McFarland and Company, 2000.

McNary, Kyle. *Black Baseball*. New York: Sterling Publishers, 2003.

Meany, Tom. *There've Been Some Changes in the World of Sports*. New York: Thomas Nelson & Sons, 1962.

Meany, Tom and Tommy Holmes. *Baseball's Best*. New York: Franklin Watts, 1964.

Miller, Marvin. *A Whole Different Ballgame*. New York: Birch/Lane Press, 1991.

Moffi, Larry. *This Side of Cooperstown*. Iowa City: University of Iowa Press, 1996.

Monteleone, John. *Branch Rickey's Little Blue Book*. New York: Macmillan, 1995.

Nelson, Kevin. *The Golden Game*. Berkeley, CA: Heyday Books, 2004.

O'Neil, Buck. *I Was Right on Time*. New York: Simon & Schuster, 1996.

O'Neil, William J. *Sports Leaders and Success*. New York: McGraw Hill, 2004.

Orodenker, Richard. *The Phillies Reader*. Philadelphia: Phillies Reader, 1996.

Parrott, Harold. *The Lords of Baseball*. Atlanta: Long Street Press, 1976.

Peary, Danny. *Baseball's Finest*. North Dighton, MA: J.G. Press, 1990.

———. *We Played the Game*. New York: Hyperion, 1994.

Peary, Danny and Mary Tiegreen. *1,001 Reasons to Love Baseball*. New York: Stewart, Tabori & Chang, 2004.

Peterson, Robert W. *Only the Ball Was White*. Englewood Cliffs, NJ: Prentice-Hall, 1970.

Phalen, Rick. *A Bittersweet Journey*. Tampa, FL: McGregor Publishing, 2000.

Plaut, David. *Speaking of Baseball*. Philadelphia, PA: Running Press, 1993.

Poling, Jerry. *A Summer Up North*. Madison: University of Wisconsin Press, 2002.

Rader, Benjamin. *Baseball: A History of America's Game.* Urbana: University of Illinois Press, 2002.

Rampersad, Arnold. *Jackie Robinson: A Biography.* New York: Random House, 1997.

Reisler, Jim. *Babe Ruth Slept Here.* South Bend, IN: Diamond Communications, 1999.

Rickey, Branch and Robert Riger. *The American Diamond.* New York: Simon & Schuster, 1995.

Roberts, Robin. *My Life in Baseball.* Chicago, IL: Triumph Books, 2003.

——. *The Whiz Kids.* Philadelphia: Temple University Press, 1996.

Roberts, Robin and Paul C. Rogers. *The Whiz Kids and the 1950 Pennant.* Philadelphia: Temple University Press, 1996.

Robinson, Jackie. *Baseball Has Done It.* Philadelphia: J.B. Lippincott, 1964.

——, with Alfred Duckett. *I Never Had It Made.* Hopewell, NJ: Ecco Press, 1995.

Robinson, Rachel and Lee Daniels. *Jackie Robinson: An Intimate Portrait.* New York: Harry N. Abrams, 1996.

Robinson, Sharon. *Jackie's Nine.* New York: Scholastic Press, 2001.

——. *Promises to Keep.* New York: Scholastic Press, 2004.

Roeder, Bill. *Jackie Robinson.* New York: A.S. Barnes, 1950.

Rowan, Carl T. and Jackie Robinson. *Wait Till Next Year.* New York: Random House, 1960.

Ruck, Rob. *Sandlot Seasons.* Urbana: University of Illinois Press, 1993.

Schieffer, Bob. *Face the Nation.* New York: Simon & Schuster, 2004.

Schoendienst, Red and Rob Rains. *Red: A Baseball Life.* Champaign, IL: Sports Publishing LLC, 1998.

Schoor, Gene. *Roy Campanella: A Man of Courage.* New York: G.P. Putnam's Sons, 1959.

Scott, Richard. *Black Americans of Achievement: Jackie Robinson.* New York: Chelsea House Publishers, 1987.

Shapiro, Michael. *The Last Good Season.* New York: Doubleday, 2003.

Shaugnessy, Dan. *The Curse of the Bambino.* New York: Dutton, 1990.

Silber, Irwin. *Press Box Red.* Philadelphia: Temple University Press, 2003.

Simon, Scott. *Jackie Robinson and the Integration of Baseball.* Hoboken, NJ: John Wiley & Sons, 2002.

Smith, Curt. *Voices of the Game.* New York: Simon & Schuster, 1987.

Smith, Red. *Red Smith on Baseball.* Chicago: Ivan R. Dee, 2000.

Smith, Robert. *Heroes of Baseball.* Cleveland, OH: World Publishing, 1952.

Smith, Wendell. *Jackie Robinson: My Own Story.* New York: Greenberg, 1948.

Snyder, Brad. *Beyond the Shadow of the Senators*. Chicago: Contemporary Books, 2003.

Sokolove, Michael. *The Ticket Out*. New York: Simon & Schuster, 2004.

Stanton, Tom. *Hank Aaron and the Home Run that Changed America*. New York: HarperCollins, 2004.

Stout, Glenn. *The Dodgers*. New York: Houghton Mifflin, 2004.

Thomson, Bobby. *The Giants Win the Pennant! The Giants Win the Pennant!* New York: Zebra Books, 1991.

Thorn, John. *Total Baseball*. Toronto: Sport Classic Books, 2004.

Turner, Frederick. *When the Boys Came Back*. New York: Henry Holt, 1996.

Tygiel, Jules. *Baseball's Great Experiment*. New York: Oxford University Press, 1997.

——. *Extra Bases*. Lincoln: University of Nebraska Press, 2002.

——. *The Jackie Robinson Reader*. New York: Penguin Group, 1997.

——. *Past Time*. New York: Oxford University Press, 2000.

Vecchione, Joseph J. *The New York Times Book of Sports Legends*. New York: Times Books, 1991.

Vincent, Fay. *The Last Commissioner*. New York: Simon & Schuster, 2002.

Wallace, Joseph. *The Baseball Anthology*. New York: Harry N. Abrams, 2004.

Weber, Louis. *Baseball Legends*. Lincolnwood, IL: Publications International, 1997.

Williams, Dick and Bill Plaschke. *No More Mr. Nice Guy: A Life of Hardball*. San Diego: Harcourt Brace Jovanovich, 1990.

Winehouse, Irwin. *The Duke Snider Story*. New York: Julian Messner, 1964.

Young, Doc. *Great Negro Baseball Stars*. New York: A.S. Barnes, 1953.

Ziegel, Vic. *Summer in the City: New York Baseball, 1947–1957*. New York: Harry N. Abrams, 2004.

Zimmer, Don and Bill Madden. *Zim: A Baseball Life*. Kingston, NY: Total Sports Illustrated, 2001.

Zimmer, Don. *The Zen of Zim*. New York: St. Martin's Press, 2004.

Zoss, Joel and John Bowman. *Diamonds in the Rough*. Lincoln: University of Nebraska Press, 2004.

Credits

❧

I sincerely wish to thank the men and women listed below who responded to my requests to share their insights, reflections and feelings about Jackie Robinson. When I started this project in 2001, there were 870 major-league ballplayers still living from the Robinson decade (1947–56). I was honored that 770 of these gentlemen made contact with me.

Also included below are family members and friends of Jackie, scholars, historians, sportswriters, admirers, and just plain fans. If I have omitted any names, I sincerely apologize. I ended up conducting about eleven hundred interviews, and my only regret is that I didn't get to talk to thousands of more people who have strong feelings about Jackie Robinson.

BILL ABERNATHIE
TED ABERNATHY
CAL ABRAMS
ELLIOT ABRAMSON
ERNIE ACCORSI
THOMAS ACKER
DICK ADAMS
HERBERT ADAMS
J.A. ADANDE
BOB ADDIS
MARY ADLER
MARV ALBERT
DAVID ALDRIDGE
MAURY ALLEN
MEL ALLEN
PERCY ALLEN
GAIR ALLIE
JOE ALTOBELLI
JOHN AMALFITANO
DAVE ANDERSON
DR. ELIJAH ANDERSON

SPARKY ANDERSON
HERB ANDREWS
MAYA ANGELOU
JOHN ANTONELLI
MARTY APPEL
JOE ARBENA
RINALDO ARDIZOIA
HANK ARFT
DICK ARMSTRONG
GEOFFREY ARNOLD
RICHIE ASHBURN
JEANNE MOUTOUSSAMY-ASHE
BOB ASPROMONTE
JOE ASTROTH
JAMES ATKINS
TOBY ATWELL
ELDON AUCKER
TURK AULDS
EARL AVERILL
EDSON BAHR
ED BAILEY

LOU BRISSIE
MARINER BRITO
DICK BRODOWSKI
BOB BROEG
TOM BROKAW
JIM BROSNAN
ALTON BROWN
JAMES BROWN
LARRY BROWN
BOBBY BROWN
EARKE BRYCJER
JACK BRUNER
HOWARD BRYANT
JAY BUCHSBAUM
DON BUDDIN
GEORGE BULLARD
STEVE BULLOCK
CURTIS BUNN
JIM BUNNING
LEW BURDETTE
TOM BURGESS
MACK BURK
ERNEST BURKE
KEN BURKHART
WALLY BURNETTE
KEN BURNS
PETE BURNSIDE
JOE BURRIS
ED BURTSCHY
BRYAN BURWELL
DR. STEPHEN BUTLER
BUD BYERLY
TOMMY BYRNE
RALPH CABALLERO
SAM CALDERONE
ROY CAMPANELLA JR
BILL CAMPBELL
FRANK CAMPOS
DON CARDWELL
ANDY CAREY
DON CARLSEN
BOB CARPENTER
CHICO CARRESQUEL
JOHN CARROLL
SCOTT CARY
BILL CASH

JACK CASSINI
PETE CASTIGLIONE
WAYNE CAUSEY
PHIL CAVARRETTA
ART CECCARELLI
BOB CERV
BOB CHAKALES
CLIFF CHAMBERS
ED CHANDLER
SAM CHAPMAN
ED CHARLES
ROBERT CHERRY
CHARLES CHRONOPOULOS
BUBBA CHURCH
GINO CIMOLI
FRED CLAIRE
ALLIE CLARK
JIM CLARK
TRUMAN CLEVENGER
GIL COAN
JIM COATES
HOWIE COHEN
ROCKY COLAVITO
DAVID COLBURN
DAVE COLE
DICK COLE
JERRY COLEMAN
WALTER COLEMAN
LEONARD COLEMAN
BUD COLLINS
JACK COLLUM
DANNY COLONA
JIM COMMAND
CLINT CONATSER
GENE CONLEY
BOB CONROY
BILL CONSOLO
ROBERT COPE
ELMER CORWIN
BOB COSTAS
GLENN COX
ROGER CRAIG
RUFUS CRAWFORD
SHAG CRAWFORD
RICHARD CREPEAU
JACK CRIMIAN

RAY CRONE
FRANK CROSETTI
JOE CUNNINGHAM
BILL CURRIE
PERRY CURRIN
ANGELO DAGRES
JEROME DAHLKE
PETE DALEY
HAL DANIELS
CLIFF DAPPER
AL DARK
HARRY DAUGHERTY
BOB DAVIS
BRANDY DAVIS
TOMMY DAVIS
WILLIE DAVIS
COT DEAL
ROD DEDEAUX
BOBBY DEL GRECO
IKE DELOCK
JIM DELSING
JOE DEMAESTRI
BILL DEMARS
DON DEMETER
CON DEMPSEY
SAM DENTE
JIM DERRINGTON
RUSS DERRY
BING DEVINE
CHUCK DIERING
LERY DIETZEL
DAVID DILLARD
BOB DILLINGER
DOM DIMAGGIO
BOB DIPIETRO
ART DITMAR
JACK DITTMER
SONNY DIXON
BILL DOANE
LARRY DOBY
BOBBY DOERR
JOE DORINSON
WARREN DORN
RAYMOND DOSWELL
JACQUES DOUCET
BILL DOZIER

MOE DRABOWSKY
SOLLY DRAKE
DAVE DRAVECKY
WALT DROPO
HERM DUCKAT
MAHLON DUCKETT
GRANT DUNLAP
RYNE DUREN
JOE DURHAM
BILL DURNEY
CARL DUSER
DR. MICHAEL ERIC DYSON
GERALD EARLY
JOHN EDELMAN
MARIAN WRIGHT EDELMAN
DR. HARRY EDWARDS
CHARLES EINSTEIN
GEORGE ELDER
JOHN ELDRED
BOB ELSON
PAUL ELSTEIN
DICK ENBERG
ERIC ENDERS
DEL ENNIS
AL EPPERLY
EDDIE ERAUTT
HAL ERICKSON
PAUL ERICKSON
CAL ERMER
CARL ERSKINE
GERALD ESKANAZI
SAM ESPOSITO
GEORGE ESTOCK
ELROY FACE
GERALD FAHR
DAVID FALKNER
JOE FALLS
JIM FANNING
FRANK FANOVICH
PERRY FARRELL
JOHN FASZHOLZ
KATY FEENEY
JOHN FEINSTEIN
BOB FELLER
TOMMY FERGUSON
HUMBERTO FERNANDEZ

DON FERRARESE
BOO FERRISS
HENRY FETTER
DAVID FINDLAY
TOM FINE
BILL FISCHER
MAURICE FISHER
ED FITZGERALD
TOM FLANIGAN
CURT FLOOD
BEN FLOWERS
HANK FOILES
HENRY FONER
WHITEY FORD
ART FOWLER
PAUL FOYTACK
TITO FRANCONA
DR. JOHN HOPE FRANKLIN
HERMAN FRANKS
JOE FRAZIER
HERSHELL FREEMAN
MIKE FREEMAN
GENE FREESE
GEORGE FREESE
LINUS FREY
GEORGE FRICK
JIM FRIDLEY
BOB FRIEND
OWEN FRIEND
HARVEY FROMMER
RON GABRIEL
BILL GALLO
PETER GAMMONS
JOE GARAGIOLA
MARY GARBER
ALEX GARBOWSKI
BILLY GARDNER
NED GARVER
JIM GATES
PETE GEBRIAN
SIDNEY GENDIN
GEORGE GENOVESE
JIM GENTILE
HARV GENTRY
ALEX GEORGE
DR. LARRY GERLACH

DICK GERNERT
ALEN GETTEL
BILL GILES
JOE GINSBERG
AL GIONFRIDDO
TOM GIORDANO
LARRY GITLER
EVAN GLASS
TOM GLAVIANO
BILL GLEASON
STANELY "DOC" GLENN
SHAW GLICK
BILL GLYNN
AL GOLDIS
DR. WARREN GOLDSTEIN
PETER GOLENBOCK
MIKE GOLIAT
DORIS KEARNS GOODWIN
JIM GOODWIN
JACK GORDON
CHUCK GORIN
DR. ELLIOT GORN
EDDIE GOTTLIEB
HARLOD GOULD
FRANK GRAHAM JR
STEDMAN GRAHAM
ALEX GRAMMAS
MUDCAT GRANT
LOUIS GRASMICK
JOHN GRAY
TED GRAY
BILL GREASON
JIM GREENGRASS
MARV GRISSOM
DICK GROAT
STEVE GROMEK
DON GROSS
HARLEY GROSSMAN
ERNIE GROTH
JOHN GROTH
AL GRUNWALD
GREG GUMBEL
RANDY GUMPERT
DERRICK GUNNE
DON GUTTERIDGE
TONY GWYNN

WARREN HACKER
ROBERT HAGER
BOB HALE
AL HALL
BILL HALL
DICK HALL
BARRY HALPER
PETE HAMILL
MILO HAMILTON
GENE HANDLEY
ARNOLD HANO
MEL HARDER
ROLAND HARDIN
FRANK HARDY
CHUCK HARMON
MERLE HARMON
GAIL HARRIS
BOYD HARRIS
WILMER HARRIS
KEITH HARRISON
JACK HARSHMAN
ROY HARTSFIELD
CLINT HARTUNG
ERNIE HARWELL
LULU HARWELL
CLINT HARTUNG
GRADY HATTON
GEORGE HAUSMANN
ROY HAWES
TOMMY HAWKINS
MARCUS HAYES
DR. DOROTHY HEIGHT
MELVIN HELD
WOODY HELD
IVAN HEMETZ
TOMMY HENRICH
PATRICK HENRY
ROLAND HEMOND
SOLLY HEMUS
GAIL HENLEY
DANIEL HENNINGER
BILL HENRY
RAY HERBERT
GENE HERMANSKI
EARL HERSH
MICKEY HERSKOWITZ

NEAL HERTWECK
WHITEY HERZOG
JOHN HETKI
CLARENCH HICKS
DR. JACK HIGGS
CALVIN HILL
GRANT HILL
DARIUS HILMAN
PAUL HINRICHS
HARLEY HISNER
BILLY HITCHCOCK
LLOYD HITTLE
JOAN HODGES
ELMER HODGIN
BILLY HOEFT
DR. LARRY HOGAN
CALVIN HOGUE
KEN HOLCOMBE
MICHAEL HOLLEY
TOMMY HOLMES
DONALD HONIG
JOHNNY HOPP
RALPH HOUK
FRANK HOUSE
ART HOUTTEMAN
ARLENE HOWARD
LEE HOWARD
CAL HOWE
BILL HOWERTON
SID HUDSON
CLINT HUFFORD
BILLY HUNTER
PAUL HUNTER
MONTE IRVIN
STAN ISAACS
RAY ISUM
JERRY IZENBERG
KAREEM ABDUL-JABBAR
KEITH JACKSON
REV JESSE JACKSON
JOHN JACKSON
RANDY JACKSON
RON JACKSON
SPOOK JACOBS
STEVE JACOBSEN
BILL JAMES

LARRY JANSEN
JOEY JAY
HAL JEFFCOAT
BILL JENNINGS
VIRGIL JESTER
DAN JIGGETTS
TOMMY JOHN
BILLY JOHNSON
DARRELL JOHNSON
ERNIE JOHNSON
KEN JOHNSON
L.C. JOHNSON
EDDIE JOOST
NILES JORDAN
TOM JORDAN
SPIDER JORGENSEN
HOWIE JUDSON
ROGER KAHN
DON KAISER
AL KALINE
BILL KASHATUS
BILL KAY
TED KAZANSKI
LES KEITER
GEORGE KELL
SKEETER KELL
HAROLD KELLER
WALT KELLNER
BOB KELLY
GENE KELLY
RUSS KEMMERER
BOB KENNEDY
MARTY KEOUGH
HARMON KILLEBREW
BEN KINCHLOW
JERRY KINDALL
RALPH KINER
CHUCK KING
CLYDE KING
LARRY KING
NELSON KING
TIM KING
THORNTON KIPPER
JIM KIRBY
JOE KIRRENE
CHRIS KITSOS

BILL KLAUS
JOHN KLIPPSTEIN
DICK KOECHER
LEONARD KOPPETT
STEVE KORCHECK
TONY KORNHEISER
CHUCK KORR
BILL KOSKI
SANDY KOUFAX
AL KOZAR
STEVE KRALY
CHUCK KRESS
LOU KRETLOW
ROCCO KRSNICH
DICK KRYHOSKI
TONY KUBEK
JOHN KUCKS
STAN KUCZEK
JOHN KUENSTER
BOWIE KUHN
BRUCE KUKLICK
JOHN KUME
BOB KUZAVA
CLEM LABINE
SAM LACY
JOE LAFATA
CHRIS LAMB
NEIL LANCTOT
HOBIE LANDRITH
JOE LANDRUM
DICK LANE
DON LANG
JACK LANG
MAX LANIER
PAUL LAPALME
RICHARD LAPCHICK
DON LARSEN
FRANK LARY
TOMMY LASORDA
VERN LAW
FRANK LAYDEN
LES LAYTON
HAL LEBOVITZ
MICHAEL LEE
MIKE LEIBLE
NEIL LEIFER

JIM LEMON
DON LENHARDT
BOB LENNON
TED LEPCIO
DON LEPPERT
GEORGE LERCHEN
RICH LEVIN
LEONARD LEWIN
ALLEN LEWIS
CLAUDE LEWIS
JOHN LEWIS
KENDALL LEWIS
MARTY LIEBERMAN
LOU LIMMER
WALT LINDEN
KARL LINDHOLM
CARL LINHART
ROYCE LINT
MIKE LIPETRI
ROBERT LIPSYTE
JACK LITTRELL
DANNY LITWHILER
BUD LIVELY
EARL LLOYD
CHUCK LOCKE
STU LOCKLIN
WHITEY LOCKMAN
JOHN LOGAN
JACK LOHRKE
MICHAEL LOMAX
JOE LONNETT
STAN LOPATA
AL LOPEZ
HECTOR LOPEZ
TURK LOWN
JERRY LUMPE
DON LUND
TONY LUPIEN
JERRY LYNCH
EDWARD LYONS
HANK MAJESKI
MAL MALLETTE
BOB MALLOY
ED MALONE
FRANK MALZONE
FRANK MANCUSO

MICHAEL MANDELBAUM
FELIX MANTILLA
MICKEY MANTLE
DICK MANVILLE
BILL MARDO
JOE MARGONERI
MARTY MARION
FRED MAROLEWSKI
BOB MARQUIS
ROGER MARQUIS
FRED MARSH
CLARENCE MARSHALL
BABE MARTIN
DR. CHARLES MARTIN
MORRIE MARTIN
PAUL MARTIN
RAY MARTIN
WALT MASTERSON
EDDIE MATTHEWS
GENE MAUCH
CARMEN MAURO
BOB MAVIS
CHARLIE MAXWELL
ED MAYO
ED MAYO SR.
WILLIE MAYS
BILL MAZEROSKI
BILL MAZUR
CARL MCBAIN
WINDY MCCALL
MIKE MCCORMICK
BARNEY MCCOSKEY
LES MCCRABB
MAURICE MCDERMOTT
JOE MCDONALD
IAN MCDONALD
MAJE MCDONNELL
GIL MCDOUGALD
ED MCGAH
PAT MCGLOTHIN
MICKEY MCGOWAN
GIL MCGREGOR
JOHN MCHALE
WAYNE MCLELAND
CAL MCLISH
JACK MCMAHAN

MARTY MCNEAL
DR. JAMES MCPHERSON
SAMMY MEEKS
SAM MELE
DAVE MELTON
LARRY MERCHANT
LLOYD MERRIMAN
LEN MERULLO
CHARLIE METRO
BOB MICELOTTA
ED MICKELSON
GLENN MICKENS
ED MIERKOWICZ
LARRY MIGGINS
EDDIE MIKSIS
LENNY MILEO
BILL MILLER
BOB MILLER
BOB MILLER
JOHN MILLER
MARVIN MILLER
PATRICK MILLER
STU MILLER
RUDY MINARCIN
PAUL MINNER
MINNIE MINOSO
FRED MITCHELL
JOHN MITCHELL
HUBERT MIZELL
RON MOELLER
HERB MOFORD
BILL MOISAN
ED MONAHAN
TERRENCE MOORE
BOBBY MORGAN
GUY MORTON
JIM MORTON
LES MOSS
DON MOSSIE
RON MORZINSKI
DON MUELLER
JOE MUELLER
RED MURFF
DICK MURPHY
RAY MURRAY
BRENT MUSBERGER

STAN MUSIAL
JOHN MUSUMECI
DICK MYERS
BILL NACK
STEVE NAGY
SAM NAHEN
ROSCOE NANCE
AL NAPELS
HAL NARAGON
RAY NARLESKI
DR. DANIEL NATHAN
PETE NATON
RON NECCIAI
RON NEGRAY
BOB NELSON
GLENN NELSON
KEVIN NELSON
DON NEWCOMBE
HAL NEWHOUSER
ROB NEYER
GUS NIARHOS
MILT NIELSEN
IRV NOREN
MICKEY NORTON
JOE NUXHALL
BOB OATES
EDDIE O'BRIEN
JOHNNY O'BRIEN
BILLY O'DELL
GEORGE O'DONNELL
DANIEL OKRENT
LEN OKRIE
KEITH OLBERMANN
JOHN OLDHAM
BOB OLDIS
JOHN OLGUIN
LUIS OLMO
KARL OLSON
PETER O'MALLEY
BUCK O'NEAL
ERNIE ORAVETZ
BILL OSTER
JOE OSTROWSKI
JIM OUTLAW
MICKEY OWEN
DANNY OZARK

ANDY PAFKO
JIM PAGLIARONI
STAN PALYS
SHARON PANNOZZO
DAVE PARKER
MEL PARNELL
LYNN PARROTT
TODD PARROTT
CAMILO PASCUAL
CARLOS PASCUAL
CLAUDE PASSEAU
TED PATTERSON
STAN PAWLOWSKI
JIM PEARCE
DANNY PEARY
EDDIE PELLAGRINI
PAUL PENSON
PHIL PEPE
HUGH PEPPER
CHRIS PERKINS
HARRY PERKOWSKI
JOHNNY PESKY
JOE PETERS
RUSS PETERS
RICHARD PETERSON
PAUL PETTIT
LEE PFUND
DAVID PHILLEY
BILL PHILLIPS
DONALD PHILLIPS
HOWARD PHILLIPS
JACK PHILLIPS
TAYLOR PHILLIPS
BILLY PIERCE
BILL PIERRO
AL PILARCIK
DUANE PILLETTE
JIM PISONI
LEONARD PITTS
RANCE PLESS
HERB PLEWS
JOHNNY PODRES
GARY POMERANTZ
MONTE POOLE
RAY POOLE
ED POPE

DAN PORTER
J.W. PORTER
AL PORTO
BOB POWELL
SHAUN POWELL
VIC POWER
JOE PRESKO
DWAIN PRICE
BOB PURKEY
JIM PYBURN
TOM QUALTERS
BILL QUEEN
JOHN QUINN
MARV RACKLEY
TED RADCLIFFE
HAL RAETHER
KEN RAFFENSBERGER
BOBBY RAMOS
ARNOLD RAMPERSAD
FRANK RANEY
WILLIAM RASPBERRY
SUSAN RAYL
BILL REED
WILLIS REED
DOTTIE REESE
MARK REESE
PEE WEE REESE
RUDY REGALADO
SAM REGALADO
HANK REICH
DR. CLIFFORD REID
SCOTT REIFERT
FRANK REILLY
JERRY REINSDORF
BILL RENNA
DINO RESTELLI
DAVE REYNOLDS
HAROLD REYNOLDS
WILLIAM RHODEN
DUSTY RHODES
JIM RHODES
MARK RIBOWSKY
JIM RICE
FRED RICHARDS
BOBBY RICHARDSON
AL RICHTER

BRANCH RICKEY III
STEVE RIDZIK
BOB RINKER
STEVE RIESS
PHIL RIFKIN
LAWRENCE RITTER
JIM RIVERA
PHIL RIZZUTO
DINO RESTELLI
MEL ROACH
ROBIN ROBERTS
DON ROBERTSON
OSCAR ROBERTSON
BILL ROBINSON
BROOKS ROBINSON
DAVID ROBINSON
FRANK ROBINSON
KEN ROBINSON
RACHEL ROBINSON
RAY ROBINSON
SHARON ROBINSON
WILL ROBINSON
BURTON ROCKS
LESTER RODNEY
PREACHER ROE
ED ROEBUCK
TONY ROIG
JOHN ROMONOSKY
BILL ROSEBORO
AL ROSEN
BOB ROSEN
HARRIS ROSEN
PHIL ROSEN
ROGER ROSENBLATT
DAVE ROSENFIELD
FLOYD ROSS
SPENCER ROSS
MARV ROTBLATT
NORM ROY
ROB RUCK
RUDY RUFER
BOB RULONG
KELLY RUSINACK
BILL RUSSELL
ART RUST
JOHN RUTHERFORD

PETER RUTKOFF
MILT RUTNER
BOB RYAN
BY SAAM
TOM SAFFELL
JOHNNY SAIN
ED SAMCOFF
RON SAMFORD
JEFFREY SAMMONS
TOM SANDERS
MIKE SANDLOCK
JOHN SANFORD
FRANK SAUCIER
JOHN SAUNDERS
BOB SAVAGE
MORRIS SAVRANSKY
HARRY SCHAEFFER
ART SCHALLOCK
CARL SCHEIB
CHRIS SCHENKEL
BOB SCHERBARTH
WILLARD SCHMIDT
JOHN SCHMITZ
RED SCHOENDIENST
DICK SCHOFIELD
PAUL SCHRAMKA
JOHN SCHULIANG
ART SCHULT
BILL SCHULTZ
GEORGE SCHULTZ
HOWARD SCHULTZ
ALLEN SCHWALB
ALAN SCHWARZ
HERB SCORE
STUART SCOTT
VIN SCULLY
KAL SEGRIST
BUD SELIG
ANDY SEMINICK
SONNY SENERCHIA
TED SEPKOWSKI
ELMER SEXAUER
BOBBY SHANTZ
MICHAEL SHAPIRO
BILL SHARMAN
DREW SHARP

DAN SHAUGNESSY
SPEC SHEA
LARRY SHENK
BURT SHEPHERD
NEILL SHERIDAN
DAVID SHINER
GEORGE SHUBA
REV. FRED SHUTTLESWORTH
NORM SIEBERN
ROY SIEVERS
CHARLIE SIFFORD
BOB SKINNER
AL SILVERA
CHARLIE SILVERA
AL SILVERMAN
CURT SIMMONS
JOHN SIMMONS
PETER SIMON
BILL SIMONS
TOM SIMPSON
DAVE SISLER
SIBBY SISTI
SEYMOUR SIWOFF
BOB SKINNER
MOOSE SKOWRON
ENOS SLAUGHTER
LOU SLEATER
DWAIN SLOAT
JIM SMALL
ROY SMALLEY
BOB SMITH
CLAIRE SMITH
DICK SMITH
EARL SMITH
FRANK SMITH
HAL SMITH
HAROLD SMITH
MICHAEL SMITH
OZZIE SMITH
PAUL SMITH
RON SMITH
STEPHEN SMITH
WENDELL SMITH
DUKE SNIDER
GERALD SNYDER
JIMMIE LEE SOLOMON

STEVE SOUCHOCK
WARREN SPAHN
IRWIN SPARK
LYLE SPATZ
BOB SPEAKE
MARC SPEARS
DARYL SPENCER
GEORGE SPENCER
BOB SPICER
HOMER SPRAGINS
JACK SPRING
JERRY STALEY
JACK STALLINGS
DICK STARR
DAVID STEELE
FRED STEIN
MARY STEIN
GLEN STEPHENS
BOB STEPHENSON
DAVID STERN
CHUCK STEVENS
ED STEVENS
BILL STEWART
DAVE STEWART
CHUCK STOBBS
DEAN STONE
MILTON STRASSBERG
WALT STREULI
NICK STRINCEVICH
LOU STRINGER
JACOB STUART
PAUL STUFFEL
TOM STURDIVANT
BOB STURGEON
PETE SUDER
HAYWOOD SULLIVAN
RUSS SULLIVAN
BILL SUTTON
ART SWANSON
MRS. JOE SZEKELY
BOB TALBOT
CHUCK TANNER
TED TAPPE
DR. BILLY TAYLOR
MARC TAYLOR
VERN TAYLOR

DICK TEED
RALPH TERRY
WAYNE TERWILLIGER
BERT THIEL
FRANK THOMAS
JOHN THOMAS
RON THOMAS
ART THOMPSON
BOBBY THOMSON
DON THOMPSON
GENE THOMPSON
TIM THOMPSON
JOHN THORN
SYD THRIFT
RON TILLERY
MIKE TIRICO
BILL TOENES
ANDY TOMASIC
CHRIS TORGUSEN
JOE TORRE
CECIL TRAVIS
BILL TREMEL
GUS TRIANDOS
JOE TRIMBLE
VIRGIL TRUCKS
STAN TRULL
BOB TURLEY
JULES TYGIEL
TOM UMPHLETT
TOM UPTON
BOB USHER
HAL VALENTINE
VITO VALENTINETTI
ELMER VALO
JOHN VAN CUYK
FRED VAN DUSEN
BRIAN VANDER HEIDE
JOHNNY VANDER MEER
GLEN VARNER
GEORGE VASS
GEORGE VECSEY
BILL VEECK
GENE VERBLE
MICKEY VERNON
GEORGE VESCEY
PETE VESCEY

BOB VETRONE
TOM VILLANTE
BILL VIRDON
OZZIE VIRGIL
DAVID VOIGHT
BILL VOISELLE
CLYDE VOLLMER
BEN WADE
GALE WADE
DR. LEROY WALKER
DR. RON WALTERS
PRESTON WARD
JORAM WARMUND
MIKE WARREN
NEAL WATLINGTON
J.C. WATTS
JIM WAUGH
BOB WELLMAN
DICK WELTEROTH
BILL WERBER
BILL WERLE
MAX WEST
JIM WESTLAKE
WALLY WESTLAKE
LEROY WHEAT
DON WHEELER
AL WHITE
BILL WHITE
LARRY WHITESIDE
DICK WHITMAN
JOHN WIDEMAN
AL WIDMAR
BOB WIELAND
BOB WIESLER
BOB WIETELMANN
DAVID WIGGINS
BILL WIGHT
DEL WILBER
MICHAEL WILBON
RALPH WILEY
HOYT WILHELM
LENNY WILKENS
DR. ROGER WILKINS
GEORGE WILL
ANDRE WILLIAMS
BILL WILLIAMS

BILLY WILLIAMS
DAVEY WILLIAMS
DICK WILLIAMS
PETER WILLIAMS
STAN WILLIAMS
TED WILLIAMS
GEORGE WILLIS
JIM WILLIS
MAURY WILLS
FRED WILPON
ARCHIE WILSON
ART WILSON
BILL WILSON
BOB WILSON
GRADY WILSON
KEN WILSON
BILL WINCENIAK
DAVE WINFIELD
TEX WINTER
DR. STEVEN WISENSALE
JERRY WITTE
BOB WOLFF
KEN WOOD
JOHN WOODEN
HAL WOODESHICK

FLOYD WOOLDRIDGE
EARL WOOTEN
HANK WORKMAN
AL WORTHINGTON
BRANSON WRIGHT
ROY WRIGHT
TOM WRIGHT
STEVE WYCHE
EARLY WYNN
JIMMY WYNN
LEN YOCHIM
EDDIE YOST
DR. ANDREW YOUNG
DICK YOUNG
SAL YVARS
RICHARD ZAMOFF
DAVID ZANG
GUS ZERNIAL
BOB ZICK
VIC ZIEGEL
ANDREW ZIMBALIST
DON ZIMMER
DENNIS ZIMMERMAN
GEORGE ZUVERINK

About the Author

❧

You can contact Pat Williams at:
Pat Williams
c/o Orlando Magic
8701 Maitland Summit Boulevard
Orlando, FL 32810
Phone (407) 916-2404
pwilliams@orlandomagic.com
Visit Pat Williams's Web site at:
www.patwilliamsmotivate.com

If you would like to set up a speaking engagement for Pat Williams, please write his assistant, Diana Basch, at the above address or call her at (407) 916-2454. Requests can be faxed to (407) 916-2986 or e-mailed to *dbasch@orlandomagic.com.*

We would love to hear from you. Please send your comments about this book to Pat Williams at the above address or in care of our publisher at the address below. Thank you.

Peter Vegso
Health Communications, Inc.
3201 SW 15th Street
Deerfield Beach, FL 33442

Give Your Life
the Full Court Press

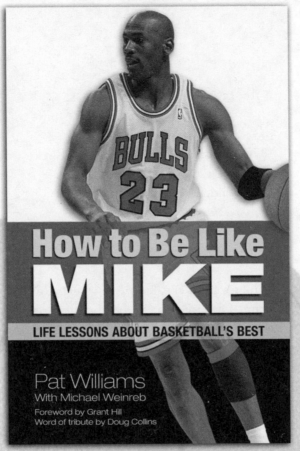

Code #9551 • Paperback • $12.95

More in the series

How to Be Like Walt
Code 2319 • Paperback • $14.95

How to Be Like Rich DeVos
Code 1584 • Paperback • $14.95

How to Be Like Women of Influence
Code 0545 • Paperback • $12.95

How to Be Like Jesus
Code 0693 • Paperback • $14.95